PUBLIC LIBRARIES IN THE KNOWLEDGE SOCIETY

An Indian Experience

Editors

S M Dhawan J L Sardana
R K Bhatt M K Jain

SHIPRA

Rs. 550; US$ 27.50

ISBN: 978-81-7541-525-6

First Published in India in 2010

Public Libraries in the Knowledge Society

Published by:

SHIPRA PUBLICATIONS

H.O.: LG 18-19, Pankaj Central Market, I.P. Ext.
Patparganj, Delhi-110092, Tel: 2223 5152, 2223 6152
Br.Off.: 115, Munish Plaza, 20, Ansari Road, Darya Ganj,
New Delhi-110002, Tel: 6594 6453, 9810522367
E-mail: info@shiprapublications.com
www.shiprapublications.com

Contents

Public Library Roles

ICT in Public Libraries

Public Library Services

Public Library Management Issues

Public Library System and Services in North Eastern India

Introduction

For long public libraries are known to have been meeting the educational, informational, and recreational needs of the people of all ages in the community. However, in the context of emerging era of knowledge society, the public libraries have arrived at a critical moment in their services. The key issue is – could public libraries be incorporated as key players in knowledge society. In the perception of general public, public libraries have traditionally been recognized as centres of popular reading materials, popular reference materials for community and business, or community information centres or community activities centres. But rarely public libraries have been considered and evaluated as serious centres for lifelong learning or self directed learning utilizing new technologies. In the context of emerging era of knowledge society, the need of the hour is to make public libraries as vibrant centres of learning and communication as well as community hubs for people to access networked information. The public libraries need to complement formal education system by providing a resource base and to emerge as platform for public to participate in lifelong learning. Investment in human capital is foundation of success in knowledge-based global economy in this century. Thus, public libraries need to look for opportunities and services to facilitate lifelong learning.

The papers in the volume focus on the current and emerging public library roles, evaluate the strengths and weakness of the public library system and the public libraries, and assess their preparedness to provide new services and facilities in the context of emerging knowledge society.

This volume comprises 23 invited and contributed papers on various topics relating to the theme of the conference such as public libraries in knowledge society, public library roles, public library development, Role of RRRLF, public library legislation, ICT in public libraries, public library services, and public library management and Public Library System and Services in North Eastern India.

The section on public libraries in knowledge society has three papers contributed by (i) Dr. Krishan Gopal, Librarian Jawaharlal Nehru University; (ii) M.P. Singh Senior Lecturer, Department of Library and Information Science, Bundelkhand University, Jhansi; and (iii) Geeta G. Gadvi, Lecturer & Head, Department of Library & Information Science, Gujarat University, Ahmedabad.

The section on public library development has three papers contributed by (i) Prof. A.C. Tikekar, Former Head of Department of Library Science, Bombay University, Mumbai; and (ii) Mrs. Moorttimatee Samantaray, Deputy Librarian, NCERT, Sri Aurobindo Marg, New Delhi (iii) Dr. R.K. Bhatt, Head, Department of Library and Information Science, University of Delhi, Delhi and Mr. Manish Kumar, Lecturer, Department of Library and Information Science, University of Delhi, Delhi.

The section of Role of RRRLF in the development of Public Libraries has only one paper by Dr. M. Sankara Reddy, Former Librarian, Telugu University, Hyderabad.

The section on public library legislation has three papers contributed by (i) Dr. Velaga Venkatappaiah, Hyderabad; (ii) Prof. M.P. Satija, Department of Library and Information Science, Guru Nanak Dev University, Amritsar jointly with Kiran Kathuria, Lecturer, Dept. of Library & Information Science, Punjabi University, Patiala; and (iii) Dr. Narendra K. Bar, Head, Library and Resource Centre, Election Commission of India, Ashok Road, New Delhi.

The section on public library roles has three papers contributed by (i) Dr. P.R. Goswami, Director, Central Secretariat Library, Delhi; (ii) Dr. Pradip Kumar Upadhyay, Technical Director, National Informatics Centre, Department of Information Technology, Ministry of Communications and Information Technology; and (iii) Devendra Kumar, Department of Library & Information Science (DLIS), CCS University, Meerut jointly with Rajkumar Singh (Librarian, Govt. Mahila Degree College, Aurai, Sant Ravidas Nagar Bhadohi) and Krishna Kumar, Faculty Member, DLIS, CCS University, Meerut.

The section on ICT in public libraries has two papers contributed by (i) Dr. Usha Mujoo Munshi, Librarian, Indian Institute of Public Administration, New Delhi; and (ii) Dr. B.N. Singh, Librarian, National Museum Institute of History of Art, Conservation and Museology (Deemed University), Janpath, New Delhi.

The section on, public library services has two papers contributed by (i) Dr. (Mrs.) Bharati Paliwal, TERI University, Delhi; and (ii) Manpreet Kaur Sohal and Prabhjeet Kaur, both Research Scholar, Department of Library & Information Science, University of Delhi jointly with Dr. (Mrs.) P.K. Walia, Reader, Department of Library & Information Science, University of Delhi, Delhi.

The section on, public library management issues has four contributed papers by (i) Dr. U.C. Sharama Head, Department of Library and Information Science, Dr. B.R. Ambedkar University, Agra, jointly with Dr. R.K. Bhatt, Department of Library and Information Science, University of Delhi; (ii) Shri Mange Ram, University Library Incharge, Dayalbagh

Educational Institute (Deemed Univ), Dayalbagh, Agra jointly with Rajbir Singh, Librarian, Vaish P.G. College, Rohtak, and Satish Yadav, Librarian, Bhadhawar P.G. College, Bah; (iii) Dr. Sewa Singh, Former Prof & Head GND University, Amritsar; and (iv) Dr. P.K.Walia, Reader, Department of Library & Information Science, University of Delhi, Delhi jointly with Ms. Esmat Momeni and Ms. Monika Gupta, both Research Scholars at Department of Library & Information Science, University of Delhi, Delhi.

The section on Public Libraries in North Eastern Region has one paper contributed by Ibohal Singh, Lecturer, Department of Library and Information Science, Manipur University, Imphal, jointly with N. Giridhari Singh, President, Ranganathan Society for Book Culture and Informatics Studies, NE Chapter, Imphal.

We are indeed very much grateful to the authors providing academic content for the volume. We are grateful to Sh. D. Kumar, Managing Director of Shipra Publications for bringing out this volume in record time.

Editors

Role of Public Libraries in Building the Knowledge Society

KRISHAN GOPAL*

1. INTRODUCTION

Literacy has been an important factor in building societies that value welfare, democracy and human rights and this is true throughout the world. Knowledge is undeniably significant in our modern society - a society that is much more complex and varied today than ever before. Society needs well-educated citizens, and wherein learning becomes a life-long activity. So long as reading and writing are basic accomplishments in a knowledge-based society, libraries will have a significant part to play in strengthening these skills.

Public libraries are among the few public meeting-places and are visited by people from all levels of society. According to Aabo's survey (*The value of public libraries* - A methodological discussion and empirical study applying the contingent valuation method) no less than 94% of the population consider it a democratic right to have a public library in their municipality. This figure is quite remarkable. The survey shows that public libraries have a value both for users and nonusers, since the majority of people assess libraries not only on a basis of self-interest but also on their value to the community as a whole. The value of personal and family use represents roughly 60 per cent of the total value. Of particular interest is the fact that cultural and social motives underlie 35-40 per cent of library evaluation. In other words, not only people consider libraries as important in their own lives but feel pleased on behalf of other users, since the social role of libraries is to disseminate culture and knowledge, preserve our literary heritage and promote democracy and equality.

The public library system is a democratic institution fulfilling a vital social function to offer everybody equal access to information and knowledge. This function must be combined with respect for the individual's right to acquire whatever knowledge and experience he or

* JNU Library, New Delhi-110067

she may choose to seek. Libraries must shift their focus and adapt their services in line with changes in the community. On the road to a knowledge based society we must develop strategies to meet the new demands of the public and thus increase the importance of libraries. It is the use of libraries which justifies their very existence.

At the present time public libraries are undergoing a process of renewal aimed at preserving basic values while adapting library services to a modem, multimedia environment. Today the debate concerning the functions of the library system and its future role as a source of culture and knowledge is wider and more intense than ever before. The background to this debate is one of cutbacks in library resources, leading to a dismantling of the system of branch libraries and a serious decline in media services compared to just a few years ago.

The library of today is digital and has perhaps gone further than any other public institution in taking advantage of technological development to improve its services, achieve more efficient use of resources and create new initiatives suited to a modem knowledge- based society. The result is an increased use of libraries by a wider public. These developments have, however, also led to greater differences between individual libraries. A debate now exists concerning the role of libraries in society, the value of literature, the dissemination of knowledge and the pleasure of reading.

2. THE PAST

As is well-known, public libraries have developed historically in tandem with the industrial society, and their formation is mostly based on enlightenment ideals of freedom of expression and of universal access to information and works of imagination. Article 19 in the Universal Declaration of Human Rights from 1948 is an eloquent and unique expression of these ideals stating that "everyone has the right to freedom of opinion and expression; this right includes freedom to hold opinions without interference and to seek, receive and impart information and ideas through any media and regardless of frontiers."

As is equally well-known, in industrial societies information is often hard to come by, and many communicative technologies are developed in order to remedy this scarcity and speed up the reliability and efficiency of distanced communication. One may just think of the immediate success of the telegraph and the telephone whose respective take-up in public and private life was centrally dependent upon their almost instant communication of data, an efficiency and immediacy that in turn fed into a development of more universal, temporal demarcations such as time zones.

Not only is information scarce in industrial society, also works of entertainment offer sought-after pastimes. Numerous autobiographies until the mid- 1970s describe how people would bike a long way to watch their favourite film at a local cinema; and public libraries were ransacked by avid users craving 'a good read' so that librarians often had to limit weekly loans for particular 'heavy users'.

Libraries in industrial societies serve to remedy the scarcity of information and (quality) entertainment and to secure universal access. The definition of information and fiction is clear, since these concepts have a physical materiality: they are books, journals, records, and films. And the role of the librarian is equally clear, if not always easy to fulfil: Librarians make explicit choices and selections amongst a known repertoire of artefacts.

Since the 1980s, a number of fundamental developments have served to change a situation of scarcity into a situation of overflow. In the early 1980s, satellite television and the VCR were introduced in many parts of the world. Notably news and entertainment went global, and this transformation was accompanied by a large-scale commodification of mediatized communication.

The commodification is mostly felt in Europe and other countries and regions that have a long tradition of public-service media, i.e. radio, television and film that serve the public good, not the interests of investors and advertisers; and media that are accountable to a diversity of output, not just popular fare that attracts the largest possible audience. Not only can people now time shift their viewing patterns, they also come to associate entertainment with commercial output, since public-service broadcasters tend to cut down on the most costly productions, i.e. entertainment including fiction.

This diversification and commodification is accompanied by a changing definition of the librarian's role. He or she is increasingly (self) defined as a 'consumer guide' assisting the individual user in making relevant choices amongst a plethora of seemingly equal cultural 'products'. This is a time when librarians begin to question received professional notions of taste and established cultural divides between art and pop even if they still prioritise their cultural function. The user becomes the focus of attention and individual service provision a hallmark of professional competence.

3. FROM INFORMATION SOCIETY TO KNOWLEDGE SOCIETY

Over the last two to three decades, information and communication technologies (ICT) have been the enabling factor in organizational change and innovation, and there is now evidence of their impact on industrial value chains. Organisations today strive to become agile and to operate profitably in an increasingly competitive environment of continuously and unpredictably changing markets. The digital age is different from the industrial age in various ways. For example, today ICT represent a substantial - and increasing-part of the added value of products and services. Their impact on the economy and on society at large has led to remarkable changes. Hence, information became an important tool.

4. INFORMATION

Information is important to any organization. Good and quality information can improve decision-making, enhance efficiency and allow organizations to gain competitive advantages. Many organizations are continuously looking for solutions to effectively seek and handle information within their internal and external environments. Business sectors also need information and effective means of managing information in order to assess their strengths and weaknesses. Porter and Miller[1] reported that one of the most important elements in competitive advantage is information.

5. KNOWLEDGE

Davenport and Prusak[2] view knowledge as an evolving mix of framed experience, values, contextual information and expert insight that provides a framework for evaluating and incorporating new experiences and information. They found that in organizations, knowledge often becomes embedded in artifacts web as documents, video, audio or repositories and in organizational routines processes, practices, and norms. They also say that for knowledge to have value it must include the human additions of context culture, experience, and interpretation.

Nonaka[3] expands this view by stating that knowledge is about meaning in the sense that it is context-specific. This implies that users of knowledge must understand and have experience with the context, or surrounding conditions and influences, in which the knowledge repository to be useful it must also store the context in which the knowledge was generated. That knowledge is context specific argues against the idea that knowledge can be applied universally, however it does not argue against the concept of organizational knowledge. Organizational knowledge is considered to be an integral component of what organizational members remember and use meaning that knowledge is actionable.

Polanyi[4] and Nonaka and Takeuchi[6] describe two types of knowledge, tacit and explicit. Tacit knowledge is that which is understood within a knower's mind and which cannot be directly expressed by data or knowledge representations and is commonly understood as unstructured knowledge. Explicit knowledge on the other hand is that knowledge which can be directly expressed by knowledge representations and is commonly known as structured knowledge, and thus easy to capture, store, and communicate. Tacit knowledge on the other hand is personal, a combination of experience and intuition, and as such the organisation's ability to capture and communicate it is heavily dependent on the individual owner's commitment to the organisation and to its need to generate value from it.

In this sense, a great deal of trust and loyalty between the individual and the organisation is necessary to leverage organisational knowledge, including its tacit dimensions.

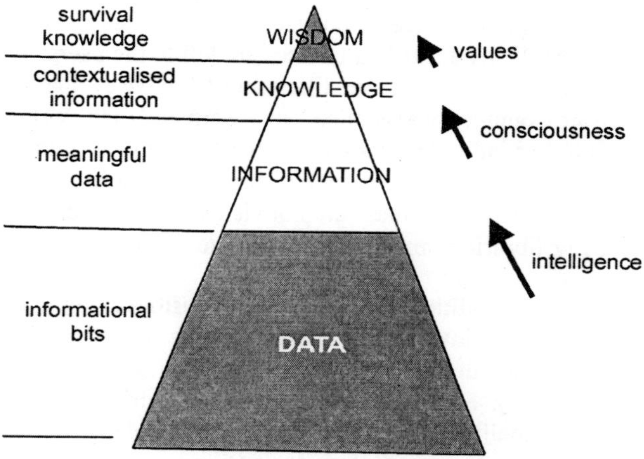

Figure 1: Relationship between Data, Information and Knowledge

It is therefore essential to make a proper distinction between the terms "data", "information", and "Knowledge" (Figure). The interchangeable use of "information" and "knowledge" tends to obscure the fact that while it can be easy and quick to transfer information from one place to another, it may often involve a very difficult and slow process to transfer knowledge. Knowledge is a human capability that can be acquired and expanded through learning.

In the 1980s, 'the information society' became a synonym of societal development. In such a society, the levers of development are information processing, i.e. efficient and reliable generation, transfer and retrieval of data, whose appropriation is often closely tied to formal sites of labour or education.

The competences necessary to advance such a society is information literacy. In its simplest form, the concept denotes the individual's ability to access, retrieve and process data of relevance to concrete problem-solving and decision- making, while in its more advanced versions, information literacy is contextualised and related to actual learning sites and wider societal and personal criteria of relevance and reflection (Kuhltau[6] 1993). Still, the concept of information literacy is closely tied to the technologies of computing and Internet access, and knowledge is defined in terms of reflexive and responsible use of information.

The definitions of libraries and of librarians change accordingly. The enormous increase in Internet-based communication serves to shift attention to the virtual, rather than the physical, library. Digital reference services, free access to large-scale data banks and secure retrieval become vital areas of professional development, and there is certainly more to come in this decisive domain of innovation.

Also, the astronomical increase in the amount of information makes the librarian's explicit choices amongst a known quantity of entities a thing of the past. Instead, explicit choices are left to the users. The many discussions on 'netiquette', Internet filters and reflexive evaluation of web information are examples of a seeming 'empowerment' of the virtual library user and his or her individual choices. Still, librarians - or rather a select group of data processing experts - make 'structural' choices as to access, storage, and retrieval - only these are not visible, and accountable, to the end user: today, librarians make selections in the first instance, not the last instance.

The librarian's traditional role as 'cultural custodian' or, in the 1980s as 'cultural guide', is downplayed in favour of the librarian's function as effective information disseminator assisting in the user's development of information literacy. Focus is on developing user friendly information searches that gradually become more and more attuned to actual problems and activities rather than stand-alone tools.

6. ROLE OF INFORMATION TECHNOLOGY

From the mid-l990s on, 'the knowledge society' began to compete with 'the information society' as a pervasive term in public discourse (Stehr[7]). While the term information society focuses on the raw materials so to speak ('information'), the term knowledge society serves to emphasise the various menus ('knowledge') that may result from people's handling of the raw materials. The change in concepts thus reflects a transformation in societal definitions of the fundamental levers of social development and of the competences necessary to bring about such developments.

In a knowledge society, the levers of development are the creation, circulation and appropriation of knowledge, i.e. non-material processes that in principle may take place anywhere and at any time. The creation of knowledge is no longer the prerogative of formal settings such as schools and work places; and hence the introduction of the term knowledge society is paralleled by a shifting emphasis from education (whose entry point is a teacher in an institutional setting) to learning (whose entry point is the learner in any given spatio-temporal context).

The competences necessary to advance a knowledge society have to do with creative ways of thinking, acting and cooperating so that existing knowledge is not only preserved and stored, but so that new forms of knowledge are developed and new types of action designed.

The development of creative competences is closely related to people's active appropriation of media and ICTs. Online interaction is a necessary means of virtual cooperation, and thus e-Learning became an important concept of the knowledge society. But so do other mediatized forms of communication such as digital storytelling, audio-visual analysis and Internet design and programming, not only as means of virtual communication, but as important ends of mediatized learning.

Today it is possible to digitise all forms of signs (e.g. text, sound, live and still pictures). Thus, the last decade has witnessed a technological and economic convergence of telecommunication, mass media and ICTs. It is becoming less and less feasible to isolate ICTs as separate technologies; and it is becoming evident that the knowledge society demands more than information literacy.

The term multimodal literacy (developed from Kress & van Leeuwen[8]) is gaining currency as a term that points to the rather complex semiotic competences that citizens need to develop in order to gain a formative influence on the knowledge society. Multimodal competences encompass the ability to access, but also to use mediatized forms of communication; it denotes the ability to retrieve and receive but also to produce such forms of communication. And, most importantly, it signals that information is but one element in a multifaceted spectrum of mediatized expressions that also encompass entertainment, interaction and performance.

7. PUBLIC LIBRARIES AS KNOWLEDGE CENTRES

If it is true that we live in a knowledge society that demands multimodal competencies most of which are mediatized, then it follows that the role of public libraries and librarians is challenged once again.

Public libraries, in their physical as well as their virtual versions, are spaces that people enter at liberty and often in their spare time. In shaping new visions for public libraries in the knowledge society, perhaps this image is their most fundamental value. For, it offers public libraries a unique chance of catching on to the multi-sited nature of learning in a knowledge society.

For example, for European children and young people informal sites of media and ICT learning are more diverse and more advanced than are the formal school settings (Livingstone & Bovill[9] and Drotner[10]). These findings imply that part of the present library public - and most of the future public - already possess a strong, informal repertoire of multimodal learning, if not collective competences.

Public libraries can build on those trends by redefining the physical libraries as informal knowledge centres and by developing their professional competences in close collaboration with other knowledge partners both in the private and public sectors. Such a development must respect the democratic principles of free access for all, principles to which public libraries are committed as cornerstones of action.

If such knowledge centres are to facilitate the development of multimodal competences demanded by the knowledge society without forfeiting the democratic foundation of libraries, then it follows that knowledge must be defined in wider terms than is the case when we speak of information literacy. As we saw, multimodal literacy encompasses both information and fiction/entertainment, reception and retrieval as well as production and performance.

To develop that kind of knowledge involves presence in the physical library, and it involves collective learning. While digital libraries certainly must and will further and finetune individual services in future, perhaps the most decisive library challenge in the years to come is to develop the physical libraries which harbour the possibilities of collective presence and hence collective learning. Ultimately, the vision must be how to develop a synergy between virtual and physical libraries with respect for the end users' frames of reference.

The challenge facing the physical libraries is intensified by the fact that many traditional services performed there are taken over by users of the virtual libraries. When the majority of mundane services leave the physical library - and the librarian's desk - then librarians in the physical library can downplay their functions in favour of virtual services; or they can redefine their role from access and individual service provision to users and facilitator of more sustained collective learning processes.

Defining the role of the librarian as knowledge facilitator is in line with the projected function of the physical library as a knowledge centre. The librarian leaves his/her desk and is present amongst users; she/he engages in sustained processes that involve groups of users offering him/her professional experiences and evaluations; and he/she interacts with partners across disciplinary and institutional boundaries.

In the knowledge-based society of today library users are becoming more self-reliant in their search for knowledge and entertainment. Librarians must develop new skills of a pedagogic nature in order to give added value to the information they supply. In a multimedia society it is necessary to acquire skills beyond those of reading and writing. Public libraries are informal centres of knowledge, defined as public meeting places by reason of both the physical library space and the virtual services they offer. Members of the public visit libraries voluntarily, usually in their own free time. The democratic principle of free access for all must be maintained. These are the values and the image we must build upon when creating new strategies for the library of the future in a knowledge-based society.

Note

Svanhild Aabo in the year 2007 obtained her doctor's degree from the University of Oslo for her thesis on the Norwegain population's views on the value of public libraries. Her survey is the first in the world to employ the methods of economists in order to assess the value of public library services on a national level.

REFERENCES

1. Porter, M.E. & Miller, V.E. (1985). How Information gives competitive advantage, *Harvard Business Review*, 63(4), 110-128.
2. Davenport, T.H., and Prusak, L. (1998). *Working Knowledge*. Boston: Harvard Business School Press.
3. Nonaka I. (1994). A Dynamic Theory of Organizational Knowledge Creation, *Organisation Science*, 5(1), 14-37.
4. Polanyi, M. (1967). *The Tacit Dimension.* London: Routledge and Kegan Paul.
5. Nonaka, I., & Takeuchi H. (1995). *The Knowledge-Creating Company: How Japanese Companies Create the Dynamics of Innovation.* Oxford University Press.
6. Kuhltau, Carol C. (1993). *Seeking Meaning : A Process Approach of Library and Information Services.* Westport, CT: Ablex Publishing.
7. Stehr, Nico (1994). *Knowledge Societies.* London: Sage.
8. Kress, Gunter & Theo van Leeuwen (2001). *Multimodal Discourse: The Modes and Media of Contemporary Communication.* London: Arnold.
9. Livingstone, Sonia & Moira Bovill (Eds) (2001). *Children and their Changing Media Environment: A European Comparative Study.* New York: Earlbaum.
10. Drotner, Kirsten (2001). *Medier for fremtiden: Born unge og det nye medielandskab* [Media for the Future : Children, Young People and the New Media Landscape]. Copenhagen: Host & Son.

Role of Public Libraries in the Emerging Knowledge Society in Challenging Change in India

M.P. Singh*

1. INTRODUCTION

The Public libraries have an important role in the emerging knowledge society in facilitating information as required for managing transition of capital oriented economy of the country to knowledge-based economy. Public library is also called the people's libraries, as the public libraries are established for the benefit of the people. Freedom, prosperity and the development of knowledge society and of individuals are fundamental human values. They will only be attained through the ability of well-informed citizens to exercise their democratic rights and to play an active role in emerging knowledge society in the challenging era of the millennium. The public library, the local gateway to knowledge, provides basic means for lifelong learning, independent decision-making and cultural development of the individual and social groups.

The public libraries are the local centres of information, making all kinds of knowledge and information readily available to its readers. The services of the public library are provided on the basis of equality of access for all, regardless of age, race, sex, religion, nationality, language or social status. Specific services and materials are provided to all users who cannot, for whatever reasons, use the regular services and materials, for example linguistic minorities, people with disabilities or people in hospitals or prisons. All age groups must find material relevant to their changing needs. Collections and services have to include all media types and modern technologies as well as traditional materials. High quality and relevance to local needs and conditions are fundamental. Materials must reflect current trends in the knowledge society as well as human endeavors and imaginations.

---

* Senior Lecturer, Department of Library and Information Science, Bundelkhand University, Jhansi-284128, Email id: mpsingh_bu@yahoo.co.in

2. DEFINITION

A public library is an organization established, supported and funded by the community, either through local, regional or national government or through some other form of community organization. It provides access to knowledge, information and works of the imagination through a range of resources and services and is equally available to all members of the community regardless of race, nationality, age, gender, religion, language, disability, economic and employment status and educational attainment.

3. PUBLIC LIBRARY OBJECTIVES

The primary purpose of the public library is to provide resources and services in a variety of media to meet the needs of individuals and groups for education, information and personal development including recreation and leisure. Public libraries have an important role in the development and maintenance of a democratic society by giving individuals in the community access to a wide and varied range of knowledge, ideas and opinions. These objectives of public libraries are essentially aimed at political, socio-economic, educational, industrial and cultural development of the society.

4. MISSION

Dr. Ranganathan, in his book on library manual, wrote about the mission of public libraries. The following are the key missions which relate to information, literacy, education and culture and these should remain at the core of public library services

- The mission of public libraries is to provide a life-long self education to each member of the society.
- To collect up-to-date, recent and current information related to each subject.
- To help in providing each and every kind of information material at various levels for the persons of the society.
- To collect and organize the material and information for education and recreation of he people of the society.
- To collect and provide all other types of reading materials for the benefit of the society.

5. ROLE OF PUBLIC LIBRARIES IN THE EMERGING KNOWLEDGE SOCIETY

To be effective in fulfilling its goals the public library must be accessible to all including its potential users. Any limitations to library access, whether deliberate or accidental, will undermine the public library and its primary role of meeting the library and information needs of the community it serves.

6. ANALYZING ACTUAL AND POTENTIAL USERS IN THE COMMUNITY

It is important to establish a clear profile of the community as to who uses and who doesn't. use the library service. It is also necessary to collect necessary data, analyze it to identify the needs of individuals and groups within the public that can be met by the public library.

7. PLANNING READER SERVICES

The public library must provide services based on analysis of library and information needs of the local community. In planning services, clear priorities must be established and a strategy developed for organizing services on medium to long term basis. Services should be developed for identified groups and provided only if such groups exist in the local community. The services of the library should not be subject to any form of ideological, political, religious or commercial pressure. Services must be able to adjust changes in the society, and reflect changes in the society, for example, changing family structures, employment patterns, demographic changes, cultural diversity and methods and media of communication. The libraries should also take account of traditional cultures as well as new technologies, for example, support for oral methods of communication as well as making use of information and communication technology.

8. TRADITIONAL SERVICES

Public libraries provide a range of services, both within the library and in the public, to satisfy their users' needs. The library should facilitate access to its services for all, including those who have difficulty in reading print. The following services, which should be easily accessible to the user in a variety of formats and media, must be provided.

- Provision of print and non print reading material for use within the library
- Loan of print and non print reading material
- Information services using print and non print reading material
- Users' advisory services including reservation services
- Community information services
- User education including support for literacy programmes
- Programmes and events.

This is not an exhaustive list but an indicative of the key services of the public libraries. Their range and depth will depend upon the size of the library and the emerging information trends in the knowledge society. Every library should aim at network participation to give user access to wide range of material. Service provision should not be confined to library building premises but also taken to users sites whenever physical access to public library is not possible. In providing services, both within the library and outside, use should be made of information and communications technologies as well as of the print media.

9. PUBLIC LIBRARY SERVICES THROUGH ICT IN CHANGING TRENDS

The rapid development of Information Communication Technologies has brought huge amount of information within reach of all those with access to non print media. Information provision has always been the key role of the public libraries. However, the ways in which information can be collected, accessed and presented have changed radically in recent years. The public library has a number of roles in providing information:

- Providing access to information at all levels
- Collecting information about the local community and making it readily accessible, often in co-operation with other organizations
- Training people of all ages in the use of information and the connected technology
- Guiding users to the appropriate information sources
- Providing opportunities for disabled people to have independent access to information
- Acting as a gateway to the information world by making it accessible to all, thus helping to bridge the gap between 'the information rich' and 'the information poor'.

The tremendous developments of the Internet have been largely unstructured and uncontrolled. The huge amount of information that can be accessed via the Internet is of varying quality and accuracy. The key role of the librarian in the public library system is to guide users to reliable information sources meeting their requirements.

10. PUBLIC LIBRARY LINKAGES THROUGH LIBRARY NETWORKS

Each library collection is in some degree unique. No collection in a single library can afford to contain all the materials that the members of public require. Libraries, therefore, can greatly enhance their service capacity and potential by organizing access to collections of other libraries. Public libraries therefore can benefit from participating in resource-sharing schemes at any level, local, regional, national and international, involving libraries of a wide range of organizations with information resources. The libraries also need to make their collections available for loan to other libraries through participation in the network, for example, in a union catalogue or in a local network of information providers, such as schools, colleges and universities. Thus public libraries must operate in co-operation with other public libraries, with research libraries and with libraries in educational establishments, as part of the national and international networks of library and information services.

Public libraries are instruments of equal opportunity and must provide a safety net against alienation and social exclusion from technological advance by becoming the electronic gateways to information in the digital age. They should enable all citizens to have access to the information to participate positively in the emerging knowledge society. The library should provide access to e-resources of the library and also of other libraries through the creation of effective electronic networks at all levels from local to international. This includes participation in community networks, programmes to develop technologically advanced communities and electronic networks linking two or more agencies. They should also be part of national information policies.

11. FUTURE PLAN

Libraries are susceptible to external forces. Developments both within and outside librarianship are likely to have impact on library services. Libraries need to anticipate such developments, effect suitable changes, particularly technological changes to shape libraries for the future. The role of policy-makers and other staff in this regard is of crucial importance.

12. CONCLUSION

In the knowledge based economy large sections of the society would certainly need access to information to address issues and problems related to knowledge creation, knowledge application, or knowledge utilization. Hence effective public library system is the need of the hour for the benefit of common man in public. Origin and growth of public libraries has been a direct outcome of societal changes brought out by driving forces such as industrial development, illiteracy eradication, widespread education, and socio-economic developments. Modern public libraries are invaluable institutions, providing free book service to every citizens of the country without any distinctions. In the present context of knowledge society, there is thus an urgent need to build wider network of public libraries in each State of India by utilizing modern information and communication technologies.

BIBLIOGRAPHY

1. Barua, B. P. (1994). Raja Rammohun Roy Library Foundation and Library Movement in India. Presented at 39th All India Library Conference. Delhi: Indian Library Association.
2. Bhattacharjee, R. (2002). Public Library Services in India: system and Deficiencies. IFLANET. Public Library Section country Report: India.
3. Pandey Sharma, S.K.. (1997). Public Libraries in India: Trends and Status. *Public Libraries in Developing Countries: Status and Trends*. Ed. P.K. Mahapatra, pp121-127. New Delhi: Vikas Publishing House.
4. *Verma, I.N. and Agrawal, U.K. (1994)* Public Library Services in India. *Udaipur): Himanshu.*
5. Zahid, Ashraf Wani. (2008) Development of Public Libraries in India. *Library Philosophy and Practice*.

Government Knowledge Centre: A Model for Public Libraries

GEETA G. GADHAVI*

1. INTRODUCTION

Developed world countries are fast becoming knowledge based economies leading to paradigm shift in the way information infrastructure including knowledge institutions, knowledge networks and telecom infrastructure are developed. By inference library becomes an essential component of the knowledge infrastructure. Public libraries can thus be envisaged as integral part of the information highway, allowing people to access the enormous, untold wealth of knowledge available any where. This also lends public libraries an opportunity to serve the humanity. As per vision statement of the Library of Congress, "The library is in the unique position to be both Catalyst and Participant in the intellectual process that transforms information into knowledge, and knowledge into wisdom". The UNESCO Public Library manifesto of 1994 has also designated public library as "The local gateway to knowledge". Public Library converges social knowledge, adds value to it, produces new knowledge and diffuses it as requested. The Library premises can be a place for gathering educated people to communicate and create tacit knowledge, and interpret tacit knowledge in to codified knowledge. At the same time public library can be a "server" disseminating information and knowledge to those out of the network reach, or by attracting people to the nearby libraries to access Internet service. Additionally, with the global networking of library community and other information servers, local libraries became globally accessible libraries. Modern public libraries became globally accessible, popular and of enduring importance to social justice and the maintenance of the democratic society. Given these new roles, public library becomes a multi-purpose agency with multiple roles covering the areas of

* Sr. Lecturer and Head, Department of Library & Information Science, Gujarat University , Ahmedabad 380 009
Email : geetmin@yahoo.co.in

information, lifelong learning, recreation and leisure, culture and research. The ICT could be harnessed to empower people. Knowledge should thus be one of the core missions of the library. Public libraries will have to grow as specialist in each discipline and make knowledge available easily for use.

2. STATE CENTRAL LIBRARY AS KNOWLEDGE CENTRE

Gujarat has a great historical and cultural past. Its literacy rate is about 70%, which lends great scope for introducing measures to reduce illiteracy and increase better opportunities for employment. These social measures can be taken only if people have access to knowledge and skills. At present, knowledge is beyond the reach of large cross-sections of the society. The ultimate library vision is that everybody should have access to knowledge.

We all know that the Internet has emerged as a major tool for churning out information and producing new knowledge. The other dimension of Internet is that it has been instrumental in creating new issues such as information overload. Online information is doubling every 6 months, where as unstructured information is doubling every three months. The same is true with corporate information; doubling every 18 months, medical information is doubling every 5 years. Hence, due to information overload knowledge is getting underutilized. Given the fact that sum total of human knowledge doubles every two to three years, world's knowledge doubling every six months, printed knowledge doubling every five years, and medical knowledge doubling every 3.5 years, this issue of information overload is far more serious than we perceive. Considering these factors the Government of Gujarat has decided to convert the State Central Library into a Knowledge Centre, the first state in India to accomplish this work.

3. TOWARDS KNOWLEDGE SOCIETY

A knowledge Society can grow only if knowledge is accessible freely. If not, even the literate will become uneducated. Mark Twain says "The man who does not read books has no advantage over the man who cannot read". We have, therefore, to transform our society into a Knowledge Society. In it every person can contribute at the local level in terms of experience, initiatives or needs. This would lead to local and national development, in terms of skilled workforce, new competencies to innovate and develop new technologies. The knowledge Centre will be collecting information on Indian and foreign R&D results, help the public with the required information about patents and unused R&D results of government managed laboratories. As the State Knowledge Centre (SKC) is established as a one-stop window, not only will the time of professionals be saved but the duplication in the creation of similar products or R&D efforts will be minimized. We expect that people will begin to specialize in disciplines, knowledge about a discovery can be made available to users at low cost of interest and its commercial applications would contribute to economic development. A poor economy can be transformed into a knowledge-driven economy. Small-scale individual enterprises can grow extensively. The economic implications of knowledge give rise to knowledge based economy. Obsolescence of technology and its replacement by improved technology would give rise to new products at lesser cost. This kind of environment, it is envisaged would give rise to competition and market expansion. Those who have access to precise knowledge would be at advantage to create new and better products, market them well, attract finance, and use raw materials effectively among other benefits. They in turn become part of the growing knowledge economy. Knowledge is thus the key to the economic development of the State. While the rich will use it for wealth generation, the poor will use it for poverty alleviation and it is this context that the State Knowledge Centre gains importance.

4. TRANSFORMING TRADITIONAL LIBRARY TO KNOWLEDGE CENTRE

A knowledge centre is an extended version of a public library, disseminating knowledge, providing useful information to the public that triggers transformation in the society. One of the foremost questions that arises is - how do we get it? It is as simple as anything. By collecting, organizing and disseminating both knowledge and information one can visualize a knowledge centre. Knowledge will be pooled systematically for wider use in various context. Knowledge will be available locally with the help of ICT, not merely matching users' needs with knowledge resources, but also assisting them in taking decisions in global and futuristic perspectives. Every day new development occurs in the knowledge sector. These have to be captured on each and every subject, preserved and presented in digital form. Knowledge centre will cull knowledge from every source of information by adopting new methods to collect information on the issues of local interest. Given the digital resources, the Knowledge Centre will serve 24 x 7. Public Library of Gandhinagar is going to turn its face as Government Knowledge Centre (GKC). The GKC will witness transformation in every sector, including personnel, service sector, physical infrastructure and knowledge resources.

4.1 *Personnel Sector*

To provide sophisticated service of the kind as required in a knowledge centre with traditional mind set, is not possible. Trained and skilled manpower is required to manage change in all aspects of services. Gujarat Knowledge Centre has to work in coordination with National Knowledge centre and apply all international standards and best practices. Staff will be selected on the basis of their potential and strengths in various operations. GKC will have Manager, Knowledge Centre, Consultants for

Content Creation Centre and for Digital Library Unit, RTI queries, State Archives and for Extension activities GKC will have Knowledge Associates and knowledge Assistants. For existing staff, GKC will provide intensive training opportunities in the areas related to their new jobs. Personnel with IT and ICT skills will be preferred. Suitable communication skills, managerial skills and office etiquettes will constitute critical criteria for key posts. Recently GKC employed 53 surpluses employees from government. More than 10 IT professionals will be recruited after one month for GKC. Government of Gujarat State has decided to promote existing staff after their intensive training. State Librarians in class I and II cadre will be recruited directly. Other professionals will be appointed on fixed pay as per State Government rules.

4.2 *Infrastructure*

Building: GKC will be the new name, face and identity of State Central Library, Gandhinagar. Existing building will be renovated to give it a modern look. It already has renovated auditorium, rare books and manuscripts section, children's library, women's library, senior citizen's section, Braille section, text book section, fumigation unit, maintenance unit, reprography unit, unprocessed books and record room, exhibition gallery, canteen and reception/personal belongings/ counter. NID, Ahmedabad has designed the floor plan. The Government of Gujarat has sanctioned Rs.2.5 crore for modernization of building and infrastructure. GKC proposes to spend 2 crore for renovation of building and 50 lakh for furniture. Furniture has been planned out for the centre. Suitable tables and chairs for staff as well as for computer terminal's utility have been selected. Good quality waiting lounge is going to be developed. In order to maintain office documents and records filing racks and storage units have been acquired. GKC has purchased CDs, DVDs and computer related stationery. GKC building will be centrally air conditioned in the near future. To maintain building, infrastructure facilities, cleaning and security will be out sourced.

4.3 *Technology*

GKC has already purchased 60 computers from RRRLF Grants. All the computers will be equipped with Internet accessibility. Intranet connectivity will be provided to staff members of GKC. To create digital contents using international standards adequate plotters, printers and related hardware and software are under plan for procurement. GKC has also planned for upgradation of technology. It has been decided that GKC will have access to books and other documents available in India and outside India by using library networks like DELNET. State Central Library has its own website which will be shortly converted in GKC's website, online service for renewing and reserving books will be provided in near future. Telephones with STD connections for senior staff, officers will be provided.

One or two coin system public telephone lines will be provided for users and others. In order to provide suitable facilities to physical challenged people, dedicated elevator facility will be provided. For auto check in/ out, book drop facility, checking loss of books, use of smart card, and to maintain patron records as well as usage tracking - RFID system will be implemented in GKC within reasonable period.

4.4 *Resources*

GKC has Rs.6 crore fixed deposits and earns Rs.54 lakh of interest. To serve clientele, GKC will purchase books from the interest amount earned on fixed deposits. Books will also be purchased from the grants released by RRRLF. There will be a separate collection of books received under the copyright Act. To identify core subjects of need, a survey of Gujarat State will be conducted. Books and journals will be purchased with the ideas of generating income. Through request and advertisement, manuscripts lying with or available with any one will be procured and GKC will preserve them for next generation. The rare books will be identified from the collection. e-books, e-journals, e-newspapers, and e-thesis with other web-based resources will be subscribed by GKC. To create an automated and user-friendly environment GKC will enrich its collection and services. GKC's chief source of income will be government grants, subscription amount, grants from RRRLF, donations in cash, kind, land and building. Each and every sector of service in GKC will have to generate its finance by offering value added services and some paid services. One of the ways of generating revenue is through innovative ideas like utilizing the unused building space for advertising / hoardings. State Central Library implemented this idea only for Rajkot city's libraries and it earns Rs. 12 lakh per annum. That library utilizes this money to purchase books/resources. Now, Junagadh, Jamnagar, Baroda and Mahesana district's library's place will be utilized gradually.

4.5 *Services*

Over and above traditional Library Services GKC requires new service providers with IT based knowledge. Online renewal and reservation of books services, Document delivery service, Ask the Librarian (Reference desk), alerting services, reprography services, resource web form, FAQs and many more non-traditional services will be offered by GKC. To furnish these services qualified staff with ample experience will be deployed.

6. GOVERNMENT KNOWLEDGE CENTRE: OBJECTIVES

The GKC will have the following objectives:

- Make the GKC inter - sectoral in due course of time so that it becomes a one-stop centre for accessing knowledge on different subjects or topics of interest to users in Gujarat;

- Capture knowledge from projects, assignments, grey literature, case studies, experts, etc. on identified subjects and make them accessible in database from;
- Develop collections on important subjects;
- Connect each component of knowledge with a set of experts and develop an active database of such experts;
- Create databases, develop an Intranet and maintain information on important knowledge repositories;
- Develop catalogues and indexes in machine readable from using international standards of physical and electronic resources;
- Develop links with resources which are both physical; such as institutions and individuals, and electronic resources available through the Internet;
- To furnish as much information to the users as the users' need to complete their assignments;
- Give knowledge and information support to the adult population and to see how they are benefited from new technology and avenues;
- Offer knowledge inputs to deprived sections of the society who come from rural and urban sectors so that they upgrade their standards of living;
- Distribute knowledge on health and family welfare;
- Train every user in accessing information and guide the users to the appropriate resource;
- Give integrated access to information available with DELNET on the subjects and collect relevant information on the subjects from other sources;
- Coordinate with National Knowledge Centre at DELNET in order to:
- Collect useful knowledge resources from India and International sources for the benefit of users in Gujarat;
- Promote awareness about the resources of Gujarat in India and outside India specially among those users who use knowledge for development; and
- Seek support and collaboration for projects to be established in Gujarat

6.1 *GKC Functions*

GKC will occupy resources based on the result of local surveys and accordingly disseminate appropriate knowledge to its clientele. As per Dr. H.K. Kaul's report the GKC will:

1. Make surveys of people living around, at least 5 kms. in radius, and find out:
    a. The number of unemployed youth and their interests and specializations;
    b. The number of women who have time to learn skills and are interested in making a living by using those skills;

   c. The number of physically challenged people who need support of knowledge and skills; and
   d. Identify all skills in which the public is interested in adopting or developing further.
2. Offer knowledge support to public;
3. Identify the languages in which content will be serviced and the relative content in English.
4. Coordinate with other departments of the knowledge centre linked up with knowledge Gateway of DELNET for giving knowledge support to the users, with the support of Department of Learning Skills, Department of Web resources/Development, Department of Training and Surveys and Department of Administration and Publicity.

7. CONCLUSION

Gujarat has the credit of having Government Knowledge Centre (GKC) first of its kind. Information technology will be harnessed for effective collection development activities, storage and dissemination of information and knowledge. There is an urgent need to exploit library material for disseminating knowledge to the public. Like GKC all other libraries can be modernized in phases using information and communication technologies. Promotion of quality in services and creation of products could be introduced gradually by the knowledge centre among the industrial community in different sectors. The knowledge centre could introduce e-commerce applications and serve the business community too. The Government of Gujarat has taken this praise worthy initiative for dissemination of knowledge and information which people of Gujarat certainly deserve. This knowledge Centre will be the role model for other State Public Libraries.

REFERENCES

1. Kaul, H.K. (2006). Public Libraries as knowledge centres, *In* Kaul, H.K. and Malhan, I.V.(ed). *Knowledge, Library and Information Networking – NACLIN 2006*, New Delhi, DELNET-Developing Library Network,2007, pp. 1-18.
2. Satija, M.P. (2007). Democracy and knowledge society in India, *In* Kaul, H.K. and Malhan, I.V.(ed). *Knowledge, Library and Information Networking – NACLIN 2006*, New Delhi: DELNET-Developing Library Network, 2007, pp. 19-31.
3. The Library of Congress in the year 2000: A Vision Management and Planning Committee, The Library of Congress, Washington DC, June 29, 1988: viii
4. UNESCO Public Library Manifesto, November, 1994.
5. Kaul, H.K. (2006). Report of the Modernisation of State Central Library, Gandhinagar.

Library Innovation for the Knowledge Society

KIRSTEN DROTNER*

As we move from a concept of the information society on to a concept of a knowledge society, the role of public libraries must undergo similar changes of priority. What should be the role of public libraries when most people have ample access to a plethora of information and entertainment? How may librarians define their professional role when users themselves perform many of the functions formerly left to the professionals?

The main contentions of the article are, first, that libraries must move from defining their professional role in terms of providers of information literacy on to a role as multimodal knowledge centres encompassing information as well as entertainment, retrieval as well as production. Second, librarians need to redefine their role in the physical library as facilitators of multimodal literacy and do so in close cooperation with other partners advancing civic society.

FROM SCARCITY TO OVERFLOW

As is well-known, public libraries have developed historically in tandem with the industrial society, and their formation is mostly based on enlightenment ideals of freedom of expression and of universal access to information and works of imagination. Article 19 in the *Universal Declaration of Human Rights* from 1948 is an eloquent and unique expression of these ideals stating that "everyone has the right to freedom of opinion and expression; this right includes freedom to hold opinions without interference and to seek, receive and impart information and ideas through any media and regardless of frontiers."

As is equally well-known, in industrial societies information is often hard to come by, and many communicative technologies are developed in order to remedy this scarcity and speed up the reliablility and efficiency

* Email: drotner@litcul.sdu.dk Reproduced with prior permission. Original appeared in *Scandinavian Public Library Quarterly*. 38 (2), 2005 Online version at http://www.splq.info/vol38_2/07.htm

of distanced communication. One may just think of the immediate success of the telegraph and the telephone whose respective take-up in public and private life was centrally dependent upon their almost instant communication of data, an efficiency and immediacy that in turn fed into a development of more universal, temporal demarcations such as time zones.

Not only is information scarce in industrial society, also works of entertainment offer sought-after pastimes. Numerous autobiographies until the mid- 1970s describe how people would bike a long way to watch their favourite film at a local cinema; and public libraries were ransacked by avid users craving 'a good read' so that librarians often had to limit weekly loans for particular 'heavy users'.

Libraries in industrial societies serve to remedy the scarcity of information and (quality) entertainment and to secure universal access. The definition of information and fiction is clear, since these concepts have a physical materiality: they are books, journals, records, and films. And the role of the librarian is equally clear, if not always easy to fulfil: Librarians make explicit choices and selections amongst a known repertoire of artefacts.

Since the 1980s, a number of fundamental developments have served to change a situation of scarcity into a situation of overflow. In the early 1980s, satellite television and the VCR are introduced in many parts of the world. Notably news and entertainment go global, and this transformation is accompanied by a large-scale commodification of mediatized communication.

The commodification is mostly felt in Europe and other countries and regions that have a long tradition of public-service media, i.e. radio, television and film that serve the public good, not the interests of investors and advertisers; and media that are accountable to a diversity of output, not just popular fare that attracts the largest possible audience. Not only can people now timeshift their viewing patterns, they also come to associate entertainment with commercial output, since public-service broadcasters tend to cut down on the most costly productions, i.e. entertainment including fiction.

This diversification and commodification is accompanied by a changing definition of the librarian's role. He or she is increasingly (self)defined as a 'consumer guide' assisting the individual user in making relevant choices amongst a plethora of seemingly equal cultural 'products'. This is a time when librarians begin to question received professional notions of taste and established cultural divides between art and pop even if they still prioritise their cultural function. The user becomes the focus of attention and individual service provision a hallmark of professional competence.

FROM INFORMATION SOCIETY TO KNOWLEDGE SOCIETY

Of more immediate impact than the globalization and commodification of mass media is the introduction from the late 1980s on of computers and later the Internet and mobile media. In the 1980s, 'the information society' becomes a synonym of societal development. In such a society, the levers of development are information processing, i.e. efficient and reliable generation, transfer and retrieval of data, whose appropriation is often closely tied to formal sites of labour or education.

The competences necessary to advance such a society is information literacy. In its simplest form, the concept denotes the individual's ability to access, retrieve and process data of relevance to concrete problem-solving and decision- making, while in its more advanced versions, information literacy is contextualised and related to actual learning sites and wider societal and personal crieria of relevance and reflection (Kuhlthau 1993, Bruce 1997). Still, the concept of information literacy is closely tied to the technologies of computing and Internet access, and knowledge is defined in terms of reflexive and responsible use of information.

The definitions of libraries and of librarians change accordingly. The enormous increase in Internet-based communication serves to shift attention to the virtual, rather than the physical, library. Digital reference services, free access to large-scale data banks and secure retrieval become vital areas of professional development, and there is certainly more to come in this decisive domain of innovation.

Also, the astronomical increase in the amount of information makes the librarian's explicit choices amongst a known quantity of entities a thing of the past. Instead, explicit choices are left to the users. The many discussions on 'netiquette', Internet filters and reflexive evaluation of web information are examples of a seeming 'empowerment' of the virtual library user and his or her individual choices. Still, librarians – or rather a select group of data processing experts – make 'structural' choices as to access, storage, and retrieval - only these are not visible, and accountable, to the end user: today, librarians make selections in the first instance, not the last instance.

The librarian's traditional role as 'cultural custodian' or, in the 1980s as 'cultural guide', is downplayed in favour of the librarian's function as effective information disseminator assisting in the user's development of information literacy. Focus is on developing userfriendly information searches that gradually become more and more attuned to actual problems and activities rather than stand-alone tools.

MULTIMODAL LITERACY

From the mid-1990s on, 'the knowledge society' (Stehr 1994) begins to compete with 'the information society' as a pervasive term in public discourse. While the term information society focuses on the raw materials so to speak ('information'), the term knowledge society serves to emphasise the various menus ('knowledge') that may result from people's handling of the raw materials. The change in concepts thus reflects a transformation in societal definitions of the fundamental levers of social development and of the competences necessary to bring about such developments.

In a knowledge society, the levers of development is the creation, circulation and appropriation of knowledge, i.e. non-material processes that in principle may take place anywhere and at any time. The creation of knowledge is no longer the prerogative of formal settings such as schools and work places; and hence the introduction of the term knowledge society is parallelled by a shifting emphasis from education (whose entry point is a teacher in an institutional setting) to learning (whose entry point is the learner in any given spatio-temporal context).

The competences necessary to advance a knowledge society have to do with creative ways of thinking, acting and cooperating so that existing knowledge is not only preserved and stored, but so that new forms of knowledge are developed and new types of action designed.

The development of creative competences is closely related to people's active appropriation of media and ICTs. Online interaction is a necessary means of virtual cooperation, and thus elearning becomes an important concept of the knowledge society. But so do other mediatized forms of communication such as digital storytelling, audio-visual analysis and Internet design and programming. And not only as means of virtual communication, but as important ends of mediatized learning.

Today it is possible to digitise all forms of signs (e.g. text, sound, live and still pictures). Thus, the last decade has witnessed a technological and ecomic convergence of telecommunication, mass media and ICTs. It is becoming less and less feasible to isolate ICTs as separate technologies; and it is becoming evident that the knowledge society demands more than information literacy.

The term multimodal literacy (developed from Kress & van Leeuwen 2001) is gaining currency as a term that points to the rather complex semiotic competences that citizens need to develop in order to gain a formative influence on the knowledge society.Multimodal competences encompass the ability to access, but also to use mediatized forms of communication; it denotes the ability to retrieve and receive but also to produce such forms of communication. And, most importantly, it signals that information is but one element in a multifaceted spectrum of mediatized expressions that also encompass entertainment, interaction and performance.

KNOWLEDGE FOR WHAT AND FOR WHOM?

If it is true that we live in a knowledge society that demands multimodal competencies most of which are mediatized, then it follows that the role of public libraries and librarians is challenged once again.

Public libraries, in their physical as well as their virtual versions, are spaces that people enter at liberty and often in their spare time. In shaping new visions for public libraries in the knowledge society, perhaps this image is their most fundamental value. For it offers public libraries a unique chance of catching on to the multi-sited nature of learning in a knowledge society.

For example, for European children and young people informal sites of media and ICT learning are more diverse and more advanced than are the formal school settings (Livingstone & Bovill, 2001; Drotner, 2001). These findings imply that part of the present library public - and most of the future public - already possess a strong, informal repertoire of multimodal learning, if not collective competences.

Public libraries can build on those trends by redefining the physical libraries as informal knowledge centres and by developing their professional competences in close collaboration with other knowledge partners both in the private and public sectors. Such a development must respect the democratic principles of free access for all, principles to which public libraries are committed as cornerstones of action.

If such knowledge centres are to facilitate the development of multimodal competences demanded by the knowledge society without forfeiting the democratic foundation of libraries, then it follows that knowledge must be defined in wider terms than is the case when we speak of information literacy. As we saw, multimodal literacy encompasses both information and fiction/ entertainment, reception and retrieval as well as production and performance.

To develop that kind of knowledge involves presence in the physical library, and it involves collective learning. While digital libraries certainly must and will further and finetune individual services in future, perhaps the most decisive library challenge in the years to come is to develop the physical libraries which harbour the possibilities of collective presence and hence collective learning. Ultimately, the vision must be how to develop a synergy between virtual and physical libraries with respect for the end users' frames of reference.

The challenge facing the physical libraries is intensified by the fact that many traditional services performed there are taken over by users of the virtual libraries. When the majority of mundane services leave the physical library – and the librarian's desk – then librarians in the physical library can downplay their functions in favour of virtual services; or they can redefine their role from access and individual service provision to users and facilitator of more sustained collective learning processes.

Defining the role of the librarian as knowledge facilitator is in line with the projected function of the physical library as a knowledge centre. The librarian leaves her desk and is present amongst users; she engages in sustained processes that involve groups of users offering her professional experiences and evaluations; and she interacts with partners across disciplinary and institutional boundaries.

A good many library projects, also in the Scandinavian countries, already make important insights pointing the way ahead – as is evident from e.g. the report issued by the Nordbok project.

Strategies on Information Literacy in Nordic Public Libraries

In a sense, the issues involved in developing public libraries as informal knowledge centres in the manner sketched out above, takes us back to some of the old, yet recurring questions of library service: what is the role of public libraries in furthering civic society and citizenship? How should librarians be trained and how should they operate in their daily work in order to make the institutional ideals materialise? The answers to be found, however, belong to our own present and immediate future.

Table 1: Library Innovation and Socio-cultural Conditions

	Industriel society	*Information society*	*Knowledge society*
Aim of library use	Cultural discrim-ination (taste)→ Personal relevance of cultural choice	Universal and free access to information→ Information literacy	Universal and free use of information and fiction → Multimodal literacy
Definition of library/librarian	Cultural custodian → Cultural guide	Information disseminator	Knowledge faciliator
Definition of material/content	Material enity, physical artefact	Non-Material Process →Effec-tive, reliable infor-mation processing	Material artefacts and Non-Material Processes→ Information and fiction
Definition of user	Receiver of choice → cultural consumer	Information pro-ducer and evaluator	Knowledge pro-ducer, cooperator and cultural citizen

Public libraries can build on those trends by redefining the physical libraries as informal knowledge centres and by developing their professional competences in close collaboration with other knowledge partners both in the private and public sectors

REFERENCES

Bruce, Christine (1997) *The Seven Faces of Information Literacy* Blackwood: Auslib Press.

Drotner, Kirsten (2001) *Medier for fremtiden: børn, unge og det nye medielandskab* [Media for the Future: Children, Young People and the New Media Landscape] Copenhagen: Høst & Søn.

Kress, Gunter & Theo van Leeuwen (2001) *Multimodal Discourse: the Modes and Media of Contemporary Communication* London: Arnold.

Kuhltau, Carol C. (1993) *Seeking Meaning: a Process Approach to Library and Information Services* Westport, CT: Ablex Publishing.

Livingstone, Sonia & Moira Bovill (Eds) (2001) *Children and their Changing Media Environment: A European Comparative Study* New York: Earlbaum.

Stehr, Nico (1994) *Knowledge Societies* London: Sage.

Road Map for Development of Public Libraries in India

A.C. TIKEKAR*

1. PUBLIC LIBRARIES

In the world of libraries public libraries assume a special significance. Among the different types of libraries, public libraries are unique in their nature, objectives, scope of services and governance. In academic libraries the services are offered to the students enrolled; in special libraries they are limited to the inmates of the respective institutions. The public libraries function as a system comprising of several libraries of distinguishing nature like the National Library, State Libraries, District Libraries, Taluka/ Village Libraries. All these libraries work together in the sphere of assigned roles and responsibilities. The clientele of public libraries, moreover, can use their services for indefinite period even lifelong. "*Once a Reader Always a Reader*" is experienced only in case of public libraries. The range of clientele of a public library is vast and varied. Children, youth, elders, physically challenged; literate, neo literate, educated, scholars, persons from different vocations and professions can avail of the services of public libraries. Caste, creed, sex are no bar for the membership of public libraries. The public library services are available free of cost or at nominal charges. This unique nature of public libraries bestows on them the status of social institutions catering to the educational and cultural needs of public at large, and this peculiar status injects in them the import of developing personalities of individuals as well as the communities and countries. In view of the important role of public libraries in social and national development, it is no wonder that the international bodies like UNESCO have taken up the cause of establishing public libraries throughout the world, and framing norms and standards for their proper functioning. Public libraries are considered as the *People's Universities* and the *Sites of lifelong learning*.

---

* Retd. Professor & Librarian, University of Bombay, Mumbai

2. PUBLIC LIBRARIES SCENARIO IN INDIA

2.1 Pre-Independence

The Public libraries scenario in India during the 19th and 20th centuries is well described by D R Kalia in his article on Public Libraries appeared in "50 Years Library and Information Services in India, Ed. by M K Jain (1998). The Guidelines for Public Libraries and Systems prepared by him in 1988 for RRRLF gives in detail the authoritative data on Public Libraries in India during the time. The main revealed in them are as below:

- During 185 years of British Rule in India no remarkable progress was done in respect of establishment and development of public libraries. The British pattern of '*Local Library Authority*', granted to counties was not introduced in India. Though Municipal Corporation Acts were enacted since 1688, *public libraries* appeared as one of their responsibilities only in the 1882 Act. As this was not obligatory one the outcome was not satisfactory. On the eve of our Independence in 1947, out of 2,843 local governments in the country only 950 had established public libraries.
- The public spirited philanthropists established *Free Reading Rooms* extending reading facility to general public.
- There were *Subscription Libraries* offering facility of lending of books for home reading at cost in the form of subscription, and a refundable deposit for security of books borrowed. As a consequence, these services remained confined to urban upper classes only. The number of such libraries too was small.

2.2 Post Independence

While reviewing the public libraries scenario in the post independence era it is worthwhile to note the initiatives of Princely States like Baroda and group of individuals and the NGOs in the fields of education and public libraries aiming at the enlightenment of public at large necessary for attaining independence. The Library Movement in Baroda in the first decade of the twentieth century, the formation of the Library Associations at the State and national levels, efforts at providing training in librarianship, and establishing, sustaining and continuing public libraries not only in urban but also in rural areas ...all of these have certainly contributed to the post independence development of public libraries in India. The achievements through the enactment of Public Libraries Acts after independence are due to these initiatives taken well before independence. In Maharashtra State, the Library Development Report of Professor A A A Fyzee produced in 1940 gave way to establish a public library system in the State before and after independence. As of now, there are around eighty public libraries scattered all over the State completing hundred and more years of their useful existence.

The post independence era is marked with the establishment of the National Library of India in Kolkata (1948), Delhi Public Library as a pilot project of UNESCO (1951), K P Sinha Committee Report reviewing the status of public Libraries in the country (1959), establishment of the Raja RamMohun Roy Library Foundation (1972), enactment of Public Libraries Acts in sixteen States (1948–2008), D P Chattopadhyaya Committee Document on *National Policy on Library and Information System* (1986) and the National Knowledge Commission Report (2007), entitled *Libraries: Gateways to* Knowledge. Delivery of Books and Periodicals Act (1954,56) and taking over the financial responsibilities of a few old libraries in the country designating them as *those of national importance* played a complementary role in the development of public libraries in the country.

3. ROAD MAP FOR THE DEVELOPMENT OF PUBLIC LIBRARIES IN INDIA

A road map is a directorial design of development prepared after taking into account the changing environment and changing times. In the earlier part of the article the past and the present scenario of public libraries in India has been described in brief. The unique feature of public libraries is that they work in a system and there is an inherent hierarchy of them. The public library system evolved in India comprises of a National Library, State Libraries, Regional/Divisional Libraries, District libraries, Taluka/ Village Libraries. While preparing the road map for their development every component of the public library system entails a fresh look and improvements necessitated by the change in times and environment. Lacunae, deficiencies and road blocks, if any, are identified and removed. The scenario described above mainly reflects the situation in the last two centuries. With the advent of the 21st century dominated by Information and Communication Technology (ICT) various aspects of public libraries warrant change. They include collections, their organization for use and services. The modes and methods to be employed for fulfilling the respective objectives of them are also changing. The road map for public libraries should take note of these changes and draw a development plan accordingly.

For drawing a road map the following changes common to all the kinds of libraries in the System are indicated:

- The collections of library materials are now of both print and electronic. In this sense the 21st century public libraries are becoming *hybrid* in nature. Situations like print and digital versions of the same documents, digitally born material, CDs, DVDs, online INTERNET resources along with the printed material prevail on larger scale than earlier.

- ICT applications to the various library tasks and services are more and more desired and adopted. Libraries in the system will be computerized and their functioning will be automated.
- ICT based library tools like catalogues, union catalogues, retrieving methods like indexing, searching, consolidation of information and services like reference, and documentation entail new competencies for library and information professionals.
- The management of libraries will have to be modernized in terms of adopting e-governance, marketing techniques and devising suitable strategies for making the management more reader/user friendly. The old restrictive rules and regulations of the library will have to be changed to suit the new environment.
- The role of a public library is changing from '*A Temple of Learning*' to '*A Knowledge Centre*'

ROAD MAP FOR LIBRARY WISE DEVELOPMENT

3.1 National Library

The National Library of India has a long past. In the compendium of proceedings of International Conference on National Library Services (ICONLIS)[2] brought out in 2004 the centennial assessment of the National Library of India was made by various authors. The major observations useful for the road map are listed below:-

- The National Library should function as an Apex Library of the country and discharge duties and responsibilities accordingly.
- It should function as a Leader Library of the Public Library System of the country and provide other libraries with directional guidance for their all round development.
- It should keep before it a large picture of a National Library as such, and endeavor to fulfill its obligatory, and allied objectives in full.
- From among them some specific are Bibliographical control of Indian Publications, strengthening the special subject national collections and also the three designated libraries receiving Indian publications through the DB Act. For a cent percent collection of the material not only the Awareness campaigns be held but the special drive to obtain gaps be launched. A special effort be made to procure e material by amending the DBA. These collections be processed, organized for use and made available to public at large.
- Some areas so far not undertaken like formulation of norms and standards for the proper functioning of all types of public libraries in the System, establishment of a *Centre for the Book* for promoting reading habit among all, after the pattern of that established in the Library of Congress, US in 1977, be attended to.

- With the adoption of ICT linkages/portals be established for making available the material in the collections of other libraries outside the country, useful for Indian studies and researches.
- The concept of *Virtual Library* be introduced and monitored so as to increase the use of old material lying unused in several public libraries in the country.

3.2 State Central Libraries

State Central Libraries (SCL) are next to the National library in importance. They are established by State/UT governments through Public Library Acts or without them. They are the top libraries in the State Public Library System. A publication (2003) '*Status of State Central Libraries in India, An Analytical Study*' authored by Dr. R Ramasamy[3], offers authoritative information helpful for drawing a road map for the development of State Central Libraries in India. It is interesting to note that out of 27 SCLs 7 were established before 1947.

Based on the data collected in 1998 i.e. a decade ago only 7 SCLs out of 27 had initiated the application of ICT and that too partially. It is not a very encouraging situation as regards the Libraries supposed to be the ones leading the other libraries in the system of the State. Even after a decade in 2009 the situation of SCLs in respect of buildings, infrastructure, collections and their organization for use, services, modernization is far from satisfactory. Their development is related to the respective Govt's perspectives and priorities. The countrywide situation of SCLs, therefore, remained uneven. As an important kind of libraries in the country they need more attention in terms of finances, guidance and monitoring. As public libraries are a State subject a central body like RRRLF has to take lead in their development in the right direction.

3.3 Other Libraries in the System

This category of libraries comprise of Regional, Divisional, District, Taluka/Town and village libraries. The concept of Regional libraries was originated in the Fyzee Committee Report to meet the multilingual parts of a Province. That continued even after the formation of States on linguistic basis. Following this pattern the bigger States were encouraged to establish the Divisional Libraries as per administrative divisions of the State. Regional and Divisional Libraries are of Govt's own, and hence they are financed fully by the Govt. The time has come to review the concept of regional and divisional libraries along with their utility. They should not continue existing as weak links and not much used entities in the System.

The District and Taluka/Town libraries are the core of public libraries established and continued with the public support. It is always pointed out that they are essentially subscription libraries and not the free public libraries. As a part of the State Govt. Public Library System authenticated by legislature or otherwise District and Town libraries get stipulated financial assistance. But that is not enough to meet various expenses to be met for running these libraries. In Maharashtra four decades have passed the enactment of the Public Libraries Act, the library staff working in public libraries do not get adequate salaries and other service benefits. Their charging nominal subscription is therefore justified. To give an example of Maharashtra State again one more District library is established by Govt. itself, even though another District Library run by a registered Society recognized by the State Govt. for substantial financial aid has been functioning there for a long time. These Govt. Regional/Divisional and District Libraries are the work places of the Directorate of Libraries administrative offices and officers. The utility of these Govt. District Libraries too need a fresh look and improvement.

3.4 Rural/Village Libraries

The success of the public library movement depends much on the coverage of the vast and scattered rural area of the States and the country, by some sort of library service. Establishing a public library in an area of 10,000 habitants is an ideal situation. Some surrogate arrangements of circulation of boxes containing books, visits of mobile libraries were attempted in the past. Now a new concept of attaching a library to the community centre is emerging. The 73rd Amendment to the Constitution has empowered *Panchayats in villages* to undertake educational programmes for villagers. Public libraries are one of them. There are attempts made by States to harmonize this provision with their prevailing Public Library Acts. The National Knowledge Commission has recommended a Knowledge Centre to be established in villages extending library services too. In the din of these different approaches to the nature and functioning of village libraries much has remained to be done. A road map for public libraries must take cognizance of this and settle on an appropriate pattern of village library. It should be remembered that the village libraries are the base libraries in the public library system of States and the country. Due attention will have to be given to them lest a big chunk of population will be deprived of the desired library services.

3.5 Other Issues Related to Public Libraries

There are a few miscellaneous but important issues related to the development and growth of public libraries in the country. These are public library legislation, modernization of library functioning and services, computerization and automation of libraries, new ITC based preservation methods, scanning and digitalization of old library materials, library networking at local, state and national levels, transformation of traditional public libraries into modern ones involving retrospective conversion projects, using library software meeting Indian languages requirements and scripts, and electronic security systems. Each of such areas of expansion and development of libraries need consideration and implementation taking into account the customization factor so important to assimilate these new things effectively in the original systems. The training of the library personnel to absorb these changes well and continuing with them is also an important issue to be dealt with.

4. CONCLUSION

The Road Map for the public libraries development in India has to take into account the various kinds of libraries as existing in the library systems of the State as well as the Govt. of India's perspective of libraries in the country including the National Library of India. The portfolios of public libraries are found attached to different ministries at the State and the Central Govt. level: Culture, Sports, Higher Education, & Secondary Education. Out of over thirty State/UTs only 16 have library legislation. Only five of them have a cess facility in them. While reaching the first decade of the 21st Century dominated by e-governance and ICT applications in various service sectors public libraries cannot afford to lag behind. In the development of road map for public libraries these factors should be taken into account as well as a well harmonized path to forge ahead will have to be found out.

REFRENCES

1. Jain, M. K. Chief Ed. (1998). *50 Years Library and Information Services in India*. Delhi, Shipra Publications.
2. Kaul, H. K. Ed (2004). *National Library Services ICONLIS 2004*. Kolkata, The National Library.
3. Ramasamy, R. (2003). *Status of State Central Libraries in India: An Analytical Study*. Delhi, Gyan Publishing House.

Connecting School and Public Libraries: Need of the Hour

MOORTTIMATEE SAMANTARAY*

1. INTRODUCTION

The best ways to improve the quality of education is to make it respond to the demands of the society, to usher in the social change, development and to do away with outdated social practices. At the time of birth, human infant is just a biological organism with only animal needs and impulses. He knows nothing about the society or social behaviors. Human child has an innate capacity to learn and to communicate social institution like the community, peer group, school etc. The need is to educate the human child to be a responsible and useful member of the society. The learning to live in society is the process of socialization. The characteristics of socialization is a lifelong process, it enables to enact certain roles, helps in inculcation of principles, values and symbols of the social system. Again, socialization can be divided into primary and secondary. The basic physical needs are primary needs, whereas need for learning skills to earn livelihood is the secondary need. Family meets the primary needs, whereas the secondary needs of a child are met by the schools. In this modern society, social mobility and groups take place so frequently that individual's loyalty to a particular social group weakens. Several social agencies or institutions in which he or she participates viz. his /her family socialize the child, school, peer group, neighborhood etc. Family is the locus of early socialization or internalization of basic values of culture because the child is most plastic and exposed longest in dependent relationship with parents. Due to various reasons, the role of family in socialization process and education is being taken over more and more by other agencies, mainly the school.

The child also learns many things from the peer group. In modern society school system has emerged as one of the most potent agencies of

* Deputy Librarian, NCERT, Sri Aurobindo Marg, New Delhi-110016
Email: murtimati.rath@gmail.com

socialization. Besides the family, peer group and school, now-a-days mass communication such as television, radio, cinema, newspaper, books and audio-video cassettes, have become an integral part of life. These means of mass communication have a greater impact on the process of socialization and it assumes greater significance. Education helps the child to train for the future role of an adult. The children have to learn to be fathers or mothers, teachers or civil servants, shopkeepers or priests. They have to learn to be members to more than one institutional group also. The child receives informal education at family or peer group but receives formal education at school. They have a major role in changing the existing social modes. Education provides a link between the individual and the society. Education is the main component in achieving a status in the social system. The relation between education and social stratification is very complex and can only be understand in relation to the concept of social mobility. Education plays an important and dynamic force in the life of individual, influencing his social development. Education determines the levels of prosperity, welfare and security of the people. On the quality and number of persons out of our schools and colleges will depend our success to the great enterprise of natural reconstruction. According to UNESCO, education leads the social revolution. It was Lakshmana Swamy Mudaliar Commission of 1953, which made the school as a centre for teaching – learning cum activity centre. Based on Mudaliar commission report, the aim of secondary education shifted to producing ideal democratic citizens by emphasizing the all round development of the learners. A major shift in India's education policy was in 1986 when the New Education Policy (NEP) and its later modification into the programme of action (1992) targeted all children up to 14 years with quality educational provision before the start of the 21st Century. Independent India gave much importance to elementary education, which saw the enrollment in elementary schools increased from 42.6 per cent in 1951 to 94.90 per cent in 1992.

2. ROLE OF SCHOOL LIBRARY

The school library is the temple of learning, home of affection and a playground to perform. The school has been chiefly concerned with the teaching of subjects specially designed in the curriculum. Educators are aware that, learning needs to accelerated by the use of many and varied devices and materials, which include both print and non-print media, in which the library plays an important role. Collection of books pictures, pamphlets, maps, films, filmstrips, recordings and any other printed media make the library a goldmine for each teacher and learner. As a child progresses with reading, his/her curiosity is stimulated to seek answers through print, which leads him/her to visit the library. Through extensive reading, the child enables himself to make proper judgment in all lifestyles.

Thus, the use of library provides proper opportunity to explore and gain in-depth knowledge, develop a taste for reading and learn how to choose the right books to read, to absorb and widen the horizon of knowledge. Books not only teach children a few facts but also enrich their imagination, widen their outlook, develop a fact-finding attitude and train them to use their leisure time properly. The social and educational significance of books for children cannot be underestimated. The school library equips students with life-long learning skills and develops the imagination enabling them to live as responsible citizens. Books have always been a source of information, comfort and pleasure for those, who know how to use them. The habit of using books needs to be developed for the childhood. The librarian and the teacher both give the child proper instruction and direction in order to develop an independent reading habit and prepare their own projects. As a result, the child learns how to study, how to discover, how to answer and to get familiar with the contents of many books.

3. COMMUNITY PARTICIPATION IN EDUCATION

Education is a social process. The participation of community in the education process is a precondition. Schools of the past in the forms of "Pathashalas" and "Madarsas" show the link between the education and community participation. The society transmitted knowledge and skills through these institutions. However, with growing formalization and govermentalisation of education, the linkage between the community and school has sickened leading to widening gap. National educational policies have been formulated recommending active involvement of local community members in the functioning of educational institutions. The word "community" is an expression of the unity of life of a group of people. Like "community", the term "participation" is also used in different ways. In simple term, by participation means "taking part" or "involvement of people". Community participation may be highlighted for different points of views out of which participation by providing information or materials contribution is one important aspect of life.

Community participation has been translated into reality with the creation of various grass root level structures in education such as Village Education Committees, School Management Committees, Mother Teacher Association, and Parent-Teacher Association which represent both the school and the community. The community participation process helps in community mobilization and community empowerment.

4. SOCIAL ORGANIZATION OF KNOWLEDGE

Organization of knowledge includes knowledge creation, knowledge accumulation and knowledge dissemination. Knowledge can be expressed in terms of tacit, explicit, received, subjective, procedural and constructed knowledge. Knowledge can be transferred in different modes, which can be expressed in terms of information technology, migration of individuals across the globe, re-interpretation of knowledge, recorded devices and easy availability and use of ICT gadgets.

5. NEED OF PUBLIC LIBRARY

At the dawn of Indian Independence in 1947, the rate of literacy was mere 16 per cent which in 1991 surged to 52.19 per cent. It further increased to 60 percent due to the initiatives taken by the Government. In the wake of the slogan "Education for all", comes in the complimentary battle cry of "Books for All". Education is a complex affair starting from the embryo in the mother's womb and ending on the burning ground. Those, who complete their school education, are in need of continuous learning as knowledge is dynamic, tumultuous, and infinite in nature. Thus, public libraries become the centres of self-learning, continuous learning, facilitating learning at one's own pace, leisure, and intellect level. The public libraries play a vital role not only for the school dropouts but also for the school children. It is obligatory on the part of the states to establish free access to public libraries along with the primary schools. As a consequence of making education, a fundamental right, 'free unhindered access to libraries' also becomes collaterally and justifiably fundamental right to education. The public library acts as:

- The institution of the masses,
- Movement of new type of libraries and libraries system,
- Growth of the movement for awakening,
- Programmers for adult education and literacy,
- Catalyzing growth in literacy rate,
- Thrust on rural libraries and community resource center,
- Provide information services at grass root level,
- Inculcation of reading habit,
- Procurement of good books for children and women,
- Networking of rural libraries with district libraries,
- Cater to the needs of the student community,

6. PUBLIC-SCHOOL LIBRARIES CO-OPERATION

Countries like USA have established programmes for collaboration between public libraries and school libraries wherein public library system is viewed as an integral partner with schools helping students to achieve academic success. Sharing of resources and activities in both schools and public library set-up can help achieve common goals. In the times of tightened budget conditions, libraries do need allies. School libraries with limited budget feel helpless to serve the teens. On the other hand, public libraries, viewed as serving the informational, cultural educational and recreational needs of the entire community, do have funds to fill gap. The public library's primary role is to facilitate the informal self-education of the individual from the pre-schooled to the senior citizen whereas the school resource center is designed as an integral part of the instructional system, and required to plan and develop curricular with teachers and teach units of study. The school and public libraries may co-operate in the following areas.

- Collection development,
- Providing information services and instruction,
- Encouraging reading and literacy,
- Library related activities and projects;

7. CONCLUSION

Public and school libraries are the key institutions that can provide collection and services to meet the information needs of the youth. However, the pre-requisite in this regard being that planning for collection and services must be community based. Project evaluation studies must also be planned and undertaken to understand the impact of such projects on the community. For working out action plans, it is important to conduct first of all a series of studies to understand user needs. Further, co-operation, communication and collaboration between public and school libraries will improve the services and help in the implementation of educational reforms and promote and accelerate student learning.

BIBLIOGRAPHY

1. Auld, Hampton and others (2002). Combined school-Public Library facilities: opinions, case studies and questions to consider, Part 2 *Public Libraries,* 41(6), Nov-Dec., 310-16.
2. Bush, Gail. (2006). Walking the road between libraries: Best practices in School and Public Library Co-operative Activities. School Library *Media Activities Monthly*. 22 (6), February, 25-28.
3. Deshpande, K.S. and Hungund, B.B (2001). Raja Rammohun Roy Library Foundation and its role in galvanizing public library movement in India. *SRELS Journal of Information Management*. 38 (3), September, 179-200.
4. JOYS School and Public Library Cooperation special issue. Ed. by Jana Fine. *Journal of Youth Services*. 4, Spring, 3-22.
5. Kaula, P.N. (2006). Need and development of libraries in rural India. *Herald of Library Science*. 45 (1-2), Jan-April, 52-59.
6. Muir, Maya (2003). Community Connectivity Partnerships with Public libraries: Extend the Reach and expand the Resources of School Libraries. *Northwest Education.* 9, Fall, 30-32.
7. Rutherford, Dawn and Brenna Shanks. A (2004). Fantastic Team Schools and Public Libraries. *VOYA*. 27(5), December, 32-33.
8. Samantaray, M. (2006). School Library-A centre of Learning. *The Primary Teacher*, VXXXI (1-2). Jan & April, 61-65.

Public Libraries in Delhi: A Historical Study

R K BHATT[1]
MANISH KUMAR[2]

1. INTRODUCTION

Public library is one of the greatest educational, cultural and social treasures of a country. It represents the cultural and intellectual status of a community and is a mirror of the society. The Father of Librarianship in India Dr. S.R. Ranganathan defined public library as a "library owned and maintained by the public of its area for the socialization of its books and other kind of materials for free service to the people."[1] Thus, its services are free for all, irrespective of age, profession, race, sex, colour or creed. Unesco in its public library manifesto 1994 defines public library, "as a library which is established under the clear mandate of law, which is maintained wholly from public fund, which levies no fees from its users for any of its services and which is open for free and equal use by all members of the community regardless of race, colour, caste, creed, religion, age, nationality, language, status or level of educational attainments"[2]. However, the concept of public library has undergone tremendous change over time mainly due to advancement in the frontiers of knowledge, technology and the way people now think about their attitudes towards life, goals and mission. That public library is an essential organ of any modern society for its prosperity and development, is a well accepted message world over. Every country is ensuring for systematic development of public libraries and to a large extent this is also true for India. Public libraries in India are spread all over the country and state- wise these are structured as state, district, city, and village libraries. To ensure the development of public libraries in India the State governments and the Central government of India have been launching several programmes, in addition to passing and enacting the library legislation to ensure such libraries constant source of income and proper financial support.

---

1. Reader & Head, Department of Library and Information Science, University of Delhi
2. Lecturer, Department of Library and Information Science, University of Delhi

2. PUBLIC LIBRARIES IN DELHI

Delhi, being the capital of Independent India, has been truly transformed post-independence from a city of virtually no library worth its name to the pre-eminent position of a center of library and information networks. There are so many public libraries in Delhi. They are small in terms of collection, staff and services and yet to certain extent they are able to serve people from several fields. Most of these libraries function under the patronage of private bodies. Some receive grant from the philanthropic societies. Some others receive grants-in-aid from Delhi Municipal Committee or Central government. Unfortunately, no systematic attempt has so far been made to compile a list of public libraries in Delhi. Hence, this study is restricted to only those libraries which in one way or the other were located or information about them was found in the literature on public libraries in Delhi. Majority of them are managed by local bodies. Their condition, in the absence of proper financial and manpower support, is very poor but they are managing to sustain their activities. To best of our efforts, we could find out the existence of following public libraries in Delhi out of which a few have been selected for detailed description on the basis of the source material available on them. They are: Babu Purshotam Das Tandon Library; Bal Krishan Library; Bhai Vir Singh Public Library; Birla Line Public Library; Dayanand Vedic Library; Deen Dayal Upadhyay Smark Samiti Library; Delhi Muncipal Corporation Central Library; Delhi Public Library (Sarojini Nagar, New Delhi); Desh Bandhu Chittranjandass Library; Desh Hitaishi Public Library; Dr. Zakir Hussain Memorial, Educational and Cultural Foundation Library; Dyal Singh Public Library; Fatehpuri Muslim Public Library; Gita Bhawan Sabha; Guru Nanak Foundation Library; Hardayal Muncipal Public Library; Harish Chandra Public Library; Jain Public Library; Jain Sarva Janik Pustakalaya; Kafia Public Library; Kalicharan S.D. Library; Katra Neel Public Library; Kayastha Reading Room and Library; Marwari Public Library (Chandni Chowk); New Delhi Municipal Committee Library; Nanhamal Jain Public Library; Rachna Path, Bapu Library; Raghumal Vedic Public Library; Rama Krishna Mission Library; Ramana Kendra Library; Saini Public Library; Sardar Vallabhbhai Patel Public Library; Shri Jawahar Lal Nehru Public Library; Shri Mahavir Jain Public Library (Chandni Chowk); Sriram Natak Sankriti Mandal Library; Swami Ram Tirath Mission Library; and Vardhavan Public Library,

3. THE MARWARI PUBLIC LIBRARY

Delhi, even in the past, was agog with trade and commerce. Marwaris form an important segment in this commercial activity. Although there is some evidence to indicate the Marwari movement eastward towards Shahdara in the early 19th century, Marwaris not only continued to inhabit the walled city but also inhabited Traevelyanpur a residential area carved out by Charles Trevelyan out of his estate in 1840's. Marwaris had grown to be an affluent community by the turn of the century. Their community participation in organized social activities reflected a concern for social welfare. It was in 1915 that the Marwari Library, the first library of any type established through community awareness in Briish India, was set up by a Marwari Seth Kedar Nath Goenka in the Chandni Chowk area of Delhi. What is often ignored is the fact that the establishment of this library not only marked the onset of a real library consciousness, if not a movement, but also that this was a true public library opened as a public institution with no governmental funding. It seems the financial resources of the library have, since its inception, been drawn from donations of the Marwari patrons. It is unfortunate that this historically important library of the early 20th century is in a precarious condition seventy-five years after its establishment. With more than 50,000 books,[3] mostly in Hindi the library caters to more than 300 members and researchers scholars who find mines of information in its several collections. The yearly allocation at present is rupees one lakh of which half is contributed by the Government and the rest is raised through donations from the prominent Marwaris.

4. THE HARDAYAL MUNICIPAL PUBLIC LIBRARY

The Hardayal Municipal Public Library of Delhi is one of the oldest public libraries in Delhi. Although initially it was not meant to be a public library, later, it has grown into a big public library system in Delhi. Previously known as the Hardinge Library (Delhi), renamed as the Hardayal Municipal Library. It was set up in 1862 and housed in a portion of the Town Hall. With a small set of books and other reading material, the library later shifted to the Honorary Magistrate's Court, where the present Pension Cell is situated[4], and it remained there till 1916. Now it is housed in a separate building. High officials of the British Government used to come to the Institute for about five years. During that time, since the Suez Canal was not in existence, ships from England to India used to traverse round the Cape of Good Hope. It took 7 to 8 months to reach India. As a result, British officers used to carry a large number of books for their voyages, which were later handed over to the Institute. This collection was eventually known as the Institute Library. It is evident from the accession number on a book in its holdings that the Institute Library as such started functioning in 1862. The building of the Institute which now houses the Town Hall was constructed during 1861 to 1866. In 1902 the Library was named the Delhi Public Library and a librarian was appointed to look after its management. An event in 1912 had its influence on the growth and development of this library. On December 23, 1912 Lord Hardinge, mounted on an elephant, was passing in a procession through the Chandni Chowk, when some members of the Ghadar Party threw a bomb. Although Lord Hardinge survived, his body-guard died. It was then that some 'elite citizens' of Delhi raised a fund to construct a building for the Delhi Public Library. The

Library was, thus, shifted to this building, which was named as the Hardinge Library Building in 1916. It was, thus, the people started calling it the Hardinge Library. In 1942 the Delhi Municipal Committee in an agreement with the Hardinge Library Management Committee agreed to provide hundred percent grant with the condition that the word 'Municipal' be added to its name. It was after this that the library's name was changed to the Hardinge Municipal Public Library. In 1970 the library was rechristened as the Hardayal Municipal Public Library after the famous freedom fighter and intellectual Lala Hardayal.

Over a century of its history the Hardayal Municipal Public Library has grown to be one of the major public libraries of Delhi. With about one lakh fifty thousand books, out of which about ten thousand books have been categorised as rare collection of the library and are kept in the 'Rare Books Section' of the library. More than five thousand of the books in its collection are those which were published before 1850,[5] and there are a large number of those that were published before 1900. The library also has about 400 manuscripts in its collection. According to information collected from the Librarian, the yearly allocation of the library is about Rs. 50 lakh including the funds for the branch libraries in different municipal wards.

5. THE DELHI PUBLIC LIBRARY

After the Second World War, international organizations, especially the United Nations Educational Scientific and Cultural Organization (UNESCO), entered the field, propagating the idea of' fundamental education', which aims at stimulating and guiding the people in the under-developed regions of the world to economic progress, and then accompanying and sustaining that progress. Its aim is "to help people to help themselves.[6]. This idea became popular in independent India, and the UNESCO is active in many areas of the literacy campaign..

In 1955, the UNESCO began a project to aid in the production of reading materials for South Asia. The project area included Burma (now Mynamar), Sri Lanka, Iran, Pakistan and India. Financed by the regular UNESCO budget as well as by the technical assistance funds, its activities were to help the improvement of book production and book distribution. While its primary aim was to stimulate the production of materials for the neo-literates, it did not envisage the neo-literate in a stationary position, but "aimed at establishing his reading skill so that literacy did not remain his goal by only a means to reach better ends[7].

The Delhi Public Library was, thus, established in 1951 by the Ministry of Education, Government of India, with financial and technical assistance from the UNESCO as a Pilot Project. Started as a small unitary library in old Delhi, it has since developed into a premier Public Library System in the metropolitan city of Delhi. Delhi Public Library has a network of Zonal Libraries, Branches & Sub-branches, Resettlement Colonies Libraries for weaker sections of the society, Community Libraries, Deposit Stations, Sports Libraries, Mobile Library, Braille library for blinds, etc. spread all over Delhi. The library is well stocked with collection of over 14 lakh books in Hindi, English, Urdu, Punjabi & other Indian Languages—almost all subjects are represented in its collection. The Delhi Public Library is also one of the 4th recipient libraries under the provision of Delivery of Books & Newspaper (Public Libraries) Act 1954. The Library provides free library services to the residents of Delhi. Circulation of books is one of the major activities of the library. The library offers services to children and also organizes cultural activities such as lectures, debates, exhibitions etc. Some of the outstanding features of the library activities are services to Blind, Prisoners and offers Mobile Library service also. Delhi Public Library is the biggest Public Library System and was the busiest Public Library in South East Asia

Now the library has approx.14 lakh books and other reading materials in almost all subjects and Delhi Public Library had started automation of library activities in the year 1995 by installing computers. From the year 1997 onwards Computer Division has started creating Database of books received under D B Act using CDS/ISIS Software. Up to November 2007 about 38650 records were created in English Language and 26918 records in Hindi language. It is governed by the Delhi Library Board and is fully financed by the Ministry of Culture, Government of India.

It has been providing free library service to the children and adults, irrespective of any distinction of caste and creed. It is the only organization in India which is actively concerned with the production of reading materials for the newly literate adults. In fact, one of the functions of the library is to provide service for the neo-literates living in Delhi proper and in the outlying areas of the Union Territory. In 1952, it started the production of prototype reading material and since then it has published about forty booklets written in simple language. According to Jogesh Misra, it also aims at providing "information on the problems of public library service for other parts of India and for Asia generally.[8]

Thus, the Delhi Public Library has been making rapid strides as a centre for dissemination of knowledge and culture. It is increasingly felt that the library should not merely serve as an efficient centre for lending of books but should grow as a living organism, devoted to promote intellectual quests, a sense of belongingness among the readers, and motivated by a deep sense of social commitment. Although the Delhi Public Library is doing well as far as the public library and its functioning is concerned, yet it is unfortunate that after four decades of Independence, Delhi is still awaiting the legislative measures for the growth and development of public libraries, especially when it has a very important and significant place in the nation as the epic centre of political, cultural, educational, and research and development activities.

6. RAGHUMAL VEDIC PUBLIC LIBRARY

The Reghumal Vedic Public Library was established in Delhi in 1915 and its managed by a trust. The stock, exceeding 25,000 volumes, has a concentration of sanskrit and vedic literature, though books in other languages in all subjects are also represented. The library's reading room is open to all, loan is restricted to registered members only on a nominal subscription of Rs.50/-.per annum The funds of the library are drawn mainly from the proceeds of the Trust Property, besides the grant-in-aid from the Municipal Corporation of Delhi. The library receives donations of books and money from philanthropists.

7. THE FATEHPURI MUSLIM PUBLIC LIBRARY

This library was established in 1928 as a library for the school attached to the mosque in Fatehpuri, and caters to the requirements of the Muslim community of the locality. It is managed by the Delhi Wakf Board. The stock of books, exceeding 16,000 volumes in Arabic, English, Hindi, Persian and Urdu, specializes in Islamic culture. The reading room facilities are free but loan facilities are restricted to registered members on a very littlel subscription.

8. SHRI MAHAVIR JAIN PUBLIC LIBRARY

Shri Mahavir Jain Public Library and Reading Room is another example of private philanthropic action. The Jain Sahitya Sadan (Jain Literacy Society) established a library at Chandni Chowk for popularizing literature on religion, particularly on Jainism. The stock of the library exceeds 30,000 books and bound volumes of periodicals and includes 453 manuscripts and 91 current serials. About 350 readers visit the library every day, they consult, 20,000 books and borrow 18,000 books every year. The total budget of the library is about Rs. 15,000. The library has a very good collection of rare literature on Jainism. It is popular because it is centrally located and is housed in a place of worship.

9. RAMA KRISHNA MISSION LIBRARY

Rama Krishna Mission is situated at the Ramakrishna Asharam Marg, New Delhi. It has a library where average daily attendance of the readers in the Reading Room is 310. It also has a lending section for the benefit of borrowers. Its collection has exceeded 45,000. There is a separate section for the children in the library. This library also caters to the spiritual studies. The annual grants-in-aid received from the New Delhi Municipal Committee was Rs. 5000/- and from Municipal Corporation of Delhi it was 10,000/-. The Reading Room receives 15 newspapers and 106 periodicals annually. It has now an MOU with the University of Delhi and caters to the needs of the undergraduate students as a undergraduate library of the Delhi University Library system.

10. DELHI MUNICIPAL CORPORATION LIBRARIES

The Delhi Municipal Corporation organizes nearly 25 small libraries and reading rooms in different parts of the city. This is done as part of the social education programme.

11. GITA BHAWAN SABHA

Hauz Khas Enclave, has a library attached to it. It receives annual grant of Rs. 5,000 from Delhi Administration and has a collection of 16,000 volumes.

12. NEW DELHI MUNICIPAL COMMITTEE LIBRARY

NDMC serves its readers through a mobile library and receives an annual grant of Rs. 1,50,000. It also has a library section for the children for which the annual grant is Rs. 1,50,000.

13. OTHER LIBRARIES

In addition, following public libraries need a brief description due to the role they are playing in the promotion of education, learning and literacy in Delhi. These are the British Council Division Library and American Information and Resource Centre (earlier known as American Centre Library).

13.1 The British Council Division Library

The British Council Division is the division of the British High Commission in India which deals with cultural affairs and technical co-operation. It represents Britain in the arts, sciences, and technology. The main aim of the Council is to find, and enlarge, common ground between Britain and India. Accordingly it seeks:

- to make and maintain technical co-operation projects in science, technology, medicine, education, agriculture, fisheries, management, coal, power;
- to make and maintain academic links between the British and the Indian universities;
- to establish structured programmes of specialist, scientific and professional exchange between Britain and India;
- to provide information about Britain, British books, and British resources;
- to bring British art, film, drama, music, and dance to India; and
- to provide special support for the English literature studies in India.[9]

The British Council provides a wide range of library and information services through its network of four British Council Division regional libraries at Delhi, Bombay, Kolkatta and Chennai and nine British libraries at Ahmedabad, Bangalore; Bhopal, Hyderabad, Lucknow, Patna, Pune,

Ranchi, and Thiruvanthapuram. These libraries are run jointly by the Council and the Indian Council of Cultural Relations. The British Council Library at Delhi has a rich collection in the fields of literature, history, and science. The types of materials in the collection include books, play-sets, and periodicals. It subscribes to about 117 current periodical titles in various disciplines such as architecture and design, books and information, computer, economic development, education, the English laugnage and literature, engineering and technology, environmental sciences, librarianship, management and mass media.

The special feature of the British Council Division Library is its in-house video educational software and film library. The library provides on-line bibliographic search service, access to the British Library Document Supply Centre, UK, current aware- ness service etc. Besides these services, it provides good reference service. It is open for general public irrespective of their caste, religion, age and sex. In other words, it is a public library managed by the British Council Division which to an extent is meeting the information requirements of the people of Delhi.

The collection of the library consists of 24000 books, 3200 children's books, 900 E-Zone books, 450 educational videos, 1500 home videos, 2800 IT books. The collection consists of books, play-sets, and periodicals. It subscribes to about 117 current periodical titles. The British Council Division Library network provides the users with access to contemporary British ideas and expertise. Membership to the Library has provided benefit to individuals in the organization as well as the organization as a whole. The Library provides access to the latest ideas in ones areas of study, in professional life and career development. If the user simply wants to read books, the Library has something for them - The Best of Books and E-resources. The network of 9 libraries provides the user with access to a vast array of resources. At the Library one can borrow books, access an increasing electronic resource collection, get information about studying in the UK, apply for a scholarship programme, or network with other professionals in area of interest.

The Library endeavors to offer a combination of online and off-line information resources designed to provide one with a holistic and comprehensive service and Online Information Resources. One can also access selected web-based online information resources from the Library. The staff helps the users to use these resources. Some of these resources one can even access from one's home or office. The library plans to introduce additional online resources. The fully automated library is designed to make one's experience in the library smooth and efficient. The online catalogue helps the user to find the book one is looking for, the automated check-in and check-out facility for the issue and return of books means no queues or waiting time. One can reserve or renew the books over phone, fax or email.

13.2 The American Information And Resource Centre Library

Another library of this kind is the Library of American Information and Resource Center managed by the United States Information Services.The United States of America (USA) is credited with establishing an American Public Libraries Network by opening a series of libraries in over 90 countries to reach the public directly to promote understanding and goodwill through diplomatic contacts. In India, the USA Government established a public library at New Delhi on November 21,1946. It is a library in the best traditions of a free public library. Anyone who walks in can become a member. At present the library has more than thirty thousand members belonging to various categories, like students, government officials, and general users.

The American Center Library celebrated its 25th birth anniversary on November 21,1971. During a span of about sixty six years of its existence, it has grown as a highly effective public library system in Delhi. The library in its early stage was housed in a single room on the first floor of a Janpath Building. At that time it could provide seating accommodation only for a few readers. It had only 3,000 books, 2,000 pamphlets, and 200 periodicals[10]. In 1951, five years after its functioning, the book collection totalled to about 6,000 volumes. To meet the growing demands, it started lending books on the pattern of United States Public libraries to bonafide members. In addition to Delhi, people living in Haryana, Himachal Pradesh, Punjab, Rajasthan, Uttar Pradesh were also served with book- lending service.

In 1952, the library moved to a much bigger building on Curzon Road, and finally shifted to its present house at Kasturba Gandhi Marg, New Delhi. The main purpose of the American Center Library is to provide information on the United States, its institutions, its history, its art and literature, and its people. The most attractive and interesting feature of the American Library is its Reference Service. Thousands of reference queries are received by the library from administrators, businessmen, legislators, writers and other class of users. The staff of the library provides prompt answers even on phone. Inter-library loan service is another major service which is found highly useful by the users of this library. Close relations with the Indian libraries in Delhi and all over Northern India allow the American Library to exchange material with other organizations. Similarly, over 90 percent of journals and newspapers received by the library are indexed properly. Thousands of copies of back issues of journals are available for use, once an article is located through an index. As many as 30 indexes available with the library enable users to locate articles on specific subjects. The microfilms and videotapes and audio-cassettes are also available with the library for viewing. It also provides photocopying service to its readers at very nominal rates.

The collection consist of American books, journals, reference materials, U.S. government publications, and think tank reports. The four Libraries in India have a total collection of about 82,721 books, 586 print periodicals with over 10,000 journals in electronic format, 2,425 videocassettes, and subscriptions to several leading American newspapers. Their resources range from general reference and circulation collections to specialized collections of business management materials, American studies. The collections address issues such as encouraging Indo-US trade, promoting economic reform, infrastructure development, sustainable development, drug abuse, AIDS prevention and reduction, human rights, democracy, the global information infrastructure, multiculturalism, American society and values, history and politics. Each thematic area is supported by books, periodicals and videocassettes. In addition to print materials, all the four Libraries in India provide access to information in several electronic formats: CD-ROMs and online databases.

The ESL Corner, a new section of the Library aims to promote the teaching of American English by providing audiovisual materials to improve spoken English and resource materials to help English teachers. Reference resources available at the American Libraries in India include dictionaries, directories, encyclopedias, almanacs, periodicals, periodical indexes, CD-ROM databases and online databases. In most cases, the reference collection is best used through a personal visit where professionally trained librarians provide customized service. However, if one cannot visit the library, the Library staff responds to research and reference queries submitted through telephone, fax, mail, or e-mail. The Library holdings can be accessed by a computerized Online Public Access Catalog (OPAC). It allows searches for materials by key words, or through several access points like author, title, and subject. The OPAC allows them to share resources among the four Libraries. This enables a book located in one Library to be easily lent to a patron at any other American Library. Presently, several commercial and government online services are being used for value-added information access. The reference librarian can access these online databases for one's information needs. Some of the subscription-based online services are: The Library also offers an extensive collection of CD-ROM databases covering a broad range of resources focused on international relations, economic development & trade, management, intellectual property rights, social and political issues, and human rights.

At present, the library at Delhi has a collection which includes 27,000 volumes, over 200 periodicals, 5 leading American newspapers and 70 videotapes. The New York Times from 1947 to date is available on microfilm. The collection focuses primarily on international relations, political science, economics, literature, the arts and sciences and technology. It has also a small reference collection on CD-ROM disks. These include "Facts on File", "Readers Guide to Periodical Literature", "USA's Public Diplomacy Query" and the "International Drug Library (IDL)" and Books in Print.

14. CONCLUSION

There was no significant development of public libraries in Delhi until India's Independence. In striking contrast, the erstwhile states of Baroda, Madras and many parts of Southern India witnessed intense activity in this regard. Lack of public libraries in Delhi during pre-Independent period can be attributed to several reasons. . First, social and political structures that had grown during the Delhi Renaissance period were destroyed during 1857 mutiny. This had caused an overall decline of cultural life in Delhi. Secondly, Delhi lacked in educational facilities, particularly of higher education, until the turn of the century. This is evident from the fact that even the solitary Delhi College was closed by the Government, no effort was made in this regard until the foundation of the St. Stephen's College, the Hindu College, and the Ramjas College in Delhi. Further, unnecessary delay until 1922 in the establishment of the Delhi University lends weightage to this argument. Thirdly, the attitude of administrative authorities was also responsible for delay in establishing Public libraries in Delhi. This is because we do not see manifestation of any attempts on the part of the Administration to bring in library legislation to promote public libraries in Delhi and at a time when Delhi had already been flourishing into a big centre of trade and commerce with large population to sustain. Fourthly, a proper library movement, as we witness its occurrence in many other parts of India, lacked in Delhi. The result was that Delhi did not have any public library except the Marwari Library and the Municipal Library. Considering this very fact, just after Independence Dr. S. R. Ranganathan submitted a Draft Bill to the authorities of the then Delhi Administration. However, no action was taken on it. Again, in 1954, P. N. Kaula drafted a Delhi Library Bill which was approved by the Delhi Library Association. The Bill was forwarded to the Delhi State in December 1954 for presentation to the Delhi State Vidhan Sabha. This Bill was discussed and accepted by the Law Committee appointed by the then State Government in 1954. Unfortunately, before the Bill could reach the State Vidhan Sabha, the Vidhan Sabha itself was abolished under the provision of the States Reorganization Act on the November 1, 1956[11]. Since then Delhi has been awaiting to have library legislation so that a system for public library network in the real sense could be established in Delhi. However, after independence, the political leadership, decision makers, policy makers and educationists unanimously were of the opinion that the overall development of this country, in accordance with comparative standards, can take place only if due consideration and priority is given to the development of educational sector and the libraries. This had later resulted into phenomenal growth and development of schools, colleges and universities in India.

REFERENCES

1. Mangla, P B. (1983). Public Library Law in India. *Journal of Library and Information Science*. 8(1), 7
2. UNESCO. Public Library Manifesto. 1994.
3. Ghosh (S K). (1990) Public Libraries a Painful Sight, *The Hindustan Times*, 27 June.
4. *Ibid.*
5. *Ibid.*
6. UNESCO. *Fundamental Education, Description and Programme, Monographs, on Fundamental Education*, No. 1, Paris; UNESCO, 1949, p. 15.
7. Sen (N B). ed. (1965). Development of Libraries in New India, Delhi, New Book Society of India, p. 82.
8. Misra, Jogesh. *History of Libraries and Librarianship in Modern India*, p.102.
9. The British High Commission, British Council Division, India. Cultural, Educational and Technical Co-operation, Delhi, 1992, p. 2.
10. American Center Library: Information Activities, Delhi, 1991. (a pamphlet)
11. Mishra (Jogesh). Op cit. p. 102.

Role of Raja Rammohun Roy Library Foundation in Improving Knowledge base in Rural India

M. SANKARA REDDY*

1. INTRODUCTION

Information like the other universal phenomena—land, sky, (light) fire, water and air—is a fundamental resource. Homo sapiens sans information are barbarians, information without mankind is a myth, and information is created by man and utilized by man. It is unimaginable to utilize the other resources without information resource. Mankind through its journey of a millennium or two had many paradigm shifts in their development. Information alone kept the man on the highest pedestal of civilization. The use of more and more information and for more and more purposes and more and more times made the man to bring about overall development on the earth. Today there is a dichotomy among the people as 'the information rich' and 'the information poor'. This is reflected in the uneven growth and development of the countries as well as of communities within the countries. Hence it is proven fact that the information is an important resource for the banishment of poverty, disease, illiteracy, misunderstanding and wars in the world.

The body of information in the universe has not been the creation of one person or one community or one country. It is a cumulative wealth of the mankind. It is therefore rightly said by Karal Papar that the mankind lives in three worlds—physical, mental, and the information world. The unlimited wealth of information is generally beyond the reach of every ordinary person among all the communities in the world. Therefore, today's slogan is that all men should have access to information at all places at all times. Public libraries are the gateways as stated in the UNESCO-Public Library Manifesto for accessing information. Oral communication has

* Member, Raja Rammohun Roy Library Foundation, Kolkata, Email: sankara reddy@rediffmail.com, University Librarian (Retd) Potti Sriramulu Telugu University, Hyderabad - 500 004, A.P. India

limited reach and it is like writ on the water. It is not sustainable information. Information received at the educational institutions is only basic one and limited in character because of the limitation of the academic programs and courses, whereas the public libraries of all kinds provide unlimited body of information for lifelong learning and education.

2. PUBLIC LIBRARY SYSTEM IN INDIA

During the British rule in India, libraries were completely neglected since the authorities presumed that the libraries are the centers of sedition and breeding grounds, of revolt against their rule. Even after 60 years of India's Independence libraries still have not grown and developed in the way as they should have been in a democratic set up. The position of academic libraries, except the school libraries, is a little better because of UGC's efforts. The public library system was completely neglected. Education and libraries are like two eyes but the Constitution of India had done injustice in the case of public library system. Education and public libraries were originally classified in the Constitution as State subjects. Later the Constitution was amended and the subject education was shifted into Concurrence List. It means that the Central government can act on the matter of education and allocate funds for subject areas in the Union and Concurrence Lists of powers. The State Governments which have to look after the public libraries have treated them on a very low priority. It is evident from the legislation enacted in the states for the public libraries system during the last sixty years. Out of 36 States and Union Territories around 16 States only passed library legislation and the remaining states like Uttar Pradesh, Madhya Pradesh, Punjab, Jammu and Kashmir have yet to pass it for the development of public libraries. India is a sub continent with 3,336 cities and towns and 5,57,137 villages with only 49,757 villages libraries. It amounts to only 9 per cent villages having public libraries and the remaining 91 per cent are without village library service. Nearly 85 per cent of India's population resides in rural India, and these are the people who are involved in agricultural production. They form the backbone of the national economy as India is an agrarian state. Not only are they economically poor but also poor information wise.

The village community consists of various sections like farmers, horticulturists, labor, gold smiths, craftsmen etc. In their daily activity they require knowledge both old and new to shift themselves from less productive areas to better productivity areas to meet their increasing needs. Taking an example of a farmer in a village, he would require latest information on different crops, seeds, fertilizers, pesticides, labour, weather and marketing. Without information on these areas the farmer is left high and dry. The different schemes and concessions as given by the Central and State Governments and banking institutions are not reaching to the farmers living in the remote villages as they are not aware of it. The information should reach the village folks as they are creators of wealth. The public library system should be geared to reaching the unreachable to provide knowledge.

With the advent of the computer technology, and Internet, telecommunication, networking can make information available from one corner of the world to the other within no time. The governments should seize this opportunities and make a paradigm shift in their planning and vision for taking information to all sections of people at all levels. Many reports by the committees appointed by the state and central governments stressed the importance of the information. It is a mandate on the part of authorities to implement. Dr. Damle[1] in his work entitled '*Communication of Modem Ideas and Knowledge in Indian Village[1]*' stated that "the problem of communication of modern ideas to 5,57,137 village of India is a central one. Rural roads are being built to bring into contact with the outside world. The All-India Radio has taken major programme of placing community radio sets in village centres and giving them most important programs. Yet thousands of villages are still untouched, and most of them are gradually coming into contact with the programme agencies". To quote one another such report by Archarya Rama Murthy entitled "*Towards Enlightened and Humane Society*" (1990) stated "In the backward areas

Fig: The Hierarchical Position of the Public Library System generally in Vogue in the Country

Minister In-Charge Public Libraries
↓
Library Council
↓
Directorate, Public Libraries
↓
State Central Library (Maintained by State Government)
↓
Divisional Libraries (One in each Revenue Division)
↓
Maintained by State Government
↓
Local Library Authorities
↓
District Central Library Maintained by LLA
↓
Branches of DCL in each Town
↓
Block Central Library of Rural Areas
↓
Villages Libraries as Branches of BCL
↓
Book Deposit Centers

including SC, ST habitats a network of linked libraries should be of bicycle borne mobile libraries or para schools based libraries should be brought under implementation. Theses libraries need to be enriched with creative children's literature. While the children's literature would be primarily in the regional languages, efforts should be made to increase the availability of the children's books in the local dialects or languages spoken in educationally backward areas".

3. ESTABLISHMENT OF THE RRRLF

The public libraries all over India are in pathetic condition. Their progress is not at par with the progress of the educational institutions. The State Governments are not providing adequate funds for the growth and development of the public libraries in spite of the library cess imposed by some of the State Governments. In order to set right the situation the Government of India has various options before it. Instead of taking the entire responsibility for the development of the public libraries, the Central Government opted for a lesser burden by creating the RRRLF. The RRRLF was created by the Central Government in 1972 on the occasion of the bi-centenary of the birth of Raja Rammohun Roy for "supporting and promoting a network of libraries, which could carry books and inculcate reading habits to the remotest parts of the country". Raja Rammohun Roy was a social reformer and a founding father of the Indian Renaissance. The RRRLF was inaugurated formally on May 20, 1972 at the campus of the National Library, Beelvedere, Kolkota, with a goal to ensure library facilities for all people living in both urban and rural areas. The Foundation had laid down 29 objectives for its operation. The most important one are:

- To promote library movement in the country;
- To enunciate a national library policy and to work towards its adoption by the Central and State Governments;
- To help build up a national library system by integrating the services of National Libraries, State Central Libraries, District Libraries and other types of libraries (children's academic and special) through inter-library lending system;
- To propagate the adoption of library legislation in the country;
- To provide financial and technical assistance to libraries;
- To establish in the country Regional Library Service Centers which will offer reprographic and book preservation services to assist in the reproduction and proper preservation of reading material, whether printed or in manuscript form
- To maintain a national register of qualified librarians and their fields of specialization;
- Generally to take all such measures as may be found necessary form time to time to promote library development and its utilization in the country.

Prof. S. Nural Hasan, the then Minister of Education, Social Welfare and Culture stressing the objectives of the RRRLF in detail at the inaugural function stated that "The primary objective of Raja Rammohun Roy Library Foundation will be to stimulate the library movement in India by enabling the various State and Central libraries to carry out their functions more effectively. The Foundation will make special efforts to ensure that new libraries are set-up in all districts where they do not exist and that district libraries are enabled to serve a chain of libraries in the rural areas so that these come within the reach of the common people. This would mean the setting-up of mobile units spread all over India, especially in rural areas. The mobile units will carry reading materials for the purpose of education, as well as for entertainment. The foundation will also pay special attention to the needs of children and the handicapped persons. In other words, it is going to launch a multi pronged movement in order to give a fillip to the dormant library service in the country".

The Government of India in order to implement and supervise the objectives stated above established a Directorate of Libraries in the Ministry of Culture. The RRRLF during the last 35 years had initiated many programmes for the establishment and development of public libraries in the country. The foundation had assisted about 35,000 public libraries all over the country during its 35 years of operations. Some of the important programmes initiated are:

- Enactment of library legislation in States and Union Territories.
- To evolve the national public library policy.
- Survey of the conditions of the public libraries.
- Aid to establish the public libraries in the country.
- Provision of matching grants for purchasing and distribution of books directly by RRRLF to the public libraries in the country.
- Aid for the construction of building and purchasing furniture and other requisites.
- Modernization of public libraries by applying ITC and automation.
- Pursuing the DPLs to open separate sections for women and children, physically handicapped, blind etc.,
- Arranging annual lectures on public libraries in various parts cf the country.
- Assisting Library Associations, LIS Departments, and NGO's to conduct conferences, seminars, workshops etc.,
- Announcing the best libraries awards.
- Training and retraining the library personnel working in public libraries.
- Encouraging research on public libraries issues and problems.
- Publications of Grandhana, RRRLF news letter and other publications.
- Establishment of four zonal offices in four parts of the country

3.1 Library Legislation

The RRRLF since its inception has been persuading and insisting on the State governments to enact public library legislation. Due to its efforts the public library legislation has been enacted in West Bengal (1979), Manipur (1988) Kerala (1989), Haryana (1989), Mizoram (1987), Goa (1994) Gujarat (2003) Assam (2005-2006), Orissa (2005) and Uttar Pradesh (2006). Still it is continuing its efforts to convince the State governments in the remaining states and union territories to enact the public legislation in the country.

3.2 National Policy for Public Libraries (NAPLIS)

The UNESCO in its publication *"Guidelines on information policy'*, insisted its member states to publish their policy for public libraries. The Government of India appointed a committee in 1985 under the Chairmanship of Prof. D.P. Chattapadhaya for drafting comprehensive NAPLIS[2]. The Director of RRRLF was the convenor of the committee and helped it in formulating its recommendation. The draft policy was submitted to the Government and the RRRLF has been pursuing the Government of India to adopt this policy on par with the National Educational Policy[3], the National Science Policy, and the National Industrial Policy etc. The Draft policy is still pending with the Government of India. It had recently appointed a Knowledge Commission to review the entire scenario in the country and submit its recommendations on public libraries. The Commission had submitted the report.

3.3 Survey of RRRLF on Public Libraries

The RRRLF established four Zonal Offices in the four zones of the country. The Administrative Officers in the Zonal Offices who are professional's in Library and Information Science regularly visit all the public libraries in their zonal jurisdiction and inform their Headquarters about the state of affairs on public libraries. Further the RRRLF recently got a survey conducted on the state of conditions of the public libraries by a private organization viz. A.C. Neilson Org. Marg Pvt. Ltd. The report stated that only 49,757 villages have libraries, out of 5,57,137 villages in the country. This reveals that only 9 per cent villages are having public libraries and per captia income incurred on public libraries is only Rs.0.07ps. The RRRLF based on the AC. Neilson Org. Marg report classified the States into three categories namely 1) Lagging 2) Developing 3) Developed. So the RRRLF from time to time either directly or through agencies has been conducting surveys on the public libraries in the country. *The Neilson Org.Marg Survey Report* pointed out the following perceptions towards RRRLF initiatives by the libraries

- Majority of the libraries perceived that the RRRLF schemes are instrumental to solve the problems faced by the public libraries.

- Different categories of respondents perceived that the RRRL Initiatives are the only effort in it's nature for the betterment of the public library system in the country.
- Substantial number of respondents perceived that the beneficiary library would run into deep trouble in case the RRRLF stops assistance.
- Majority advocate that RRRLF should increase assistance and take more initiatives
- Substantial number of respondents perceived that the RRRLF needs to communicate their schemes more explicitly to the beneficiaries, so that they can avail them depending upon their need and eligibility.

3.4 RRRLF Initiatives for the Establishment of Public Libraries

The RRRLF- has been pursuing the state governments to give priority and to provide funds for the establishment of public libraries in more and more villages. It provided funds for purchasing land, construction of buildings and also acquisition of required furniture. Through the efforts of RRRLF several villages libraries were established in the villages with its financial assistance to the states. The Foundation has taken long strides in promoting library services in the country. It has been spending more than 35 crores annually for the growth and development of the public libraries in the country.

3.5 Matching Grants to the States

The RRRLF provides matching grants to every state annually for purchase of books, furniture, and computers etc. If a State government gives 50 per cent of the estimated expenditure, the RRRLF provides the remaining 50 per cent of the expenditure. The RRRLF provides assistance for the following programmes of the public libraries.

- Assistance towards organization of seminars, workshops, training courses (orientation/refresher) awareness programme and book exhibitions.
- Assistance towards supply of storage and display materials and reading room furniture.
- Assistance towards development of Rural Book Deposit Centers and Mobile Library Services.
- Assistance to public libraries for increasing accommodation.
- Assistance to public libraries to acquiring TV-cum-VCP sets for educational purposes/computers for application to libraries.
- Assistance to voluntary organization providing public library services.
- Assistance to children's libraries and children's section of general Public libraries.

- Assistance towards organization of seminar/conference by National level organizations.
- Assistance to libraries towards celebration of Golden Jubilee year/ Platinum Jubilee year/Centenary year/125 year/150 year/175 year and the like.
- Assistance towards collection and compilation of library statistics through official and non-official agencies.
- Assistance towards establishment of the RRRLF children's corner.
- Assistance towards development of District Youth Resource Centers.

3.6 Aid for Construction of Building for Public Libraries in the State and Union Territories

State governments in general lack finances for the development of public library infrastructure. Building for a public library in villages is an important component. Philanthropist have been coming forward to give land for the construction of library building in the villages but the Directorate of Public Libraries are not in a position to meet the expenditure for the construction of the library buildings. RRRLF has come forward to extend financial assistance in such cases. A village library without a building is a difficult proposition. Besides the district sub-divisional and town libraries, the RRRLF has been sanctioning Rs.4 lakh for each rural libraries. During the period 2007-2008 the Foundation released building grants to 128 public libraries in the country involving an assistance of Rs.327.09 lakh. Hence, the RRRLF program to aid the construction of public library buildings is a laudable one.

3.7 Modernization of Public Libraries

The interface of computer technology with the communication technology made the flow of information easier and faster. The networking of public libraries has become essential. In order to bring the latest information to the doorsteps of the clientele, the modernization of public libraries has become inevitable. The RRRLF realized the lack of automation in public libraries. In order to fill in the gap, the RRRLF came forward to provide computers to all State central libraries (SCLs) and district central libraries (DCLs). It wants to network the SCLs and DCLs in the first phase. It also proposes ultimately to cover and link up all the public libraries, mandal libraries, village libraries and book deposit centres with the DCLs, SCLs. It aims to establish a network of Indian public libraries on the model of Jannet in England so as to satisfy the ever increasing thirst for knowledge and easy access to information by the clientele in the rural communities. The modernization of the public libraries in the villages will enable rural communities to have access to information. It is desirable to establish a photo digital library to help the public libraries."

3.8 Opening New Sections or Reading Corners in Public Libraries

The RRRLF after making various surveys realized that certain sections of rural communities like women and children have not been provided sufficient opportunities for their reading needs in public libraries. Women are important in family development. The neglect of these two sections in the rural communities would weaken the democratic foundation of the Indian society. The RRRLF has been insisting and also financing the public libraries to open separate sections for woman and children in public libraries. These sections are to be provided with required collection of books and information material. This would result generally in improving the reading habits of rural children and women. The RRRLF during the financial year 2007-2008 released Rs.32 lakh for establishing the children and women sections in the public libraries.

3.9 Annual lecture program

The RRRLF arranges annual lectures in various parts of the country in order to create the public library culture and awareness which is lacking at present. These lectures impress on the people on the importance of public libraries among the educated for life long education.

3.10 Assisting LIS Associations and NGOs

The RRRLF assists all library associations at national and state levels to hold conferences, seminars debates, and workshops on library issues. Such debates and discussions among various other things create the importance of public libraries, village libraries and community information centres in the society.

3.11 Instituting Awards for the Best Public Libraries, Best Librarians and Fellowships

The RRRLF has been giving awards annually to the best public libraries and the best public librarians to motivate the library professionals to render positive services to the people. This provides a sense of enthusiasm in the library staff to provide more and more services to the rural people.

3.12 Training and Refresher Courses to the Library Personnel

Grants are provided by the RRRLF to the Directorates of public libraries in the states to conduct refresher training courses to update the skills of the professionals in the modern technology.

3.13 Encouraging Research Programs on Problems and Issues on Public Libraries

The ultimate goal of the governments in the democratic countries is to establish an information society or a knowledge society. As stated by J.S. Mill that the worth of the State, in the long run, is the worth of the individuals composing it. The RRRLF strives through its different programmes to improve the knowledge of people and the social fabric. It provides funds for conducting research on public libraries. The young and experienced professionals are provided with grants to carry out or to conduct research on public library issues. The feedback enables the RRRLF to reorient its programmes and plans.

4. CONCLUSION

The RRRLF is the only national agency undertaking pogrammes and activities for the growth and development of public libraries in India. It is anxious to establish public library network for enriching knowledge base in rural community. The RRRLF hopes to establish libraries in backward areas, tribal areas and forest and hilly areas in order to bring the illiterates, and innocent people into the main stream of public life. The RRRLF has many splendid programs and plans. But its financial budget is scarce and limited. The Government of India should provide RRRLF at least 5 to 10 per cent of its annual budget for the development of public libraries in the country. Public libraries-should be considered as important as the educational institutions, like schools, colleges and universities. Public libraries are the gateways to information. According to the UNESCO Public Library Manifesto the establishment of public libraries, community information centres is mandatory on the part of the government. Given the poor state of public libraries in the States, the RRRLF should impress on the Central government to bring out a National Public Library Policy document at the earliest. The national policy alone can provide the direction and guidance for the overall development of the public libraries in the country. The establishment of public library network is already delayed in India. The county has already come to witness the emergence of Banks Network, Railway Network, or the INFLIBNET for the academic libraries, but there is no such network for the public libraries in the country. The programs of the RRRLF should be reoriented so that public libraries come to the reach the people at the grass root level and more explicitly.

REFERENCES

1. Damle, Y.B. (1955). Communication of Modern Ideas and Knowledge: In Indian Villages, Poona: Deccan College.
2. India: Human Resource Development, Ministry of— (1986) National Policy on library and information system; A presentation (Chairan: D.P. Chattopadhyay) New Delhi; Committee on National Policy and Information system (Mimeo).
3. India Human Resources Development, Ministry of—(1990) towards an enlightened and humane society Report of the committee for review of National Policy on education (NPE) 1986 (Chairman Ramamurti) New Delhi, The Committee.

BIBLIOGRAPHY

1. Acnielsen Org-Marg Pvt Ltd (2004). Evaluation study of states of public library with reference to the services of RRRLF, Final report, Kolkota (mimeo)
2. India. Planning Commission, New Delhi (1984). Report of the working group of the planning commission on modernization of library services and informatics for the Seventh Five Year Plan 1988-1990, New Delhi, Planning Commission.
3. Kaul, H.K. (2004). Role of public libraries as knowledge centers in modern society (paper presented at the Raja Ramamohun Roy Library Foundation National Seminar, 14Ih February 2004) (mimeo).
4. Mcarthur, Tom (1986), Worlds of reference: Lexico graphs, learning and language from the clay tablet to the computer, Cambridge; CUP
5. Mahapatra, P.K. and Thomas, V.K. eds (1996). Public libraries in developing countries; status and trends (Dr B.P. Barua Festschrift Volume) New Delhi; Vikas publishing House.
6. Raja Rammohun Roy Library Foundation, Kolkota (2008). Agenda; 73rd meeting of the Foundation, January 21, 2008 Kolkata: The Foundation (1993)
7. —Books for the Millions at their Doorsteps "Information Manual" 5th Edition, 1997.
8. —Memorandum of Association and Rules" 2nd ed, 1972.
9. —Two Decades of the Foundation, 1972-1992, Kolkata; The Foundation.

Public Library Legislation in India: Need, Evaluation and Impacts of the Existing Acts

VELAGA VENKATAPPAIAH*

1. INTRODUCTION

Public Library Legislation was originally conceived in Great Britain, and later enacted in countries like USA, Germany and in developing countries like Ceylon (now Sri Lanka), India. Dr. S.R. Ranganathan was responsible for library legislation in this country. He drafted the Model Public Libraries Act as early as in 1928, and pursued it vigorously till it was enacted and implemented. It will be surprising to note that the then Assembly made good number of modifications in the Model Act of Dr. Ranganathan and the Act was eventually passed. Dr. Ranganathan wrote a book on *Library Legislation - Hand Book to Madras Library Act (1953),* lamenting therein the situation with regard to lack of public library legislation in the States. In all, 18 States have passed the Public Library Act during 1945-2008. Of these, the princely State Kolhapur was merged in Maharashtra, after States Reorganization in 1956, and Hyderabad Public Libraries Act 1955 was merged in Andhra Pradesh Public Libraries Act in 1960.

Table 1: Indian States that Passed Library Act: 1945-2008

1	1945	Kolhapur	10	1999	Haryana
2	1948	Madras	11	1993	Mizoram
3	1955	Hyderabad	12	1994	Goa
4	1960	Andhra Pradesh	13	2001	Gujarat
5	1965	Karnataka	14	2001	Orissa
6	1967	Maharashtra	15	2005	Uttaranchal (Now Uttrakhand)
7	1979	West Bengal	16	2006	Uttar Pradesh
8	1988	Manipur	17	2006	Rajasthan
9	1989	Kerala	18	2008	Bihar

* 4-54-49, Ithanagaram, Tenali 522 201, Andhra Pradesh, Ph. 08644-228585

As of now, out of 28 States and 7 Union Territories in India, only 16 States have passed Public Library Act, but only 6 States have implemented it as yet. In Madhya Pradesh and Pondicherry library legislation is still under process. The others have yet to take initiative in this regard. Delhi is rendering public library services through Delhi Public Library System. But Delhi can hope to do better provided it mandates to have library legislation and pass it for the State.

The public library serves as a local information centre making the sources of knowledge readily available to the public. Public libraries hold the potential to stimulate neo-literates, semi-literates, non users to become readers, and serve the population with knowledge and information. Public libraries are also perceived as local gateways to national and global knowledge.

2. NEED FOR LIBRARY LEGISLATION

A public library is the "People's University". As per UNESCO Public Library Maniesto (1994), 'freedom, prosperity and the development of a society and of individuals are fundamental human values'. These values can be attained through well informed citizens, shaped through utilisation of public libraries. Education including the provision of free public libraries, is the responsibility of the Government at national, state and local levels.

India has by now established good number of public libraries maintained by local bodies and voluntary organizations, and some libraries through subscriptions. But these libraries could not come up on modern lines. In modern times, public libraries must provide services with certain standards, and with an objective of reconstruction and development of a society. These objectives cannot be achieved only through individual munificence. A library service on sound lines requires library legislation and to get a perennial source of income. Library leaders, public men, and scholars, have realised that the only way to establish and develop a public library system is through public law. Pioneers and men of vision like Edward Edwards, Dr. S.R. Ranganathan and many others spared no efforts to bring about library legislation in their respective countries. The public library manifesto emphasizes that "Public Library is the responsibility of local and national authorities. It must be supported by specific legislation and financed by national and local governments." So, if a public library is to be maintained permanently with uniform standards, integrated library service with properly laid out network of library system, a simple executive order of the State Government will not be enough as executive orders cannot generate finances. With the ever growing needs, and the escalation in prices, the task of financing will become more and more difficult in th near future. Finance as needed for the services will be possible only with a State Legislation and library cess. In brief, the main reasons for passing public library legislation can be summed up as under:

- It will constitute a proper administrative and supervisory body with executive powers essential for smooth functioning of the library;
- It will provide a well organised library system for the State, district and up to the remote village level with free access to all citizens;
- It will provide a steady and permanent source of finance;
- It will help to maintain standards in library service;
- It will be obliged to meet the objectives and remain accountable.

3. STATE POLICY FOR LIBRARY AND INFORMATION SERVICES

As per the Constitution of India, the subject of Library services forms part of the State List whereas the subject of education is a part of Concurrent List. So, it is obligatory on the part of the State Governments or Union Territories to enact laws for library legislation. The States must frame policy for public libraries before passing any Act and implement policy through statutory provision, Public Libraries Act. The developed countries had adopted this procedure. The Public Library Manifesto also stressed that "a clear policy must be formulated, defining objectives, priorities and services in relation to the local community needs". The state policy for Library and Information Services should cover the following areas:

- A public Library should render service freely to all members of the community, without any discrimination.
- The Public Libraries shall serve the community in the following order of priority: Illiterates and neo-literates, semi-literates and the participants in non-formal education programmes; people pursuing self-education, people interested in self-employment schemes; semi-skilled; children and young; casual readers, housewives; and higher education and research etc.
- For arranging free access to information they should act as Information Centres. They should provide access to all citizens for all types of information at all levels, provide information on local enterprises, associations and local interest groups, develop local histories, develop community information services, utilise the services of National Informatics Centres and introduce computer skills for achieving speed, accuracy and efficiency in service.
- The public libraries in a developing society should preserve cultural heritage, provide access to all forms of cultural expression, make efforts to foster inter cultural dialogue, favour cultural diversity and support oral tradition.
- A federal country like India needs a two-tier Public Library System in a State, that is, one at the State level as an apex body and the

other at the District level for spreading its activities to the village level with necessary infrastructure.

- The State Government/U.T. will formulate a comprehensive book selection policy for public libraries in the State. The public libraries should acquire all kinds of documents including the multimedia.
- In case of human resources, the Government should constitute a State Library and Information Service Cadre including Sub ordinate Service unit for this purpose. Recruitment rules for the said service and conditions of service shall be subject to the provisions of the Article 309 of the Constitution of India.
- Through library legislation, the State Government/U.T. will impost library cess like educational cess, as surcharge, on all possible items such as, house tax, property tax, vehicle tax, etc., as per the local conditions.
- The Government will encourage the libraries maintained by local bodies, youth organisations, voluntary agencies, Mahila Mandals, etc.

4. MODEL ACTS/BILLS

Considering the issues accepted in the draft State Policy of Public Library and Information Services, it is felt necessary to have comprehensive library legislation in each state and union territory. Over sixty two years, six Model Public Library Acts in India have been drafted on different occasions.

Table 2: Model Acts/Bills

Title of the Act	*Author*	*Year*
Union Library Bill State Level	Dr. S.R. Ranganathan	1951
MODEL LIBRARY ACT	Dr. S.R.Ranganathan (Revised number of times)	1928 to 1972
Model Public Libraries Bill	Ministry of Education, Govt. of India	1963
Model Public Libraries Bill	Planning Commission, Govt. of India	1963
Model Public Library and Information Services Act	Dr. V. Venkatappaiah Sponsored by Indian Library Association	1989 Revised in 1995 & 09
Indian Public Library Association A Model for Twenty first century	Dr. S.R. Ijari	2007

5. MODEL LIBRARY AND INFORMATION SERVICES ACT

In the wake of recent development in the country such as, New Panchayat and Municipal Acts, after amending the Constitution in 1992 as well as keeping in context the UNESCO Public Library Manifesto of 1994, Total Literacy Campaign, making information available at all levels is the emerging necessity. Model State Act needs the following essential components.

- State Library and Information Service, based on a State Policy.
- Constitution of State Library Authority at the apex level with Minister or Libraries as Chairman, as Policy making and executive body.
- Formation of Directorate of Public Libraries for streaming the administration.
- Constitution of City, District Library Authorities for rendering service from district to village level.
- Provision for a network of Public Library and Information Service from state level to village level.
- Constitution of the State Library and Information Services.
- Collection of Library cess on house tax and property tax, entertainment tax, professional tax, vehicle tax etc.
- Constitution of State Boards for education, book production, co-ordinaton etc.
- Accountability of public expenditure and services.

6. COMPARATIVE STUDY OF THE EXISTING SYSTEM

A comparative study of the existing Acts and their impact on the systematic administration has been conducted in areas such as governance system, financial management, human resources, structure of libraries, and public

Table 3: Governance System in Public Library System

S.No.	*State*	*State level body*	*District level body*
1	Andhra Pradesh	A P Granthalaya Parishad	Zilla Granthalaya Samstha
2	Tamil Nadu	State Library Committee	Local Library Authority
3	Karnataka	State Library Authority	District/City Library Authori
4	Maharashtra	State Library Council	District Library Committee
5	West Bengal	State Library Council	
6	Manipur	State Library Committee	District Library Authority
7	Kerala	State Library Council	District Library Council (elected)
8	Haryana	State Library Authority	District Library Committee
9	Mizoram	State Library Committee	—
10	Goa	State Library Council	District Library Council
11	Gujarat	State Library Development Council	District/Taluka Library Co
12	Orissa	Public Library Council Public Library Authority	District Library Committee
13	Uttaranchal	State Library Committee	District Library Authority
14	Uttar Pradesh	State Library Council	- do —
15	Rajasthan	State Library Council	Library Admn. Committee
16	Bihar	(Information not available)	

access to libraries. In any State the overall responsibility of the organization and management of public library system lies with the State Government. It will establish Departments to assist the system.

6.1 Governance System at State and District Level

In Karnataka, Orissa, there are State Library Authorities with Minister for Libraries as its Head, with executive powers. In Andhra Pradesh and Kerala, State Library Authorities are headed by non officials. In all the other States the State level bodies are advisory in nature. Except in Kerala, the Chairman of the Committee is ex-officio, but in Andhra Pradesh he is nominated by the Government.

6.2 Financial Management

The source of income for the maintenance of Public Library system differs State to State.

The position in Goa, Gujarat, Orissa, Uttarakhand, Uttar Pradesh, Rajasthan and Bihar is more or less the same. Besides, the State Governments are granting funds under their schemes for building construction, furniture etc. Along with it, the Raja Rammohun Roy Library Foundation helps with matching and non-matching schemes every year.

Table 4: Financial Management in Public Library System

S.No.	*State*	*Income Source*	*Expenditure*
1.	Tamil Nadu	1. Library Cess 2. State Funds	1. Govt. meets establishment charges 2. Other expenditure will be met by Library Cess
2.	Andhra Pradesh	1. Library Cess 2. State Funds	1. Govt. meets establishment charges 2. Other expenditure will be met by Library Cess
3.	Karnataka	1. Library Cess 2. State Funds	1. Govt. meets establishment charges 2. Other expenditure will be met by Library Cess
4.	Maharashtra	State Block Grant	Entire expenditure will be met from State funds.
5.	West Bengal	State Funds	Entire expenditure will be met from State funds.
6.	Manipur	State Funds	Entire expenditure will be met from State funds.
7.	Kerala	1. Library Cess 2. State Grant	State Library Fund of the Kerala State Library Council.
8.	Haryana	Library cess	Entire expenditure will be met from State funds.
9.	Mirozam	State Fund	Entire expenditure will be met from State funds.

6.3 Human Resources

Library staff employed in public libraries established under the Act and public libraries owned by the government are, Government servants drawing all benefits as a Government employee. But largely, staff are very poorly paid and even the payment system is most irregular and their service conditions are deplorable.

Table 5: Human Resource in Public Library System

S.No.	*State*	*Status of the Staff*
1.	Tamil Nadu	All the staff members are Government servants
2.	Andhra pradesh	1. District Librarians are Government servants 2. Other will get the benefits on par with Government servants
3.	Karnataka	All staff members are Government servants
4.	Maharashtra	All staff members are Government servants
5.	West Bengal	All staff members are Government servants
6.	Manipur	All staff members are Government servants
7.	Kerala	Staff at State Central Library are only the Government servants
8.	Haryana	Not mentioned
9.	Mizoram	All staff members are Government
10.	Goa	All staff members are Government servants
11.	Gujarat	Not mentioned
12.	Orissa	Not mentioned
13.	Uttaranchal	Not mentioned
14.	Uttar Pradesh	Not mentioned
15.	Rajasthan	Not mentioned
16.	Bihar	—

6.4 Structure of Libraries

In all the States, where there is library legislation, the same hierarchical structure is being followed except Kerala. In Kerala, State Central Library is maintained by Government of Kerala. All other libraries are maintained with the grant-in-aid by Kerala State Library Council. These libraries including those located in District head quarters are being maintained by NGOs.

6.5 Public Access to Libraries

India is the largest democratic country amongst the commonwealth nations with a population of 102.70 crore (2001). Out of which 72.22 per cent lives in rural India and 27.78 per cent in urban areas. There are 28 constituent States and 7 Union Territories. These comprise an aggregation of about 494 districts. There are about 1650 languages. About 20,000 books, monographs and periodicals are published every year in almost all

Table 6: Structure of Public Library System

S.No.	*State*	*Structure of Libraries*
1.	Tamil Nadu	1. State Central Library 2. District Central Library 3. Branch Libraries 4. Rural Libraries
2.	Andhra Pradesh	1. State Central Library 2. District Libraries 3. District Central Libraries 4. Branch Libraries 5. Mobile Libraries 6. Rural Libraries

the 15 major languages of India and in English. Half of these are fiction. Other half covers normally humanities, with a few titles in science and technology. India imports in bulk more than 100,000 titles published in English from the international market; most of these are for educational institutions. But Public Libraries do have a sizeable share of the same.

7. PUBLIC LIBRARY SYSTEM

According to Ranganathan, "Public Library system is an integrated nation-wide network of public libraries, giving free book service to one and all of the citizens, literate or illiterate." The public library system must offer

- Access to use the libraries to all the residents including illiterates without any consideration.
- Access to reading materials with a common pool from State to Village users.
- Access to information needed by the user.
- Free facilities to have the benefits from cultural heritage, arts and scientific achievements and innovations.
- Facilities for personal development.
- Periodic evaluation and feedback of service to users and their impact on administration.
- Regulation of a financial income and expenditure to meet the needs of the society.

8. COMMON FEATURES OF LIBRARY LEGISLATIONS

In all the Public Library Acts, whether implemented or not, the following are the common features:

- A formal system in administration - State Government, District Library Authority etc.
- A structure of Libraries - State Central Library, District Central Library, Taluk/Mandal Library, Rural Library etc.

- Financial support of the State Government, either from State consolidated fund or Library Cess or both.
- Provision of grant-in-aid to NGO managed libraries.
- Accountability and transparency at all levels.

9. MISSING FEATURES IN PUBLIC LIBRARY LEGISLATIONS

- A provision of State Library Authority, with Minister of Libraries as its head with executive powers conceived by Dr. Ranganathan or in the west is missing in most of the Acts. This provision was made to certain extent in Karnataka, Haryana and Orissa Acts (2001). But it has not been implemented.
- There is no clear provision to maintain or protect or save the heritage libraries, which are in existence for one hundred years, more or less in all the States. In Maharashtra there are about 150 such great libraries.
- Service to the people in slum areas, down trodden people, people living in remote areas was never thought off. But an attempt was made in Karnataka in 2007. All these years the public library service in India remains as a middle class affair.
- In our country still there about 50 per cent illiterates. There is no clear provision in the existing Acts to help them. It is to be noted library cess or taxes are being collected from them, but spending the same for the benefit of literates. This is something unsocial.
- In the States, where the library cess is being collected in all the cities, and towns and villages, but spending the same in the cities, towns, but a small amount is being spent in villages.
- In the States, where library cess is being collected, the development of libraries is linked with the income from cess. But library cess is not at all sufficient to develop the library service at full scale. That is why there is stunted growth of public libraries in Tamil Nadu, Andhra Pradesh, etc. Of course these are better than the other States. It is to be noted there is an education cess for the last several decades. But the growth of educational facilities was never linked with the educational cess. That is only educational institutions are flourished in India. The double standard policies of the State Government must be put an end to otherwise public libraries will never be developed in this country.
- Most of the Public Libraries are still suffering from the lack of minimum facilities such as —
  - a functional building, good ventilation, lighting, furniture, fittings, cleanliness, drinking water, toilets, etc.
  - a minimum core collection of books and periodicals. The concept of core collection has not been introduced in India so far;
  - most of the staff members get inadequate, unreasonable and irregular payment of salaries and do not get covered under Article 309 of the Constitution.

This is based on my experience after visiting hundreds of public libraries all over India including North Eastern States. Andhra Pradesh has 44 formal universities and deemed universities and spending 5 to 100 crore per year, but it still has not been able to set up Public Libraries which could be compared to any Public Library of standard in the West. This is the kind of treatment public libraries are accorded by the State Governments.

10. CONCLUSION: LIBRARY LEGISLATION IN INDIA– A SUCCESS OR FAILURE

Library Legislation in India is more or less photocopy of the legislation implemented in Britain or USA. These legislations have been successful abroad but not so fully in India. More than 80 per cent of the land area in India is still not covered by public library service. Besides, public library service as available in India is quite weak. India is yet to develop public libraries as Community Information Centers or make it as part and parcel of their life, the kind of service we get to see in the West.

The main reason for India not being able to develop good public libraries may be attributed to our roots in family system. From age old days to date, by nature we want to help our children and grand children by sharing our property. Our children also expect it. So, the level of philanthropy in our families is very less. Whereas in Western countries parents will not give a single penny to their children, nor children will expect it. The boys and girls leave their parents even before the marriage, and after gaining maturity they start independent living. So, these parents in twilight of the lives decide to donate their total assets to any Public Library, School, Hospital, Old age home, and so on by establishing an endowment. Library cess is a small source of income to public libraries in the West. The governments there would not give libraries even a single pie over and above the cess. However, public libraries in the West in recent years are flooded with endowments money, which is more than sufficient for better maintenance of public libraries.

The middle class group people in recent years have started settling well. The position of universities and government employees is gradually becoming better. Industrialists and business people have improved their life style. At this juncture, they have to start thinking about the public libraries in their locality. The public should develop the habit of giving, donating money to libraries. This kind of trend, if it takes place, will help India to set up good Public Libraries.

Adult Education and Public Libraries in Punjab

M.P. Satija[1] and Kiran Kathuria[2]

1. DEFINITION OF A PUBLIC LIBRARY

A library is a system which works as a social instrument to communicate knowledge and information, ideas and thoughts embodied in books, other graphic records in print and digital form. A library is a collective or communal memory of the society. According to *A.L.A. Glossary of Library and Information* Science (1983)[1], public library is, "any library which provides general library services without charge to all residents of a given community, district or region. Supported by public or private funds, the public library makes its basic collections and basic services available to the population of its legal service area free of charge to individual users, but may impose charges on users outside its legal service area. Products and services beyond the library's basic services may or may not be provided without individual charges".

Dr. Ranganathan (1940)[2] defines library as 'a public institution or establishment charged with the responsibility of collection of books, and the duty of making them accessible to those who require them. He further desired them to undertake the task of converting every person in its neighborhood into a habitual library user and reader of books. It is usually supported by local taxes and grants from government'[3].

2. DEFINITION OF LITERACY

On its website UNESCO[4] defines literacy:

1. "A literate person is one who can with understanding both read and write a short simple statement relevant to his everyday life".
2. Literacy is not the simple reading of a word or a set of associated

---

1. Dr M P Satija, Professor, Department of Library & Information Science, Guru Nanak Dev University, Amritsar-143005,India Email: satija_mp@yahoo.com

2. Lecturer, Department of Library & Information Science, Punjabi University, Patiala Email:: kirankathuriaa@gmail.com

symbols and sounds, but an act of critical understanding of men's situation in the world.

3. Literacy is not an end in itself but a means of personal liberation and development and extending individuals educational efforts involving overall inter-disciplinary responses to concrete problems.
4. A literate person is one who has acquired all the essential knowledge and skills which enable him to engage in all those activities in which literacy is required for effective functioning in his group and community and whose attaining in reading, writing and numeracy make it possible to use these skills towards his own and his community's development.

Further it defines "Literacy is the ability to identify, understand, interpret, create, communicate and compute, using printed and written materials associated with varying contexts. Literacy involves a continuum of learning to enable an individual to achieve his or her goals, to develop his or her knowledge and potential, and to participate fully in the wider society". Literacy enables everyone to live a better life. It helps fighting with ignorance to avoid getting manipulated and being left out of the mainstream. A literate person is always confident and tackles routine problems more effectively

3. ADULT EDUCATION

Encyclopedia Britannica (1977)[5] defines adult education as, "the organized provision of facilities to enable men and women to enlarge and integrate their experiences as adults". According to *Encyclopedia of Social Sciences* (1951)[6] "adult education embraces within its meaning the following varieties of activity: continuing education, corrective education; functional-group education; and folk schools or people's colleges". For Liveright[7] adult education is, "the process whereby persons who no longer (or did not) attend school on a regular and full time basis, undertake sequential and organized activities with a conscious intention of bringing about changes in information, knowledge, understanding or skills, appreciation and attitude or for the purpose of identifying and solving personal or community problems".

For Unesco, term 'adult education' has a very wide connotation. Under it comes, "the entire body of organised educational processes, whatever the content, level and method, whether formal or otherwise, whether they prolong or relapse initial education in schools, colleges and universities as well as in apprenticeship, whereby persons regarded as adult by the society to which they belong develop their abilities, enrich their knowledge, improve their technical or professional qualifications or turn them in a new direction and bring about changes in their attitude and behaviour in the two fold perspective to full personal development and participation in balanced and independent social, economic and cultural development"[8]. Thus, both formal and informal education come within its preview.

4. DIFFERENCE BETWEEN LITERACY AND ADULT EDUCATION

Adult Education is a part of literacy movement. Both have a symbiotic relationship and are parts of the larger system. Literacy provides a minimal entry point to education and through this, access to the world of information, communication, modernization and innovation. Every adult is considered to be a productive member of the human society. He/she has to be conscious, vigilant and literate to be able to participate effectively in the affairs of the family, community and society, and in the larger affairs of the nation. Eventually, acquisition of access to literacy must help in raising the level of human awareness so that they could go beyond the barriers of their own environment and establish an effective outreach with the world. The access which begins with literacy has to be reinforced and carried forward, so that it becomes a tool of continuous up-gradation of survival skills and enables every adult member of the society to prepare and face that struggle with courage and confidence. It is in this perspective that adult literacy becomes an indispensable part of a programme of adult education for illiterates.

5. BRIEF HISTORY OF ADULT EDUCATION IN INDIA

The efforts to eradicate illiteracy have a long history in India. "Unlike the most nations around the world, there were no innovative developments in the field of Indian Adult Education during the 19th century although India had a rich oral tradition since immemorial times and was renowned worldwide for its scholars and scholarship. During the 19th century, the main thrust of adult education in India revolved around basic literacy" (*An Encyclopedia of Indian Adult Education* 1999)[9].

There had been very little progress in the sphere of adult education in India which was limited to night schools in metropolitan cities till the end of World War I. Initially night schools for illiterate adults were opened by M. Visveswarya; Dewan (Governor) of Mysore in 1912, and a network of circulating libraries in the state was also established to support the programme. To popularize scientific knowledge among the masses, a science magazine 'Vigyan' was also started by him. Besides, some of the enlightened Indian rulers of the princely States of Baroda, Travancore and Mysore felt the importance of literacy among masses and extended financial support to night schools. They also set up rural libraries.

Literacy and adult education movement in India got intertwined with Independence movement. "Adult education with emphasis on literacy started during freedom movement spearheaded by Mahatma Gandhi in 1920s in which voluntary organisations played a major role"[10].

When the Congress Governments came to power in some provinces in 1937, adult literacy and education got included among the responsibilities of the Government. Mass literacy campaigns were launched in different parts of India in 1937 by the provincial governments headed by the Indian National Congress in Bengal, Bihar, Madras, and Bombay Presidencies. Furthermore, the Indian National Congress also headed Mass Literacy Campaigns at different places in Bengal, Bihar, Madras and Bombay Presidencies. Village libraries were the product of the Indian Adult Education Movement.

To collect the information on adult education programmes from various parts of India, Indian Adult Education Society was set up under the Presidentship of an eminent educationist, Shah Suleiman. The First All India Adult Education Conference was held in Delhi in March, 1938. It appointed a provisional committee to draft a constitution for Central Organization Indian Adult Education Association (IAEA).

Before Independence, there were very good public libraries. Dr. S.R. Ranganathan prepared the ground by introducing the Madras Public Libraries Bill in the Provincial Legislature of Madras in 1948. The Government of Bombay also established a central library in Bombay and three regional libraries in Poona, Ahmedabad and Dharwar.

In January, 1949, the All India Library Conference, Nagpur emphasized that the government must pay attention on libraries and library movement to enable its reach to the masses of India. Ranganathan, in his book entitled '*Library Development Plan*'[3], drew up an excellent blue print of the Indian Library Movement in its true perspective comprising Central and State Library Legislation which was also his presidential address. He worked for a nationwide educational and library system and called it 'universal mental awareness' and demanded a library system at all levels for a growing democracy. The conference also urged the government to enact public library law in each province which is essential for establishing a network of public libraries.

Government of India realized the role of public libraries in Adult Education in the 1950s. The old Imperial Library was upgraded as the National Library in 1948 by an Act of Parliament. An International Conference on Adult Education, held at Elisnore, Denmark in 1949, also recognized the importance of contribution of public libraries and museums in adult education. "It is no use teaching people to read unless at the same time an effort is made to ensure that they have books worth reading"[11]. The crucial role of education in economic and social development had been recognized immediately after getting political freedom. And efforts to increase people's participation in education and to diversify educational programmes in order to promote knowledge and skills required for nation-building have found place in successive Five Year Plans.

6. CONTRIBUTION OF DR. S. R. RANGANATHAN IN ADULT EDUCATION

Dr. Shiyali Ramamrita Ranganathan (1892-1972) 'Father of Library Science' was a creative genius and an intellectual par excellence. He was "a doyen among the librarians, a diadem in the field of education, a renowned designer of bibliographical classification and its foundation"[12]. This intellectual giant, a scholar, a dynamic library leader, a pattern maker was a crusader of free book service for all through his works. He also stressed on the need for a system of libraries to support literacy and the adult education activities and to reach everyone, whether child or adult, man or woman, rural or urban, literate or illiterate. For this purpose, he recommended extension service in the public library to attract the readers as well as non-readers. He had a faith that public libraries have an important role to play in the progress of India.[13] He was of the opinion that "there is a wrong impression that since a library consists of printed books; it cannot be of any service to illiterates. If this be so, eighty per cent of our people will be out of bounds for our library system" (Ranganathan and Neelamaghan)[14]. In his second law of library science 'Every reader his/her book', word 'every' includes children, blind and the crippled, artisans, neo-literates, farmers, factory workers, and many more. To eliminate illiteracy through public libraries, he suggested:

- To induce and maintain the interests of the illiterate people in books and in hearing books read out, it would be necessary to read to them, not only books of a religious or recreational nature, but also books of useful knowledge dealing with their daily avocation. Latter would lead to increased efficiency in their work.
- Arranging library talks, story hours, lantern talks, dramatizations to attract illiterates, literates and neo-literates.

Dr. S.R. Ranganathan said that if "a person is illiterate, it does not mean that he has no curiosity to know or that he is intellectually under-developed. Our public library should therefore adopt special methods to serve the illiterate people"[14]. He assigned the following functions to the public libraries in the promotion of adult education:

- To read out books for illiterates and neo-literates at stated hours each day.
- To produce wall pictures and charts representing the news and the latest facts and ideas.
- To use television, radio and motion pictures which are useful in Adult Education programmes.
- To arrange for discussion among literates and neo-literates.

If he were alive today he would have surely recommended the use of Internet and multimedia to the service of adult education programmes. He also advocated for the legislation of public library services in the country. Entire credit of Madras Public Library Act 1948 goes to him. Many other states also followed him. Even after 62 years of Independence, only 16 out of 28 states have Public Library Acts enacted till now. His another contribution in convincing the UNESCO for Public library pilot project at Delhi was remarkable. At present, this library is doing well for students and adults as well. "Its extention facilities include lectures, film shows, discussion groups, children group meetings, story hours, radio and television programmes". It has a well planned children section too.

7. ADULT EDUCATION IN PUNJAB

The state of Punjab was constituted as an autonomous province of India in 1937. In 1947 it was partitioned between India and Pakistan and the eastern part of it remained as Indian Punjab. On 1 November 1956, area of PEPSU (Patiala and East Punjab States Union) were integrated to form the state of Punjab. On 1 November, 1966, under the Punjab Reorganization Act, 1966, the state was reconstituted as a Punjabi-speaking state comprising the districts of Gurdaspur (excluding Dalhousie), Amritsar, Kapurthala, Jalandhar, Ferozepur, Bathinda, Patiala and Ludhiana; parts of Sangrur, Hoshiarpur and Ambala districts; and part of Kharar tehsil. The remaining area comprising 47,000 sq. km. and an estimated (1967) population of 85 lakh was shared between the new state of Haryana, Himachal Pradesh and the Union Territory of Chandigarh. The total area of the Punjab state is 50,362 sq. km. As per census 2001, total population is 24,289,296 in which 12,963,362 are males and 11,325,934 are females. 16,096,488 (66.18 per cent) are residing in rural areas whereas 8,262,511 are residing in urban areas. The decadal growth between the decades (1991-2001) is 19.76 per cent. The density (persons per sq. km) of Punjab is 482.

7.1 District-wise Present Literacy Status of the State

Punjab stands at number 16th in literacy rate in India. As per Census 2001, total population of Punjab is 2.429 crores and the literacy rate is 69.95 per cent in which 75.63 per cent are males and 63.55 per cent are females[15]. Hoshiarpur is leading in literacy rate with 81.40 per cent literates whereas Mansa is at the bottom with 52.50 per cent literates. Except Mansa, all districts have above 60 per cent males whereas Ferozpur, Mansa, Moga, Muktsar, Sangrur, Bathinda, and Faridkot districts still have less than 60 per cent literate females. Literacy wise the districts in ascending order are: Hoshiarpur, Rupnagar, Jalandhar, Nawanshar, Ludhiana, Fatehgarh Sahib, Gurdaspur, Jalandhar, Patiala, Amritsar, Moga, Faridkot Bathinda, Firozpur, Sangrur, Muktsar, Mansa.

Literacy Rates (%) in Punjab – District Wise

State/ District	*Literacy Percentage 2001**			*State/ District*	*Literacy Percentage 2001**		
	Males	*Females*	*Total*		*Males*	*Females*	*Total*
Punjab	**75.63**	**63.55**	**69.95**	Kapurthala	78.66	67.90	73.56
Amritsar	73.58	61.41	67.85	Ludhiana	80.19	72.11	76.54
Bathinda	68.31	53.76	61.51	Mansa	59.12	45.07	52.50
Faridkot	68.92	57.09	63.34	Moga	68.40	58.96	63.94
Fatehgarh Sahib	78.85	68.60	74.70	Muktsar	65.94	50.57	50.67
Firozpur	69.55	52.33	61.42	Nawanshar	83.67	69.52	76.86
Gurdaspur	80.44	67.31	74.19	Patiala	76.13	62.94	69.96
Hoshiarpur	86.97	75.56	81.40	Rupnagar	84.43	71.74	78.49
Jalandhar	82.37	72.93	77.91	Sangrur	65.97	53.29	60.04

http://punjabgovt.nic.in/Education/LiteracyRate.htm

*Excludes children in the age group 0-6 who were treated as illiterates in the 2001 Census.

India has a plethora of education schemes to literate the masses. There seems overabundance of policies, projects and missions in India. In Punjab, Government is working under *Sarva Shiksha Abhiyan (SSA)* programme to eradicate illiteracy. This scheme was launched in 2001. The Sarva Shiksha Abhiyan, a historic stride towards achieving the long cherished goal of Universalisation of Elementary Education (UEE) aims to provide useful and relevant elementary education for all children in the 6 to 14 age group by 2010. There is also another goal to bridge social, regional and gender gaps, with the active participation of the community in the management of schools.

The Abhiyan realizes the importance of Early Childhood Care and Education, and looks at the 0-14 age as a continuum. All efforts to support pre-school learning under the Integrated Child Development Scheme (ICDS) or special pre-school centres in non ICDS areas will be made to supplement the efforts being made by the Department of Women and Child Development. SSA serves to fulfill the following objectives:

- All children in school under special programs like Education Guarantee Center, Alternate School, 'Back to School'
- All children complete five years of primary schooling
- All children complete eight years of schooling by 2010
- Focus on elementary education of satisfactory quality with emphasis on education for life
- Bridge all gender and social category gaps at primary stage at elementary education level by 2010
- Universal retention by 2010

It has been successful in bringing about a huge reduction in the number of out of school children from 320 lakh in 2001-02 to about 70 lakh in

March 2007. The enrolment of girls during the same period had increased by 19.2 per cent at primary level and 15 per cent at upper primary level. 67 lakh children are presently enrolled in flexible alternative schools (India 2008)[16]. In eleventh Five Year Plan (2007-12), Government targets regarding literacy, (wikipedia)[17] are

- Reduce dropout rates of children from elementary school from 52.2 per cent in 2003-04 to 20 per cent by 2011-12
- Develop minimum standards of educational attainment in elementary school, and by regular testing monitor effectiveness of education to ensure quality
- Increase literacy rate for persons of age 7 years or more to 85 per cent.
- Lower gender gap in literacy to 10 percentage points
- Increase the percentage of each cohort going to higher education from the present 10 per cent to 15 per cent by the end of the plan.

Every state has one central state library along with district libraries in each district. Punjab state has its central state library at Patiala city, named as the M.M. Central State Library. District (public) libraries in Punjab are working under the Director of Public Instructions (DPI) who is *de facto* the director of higher education in the state. Of all the 24 districts, Punjab has public libraries only in 15 districts including the State Central Library. Nawanshahar, and Tarantaran the newly formed districts are without libraries whereas Fazilka, Ludhiana, Moga, Muktsar also are without district libraries. However, Ludhiana, Jalandhar and Amritsar have a library each maintained by respective municipal corporations. Ludhiana has a Punjab University Extension Library which also acts as a public library. The town libraries have been formally established by all municipal committees. But strictly speaking, most of them are only reading rooms with newspapers.

The 15 districts, which have district libraries, are Amritsar, Bathinda, Faridkot, Fatehgarh Sahib, Ferozepur, Gurdaspur, Hoshiarpur, Jalandhar, Kapurthala, Mansa, Mohali, Nabha, Patiala, Roopnagar (Ropar), and Sangrur.

Library services in Punjab are inadequate by and large. Except for libraries in major towns, the rest of the libraries more or less serve as reading rooms, which are kept open for a few hours each day. The rural areas have been greatly neglected. It is unfortunate that a progressive state like Punjab has lagged behind in the matter of public libraries. Punjab is, till date, without public library legislation despite many spirited efforts[18].

Literacy and libraries are complimentary and supplementary to each other. Yet this perception is missing in India. There is lack of an appropriate system for libraries. Government is spending huge amount on literacy movements and adult education in India. We need to know whether the Government has made any effort to involve libraries in this movement, or whether library professionals are doing some activities for community at their own. Therefore, we collected information from district libraries of Punjab. For this, a questionnaire was designed to collect the information from all the district libraries in Punjab. This is an effort to know, what the libraries are doing to serve the purpose. What are the reasons and problems If these libraries are lacking in providing such services. Some of the findings of the study are given below. The analysis provides information about the district libraries of Punjab:

All the 15 district libraries including the Central State Library at Patiala have total 27 sanctioned posts of library professionals (Librarians) including 8 posts in the Central State Library itself. In some libraries, there are two sanctioned posts of librarians. At present, there are only six district libraries having one full time professional/librarian. The Central State Library has four librarians working there instead of eight (sanctioned posts). Other nine district libraries are without full time professionals. A librarian working nearby are given additional charge to manage these libraries. Scarcity of staff is a big hurdle in all these libraries, so the professional staff having additional charge despite all their sincerity are unable to do the justice with this additional work. There are two such libraries which neither have any professional, nor semi-professional. Nevertheless, Some libraries having less staff are working better than the libraries having more staff.

Forty per cent of the libraries open on Sundays. Open access to library reading material provides opportunity to the users to select books of their choice in an easy way. But some libraries do not follow the same as there are 20 per cent libraries having closed access to documents. Continuation of this practice in 21st century is really sad.

A library indeed can play an important role in adult education movement. At many places, libraries are providing the services to neo-literates as well as adult illiterates. But in Punjab state, so far libraries are not involved in literacy movement, and no library is conducting any programme for adult literacy. There is no library with trained staff in adult education tasks.

Only two, i.e. 13.33 percent libraries are providing special services to the literates, neo-literates and adult literates as helping them with reading skills. And the same number of libraries are providing services to special groups. In these two libraries, only one library is arranging services to special groups such as handicapped, farmers, housewives, artisans, children of slum dwellers. It is providing audio-visual material to neo-literates and one library is providing books to neo-literates and assisting them too. Only one library is providing user education programme for adults/neo-literates. To know which libraries are providing services to the target group and organizing senior citizen programmes, it was found that 86.67 per cent libraries are not providing such services. Libraries which are providing such services are only two in number.

To serve the majority of users, especially to cover remote areas where libraries do not exist, libraries should provide mobile library service to that area. With this service library can reach those people who cannot go to the library. But no district library is providing mobile library service in Punjab. When the libraries surveyed were asked if they are providing any other service to the literates, neo-literates, the answer was negative. There is no such library doing this.

No library is providing special services like story hours for neo-literates, the target group. To serve this community, Dr. Ranganathan has emphasized on this particular service, which public libraries can easily provide. With it libraries can attract the adult illiterates too.

NGOs and Government bodies are running various programmes to promote literacy in the country. But in the Punjab state, whatever the Punjab Government and NGOs are doing for literacy, public libraries are not involved in it. It is very unfortunate that they do not understand the potential of libraries in helping adult education programmes. Libraries have no coordination with government departments such as Public Health Department, Elementary Education, Agriculture Education Programme and Special Awareness Programme in promotion of literacy.

Public libraries in Punjab are suffering from financial crunch, too. There is no provision of earmarked funds in budgets for adult education material or such activities. No library is getting any extra financial assistance or reading material from any adult education agency. However, these agencies must work with the libraries to eradicate illiteracy.

Most of the libraries do not have the adequate reading material for neo-literates. Libraries cannot provide service to these persons without appropriate reading material. There are only 13.33 per cent libraries which have shown interest in adult illiterates and neo-literates and these libraries are helping these users to some extent. But overall, the situation is not good. Till date, these district libraries are not involved by the government in the adult education programmes. Scarcity of funds, staff and adequate reading material have de-motivated the professionals to do the work for the neo-literates. Furthermore, illiterate people as well as neo-literates need environment with adequate reading material and of course some assistance from library staff. To assist them properly, library staff needs some training, too. Trained staff can be more helpful to these users.

Neo-literates need some agency with proper reading material and personal assistance to sustain their literacy. A public library can be an ideal place for the purpose. The government should recognize importance of these libraries in follow-up programmes. These libraries with trained staff and adequate reading material in adult education can provide life-long education to masses. There is a need to enact the public library law in the state with provision of all the facilities to help and sustain adult literacy programmes. Furthermore, government agencies as well as NGOs working for the adult education and literacy movements, should work in coordination with these libraries to get better results in future.

8. CONCLUSION

Public libraries in Punjab are suffering from neglect and poor resources in terms of men and material. Only 60 per cent of the district towns have come to have libraries, but they work like any government department. Most of them are without organizational heads and almost every library is understaffed. They do not have adequate funds to buy new books. Funds are just sufficient to pay for the newspaper subscriptions. This malady is due to the absence of library legislation and low priority given to libraries by the politicians and the bureaucracy. Librarians have mostly spent their energies on securing due grades and perks than on building public library services. Public, being mostly of non-readers, does not care for libraries or their pitiable state. Given the poor state of public libraries in Punjab, library legislation is the need of the hour. Secondly, public libraries must be intimately involved in the national literacy programmes at the higher level as well as and at local level. It is critical for the success and survival of the national programmes on adult education and grass root literacy.

REFERENCES

1. A.L.A. *Glossary of Library and Information Science*. (1983). Ed. Heartstill Young el al. Chicago: American Library Association.
2. Ranganathan, S.R. (1940). *Reference Service and Bibliography*. Vol.1.Madras: Madras Library Association.
3. Ranganathan S.R. (2002). *Library Development Plan*: Thirty year programme for India, with draft library bills for the Union and constituent states, Reprint, 274. Delhi: University of Delhi.
4. Unesco. http://www.nlm.nic.in/unesco_nlm.htm (Accessed on 6th March 2009)
5. *Encyclopaedia Britannica*. (1977). Chicago: Encyclopaedia Britannica, Inc.
6. *Encyclopaedia of Social Sciences* (1951). New York: The Macmillan Company.
7. Liveright, A.E. (1959). "Strategies of leadership in conducting adult education programme, New York". In 39th All India Library Conference. Delhi: Indian Library Association, 1994, 180.
8. Aggarwal, J.C. and Agrawal, S.P. eds. (1991). *Documentation Encyclopaedia of UNESCO and Education*. Vol.1. New Delhi: Concept Publishing Company.
9. *An Encyclopedia of Indian Adult Education*. (1999). Ed. S.Y. Shah. New Delhi: National Literacy Mission.
10. Kalia, D.R. (1996). "The role of Delhi Public Library in adult education: A recapitulation". In *Literacy Campaigns and Libraries*, ed. V. Venkatappaiah. New Delhi: Ess Ess Publications.
11. Trehan, G.L.(1982). *Modern Public Library: Movement and Service in India*. Chandigarh: Library Literature House.

12. Kaula, P.N. (1993). "S.R. Ranganthan as Library Scientist and Benefactor". In Ranganathan Birth Centenary Monograph. Padamshree. S.R. Ranganathan: A Creative Genius and an Intellectual par excellence by G.L. Trehan, Girja Kumar & Others. Chandigarh: Chandigarh Library Study Circle.
13. Satija, M. P. (1987). Ranganathan and the Public Library Legislation in India. *Libri,37(3),307-320.*
14. Ranganathan, S.R. and Neelamaghan, A. ed. (1972). *Public Library System*: India, Sri Lanka, UK, USA. Comparative library legislation based on the papers and proceedings of the All-India Seminar on Public Library System, Bangalore. Bangalore: Sarada Ranganathan Endowment for Library Science.
15. Punjab: Literacy rate http://punjabgovt.nic.in/Education/LiteracyRate.htm (Accessed on 6th March 2009)
16. India 2008: *A Reference Annua!.* New Delhi: Publication Division, Ministry of Information and Broadcasting, Government of India.
17. http://en.wikipedia.org/wiki/Five-year_plans_of_India(Accessed on 07-03-09)
18. Patel, Jashu and Kumar, Krishan (2004). *Libraries and Librarianship in India*. Englewood: Libraries Unlimited.

Library Legislation in India: An Overview

NARENDRA K. BAR*

1. INTRODUCTION

There are at present 28 States and 7 Union Territories is India. All of them have their own model of public library system, structure and pattern of financial assistance. Some states have taken a step further and were successful in introducing Public Library Act for the purpose. However, when we look in retrospect at what India has done in respect of library legislation in the states especially in the context of UNESCO declaration on public libraries, we get to have a mixed but discouraging picture.

The present public library system in India is organized on hierarchical model for the purpose of integrating public libraries within the state down to village library. But in reality the state of public libraries integration is different. Even in the states that have been having Public Libraries Act for the last several years, public libraries have been found to function in isolation. Necessary linkages as envisaged under the legislation exist in select states alone. Networking has no where been applied in organizing libraries. District libraries have not been given any central library functions of centralized acquisition, centralized processing, and resource sharing.

Contrary to expectations, library service in some states is still looked after by the Education Department. Still worse, in some states multiple departments are involved in the management of public library service.

Broadly, public library services in India are confined mainly to lending and reading – room services even as the scope to expand these services is much wider. Mobile library service is found to be in operation in few cities only. Not all public libraries have the capacity to keep large stock of text books to cater to the needs of the students. Audio-visual service through TV-cum-VCRs is yet another service for reaching out to community, but very few libraries have come forward to offer this service. The library service to the handicapped and disadvantaged persons is scantily rendered.

---

* Secretary, GILA, and Head, Library and Resource Centre, Election Commission of India, Ashok Road, New Delhi 110001

Given the above depressing scenario on public libraries in India, the question that arises now is – can we ever hope to have public library system of quality in India.

2. MODEL LIBRARY ACTS

On the whole, the development of public libraries in India has been very slow. The multifarious social problems in the country such as over population, poverty, illiteracy, etc. have been coming in the way of library efforts in creating and developing library consciousness among public. The progress on library development front differs from state to state. While some states have enacted library legislation, others appear to have no intention of such sorts.

The concept of legislation for libraries has been the landmark contribution of S.R. Ranganathan. In the year, 1930 Ranganathan prepared the Model Public Libraries Act and presented it at the First all Asia Education conference at Banaras. It was revised several times and the last revision was made in 1972. In addition, India witnessed four more Model Acts/Bills drafted for the purpose.

- Model Public Libraries Bill 1963, drafted by the Govt. of India under the chairmanship of Dr. D.M. Sen.
- Model Public Libraries Bill, 1965 of the Planning Commission, which was appended to the report of the working group of the Forth Five year plan.
- Model Union Libraries Act (revised in 1972) by Dr. S.R. Ranganathan.
- Model Public Library & Information Act drafted by Dr. Velaga Venkatappaiah in 1989, was revised in 1995. This Act was approved by Indian Library Association (ILA) and was in active consideration in some states; while drafting the public library bill in those states.

3. LIBRARY ACTS IN THE STATES

The public library movement received impetus by enactment of library legislation in different states of India. These Acts were aimed at ensuring perennial funding support for public libraries, defining structure of public library system in the state, powers and functions of library authorities and such other matters relating to public libraries. So far library legislation has been enacted in following16 states:

- Kolhapur state 1945

1. Madras Public Libraries Act 1948
   Having provision for library cess (10 percent) on property tax.

* Hyderabad Public Libraries Act 1955

2. Andhra Pradesh Public libraries Act 1960

Having provision for library cess (8 percent) on lands and building

3. Karnataka Public Libraries Act — 1965
   Having provision for library cess (6 percent) on lands, buildings, vehicles and profession
4. Maharashtra Public Libraries Act — 1967
   No library cess. State government meets the expenditure
5. West Bengal Public Libraries Act — 1979
   No library cess. State government meets the expenditure
6. Manipur Public Libraries Act — 1988
   No library cess.
7. Kerala Public Libraries Act — 1989
   Having provision for library cess. (5 percent) on property tax and not less than 1 percent of state expenditure on education
8. Haryana Public Libraries Act — 1989
   Local bodies to levy library cess.
9. Goa Public libraries Act — 1993
   Surcharge on IMFL 0.50 paise per ltr. and 0.50 paise on bulk ltr. of bear and 1 percent on state education budget.
10. Mizoram Public Libraries Act — 1993
    No library cess. State governemnt meets the expenditure
11. Gujarat Public Libraries Act — 2001
    No library cess.
12. Orissa Public Libraries Act. — Dec. 2001
    No library cess.
13. Uttrakhand Public Libraries Act — Feb. 2005
    No library cess.
14. Uttar Pradesh Public Libraries Act — Sept. 2006
15. Rajasthan Public Libraries Act — Feb. 2007
16. Bihar Public Libraries Act — 2008

Eight states (Haryana, Manipur, Mizoram, Orissa and Uttaranchal, Bihar, Rajasthan & U.P.) have yet to enforce the laws though they had passed the Acts several years ago.

- After the reorganization of states in 1956, Kolhapur and Hyderabad Acts were merged with Maharastra and Andhra Pradesh states respectively.

Of 28 state and 7 union territories in the country, only 16 states have enacted Public library legislation. The remaining 12 states and 7 UTs are in the process for enactment but no tangible progress has been made in this direction.

4. STATUS OF LIBRARY LEGISLATION IN THE STATES AND UTS

4.1 Arunachal Pradesh

Arunachal Pradesh after formation as a state in 1987, the government started a State Central Library at Itanagar. There were ten district libraries, twenty three block libraries and 14 circle libraries in important areas of the state. Mobile library service was introduced in the capital city through mobile van. The state is in a developing state but due to lack of proper communication and being in remote part of the country, the library education system not yet has been introduced. No effort has been made for library legislation.

4.2 Assam

The first Public Libraries Bill for Assam was drafted by Dr. S.R. Ranganathan in 1964 as per his model. In 1977 two draft bills were submitted to the Government of Assam. One was drafted by the Assam Library Association based on Ranganathan's draft bill of 1964 with minor modifications; the other was drafted by the Assam Library Services Association (Government) on the lines of the Planning Commission's Model. It is not clearly known which draft was introduced as Assam Public Libraries Bill by the Government in Assam Legislative Assembly. Unfortunately, the Bill was lost at the final stage due to the dissolution of the Sarat Sinha Ministry. As the Assam Library Association has been defunct for more than 30 years, the newly formed Guwahati Library Association should take up the issue to create public awareness in order to move for an Assam Libraries Bill in the State Assembly.

4.3 Bihar

A draft bill was prepared and submitted to the government in the year 1973. unfortunately. this draft was lost in the floods of 1975. It was resubmitted to the government for consideration in 1979. Dr. R.S.P. Singh, Librarian, State Central Library, Patna, Prof. P.N. Kaula & Shri P.N. Joshi, librarian, Bihar State secretariat library, Patna, look great initiatives in preparing the final draft. Later the draft was forwarded to Prof. P.N. Kaula for expert advice. The State Government. constituted a three-member committee to prepare a draft of Bihar Public Libraries Bill. Dr. R.S.P. Singh took the lead and drafted the bill and submitted it to the State Government. Finally, Bihar Public Libraries Act got enacted in 2008.

4.4 Chattisgarh

The state was carved out from Madhya Pradesh state on 1st November 2000 as 26th state of the Union of India. Chattisgarh means 36 forts. There was a demand for a separate state since 1964. The development of libraries in Chattisgarh is far from satisfactory. The public libraries are facing constraints for finance and other resources. An integrated approach with provision of adequate finance and adoption of uniform standards and enactment of library legislation throughout the state regarding development of public library services is highly essential.

4.5 Himachal Pradesh

Administratively the state public library system in under the control of the Director of Education. The whole system is run by the state government as there is hardly any privately managed library system. Annual budget allocation is in the form of grants, which the state government gives and the matching grants are received from RRRLF. There is no cess or any other source of income. Dr. A. S. Chandel, Professor, DLIS, NEHU, had prepared the Himachal Pradesh Public Libraries Bill in 1982.

4.6 Jammu & Kashmir

In 1951- A Library Bill for Jammu & Kashmir was prepared by Prof Kaula. This bill was not passed by the State Assembly. Such attempts by professionals however did result in preparing the authorities for the groundwork relating to library development. In 1963 the government framed rules and regulations for managing public libraries, and named this document as J & K Library and Reading Room Rules. In 1975 Jammu & Kashmir Public Libraries Bill was drafted by M.S. Randhawa. While efforts from different quarters did not make much progress in terms of getting a public library bill enactment, these did however, resulted in the appointment of a committee with Dr. M. S. Randhawa, as chairman to look into the working of the department of libraries, and to make further recommendations in improving the same. The committee submitted its report soon after and still awaits government's approval and implementation.

4.7 Jharkhand

The new state of Jharkhand was created on 15th Nov. 2000, as the 28th state of the Union of India. The new state contains 18 districts. The state has 14 Lok Sabha seats and 81 Assembly seats. There are 5 district libraries and 4 sub-divisional libraries and 1 university library, 5 special libraries and there are some public undertaking libraries. Efforts are yet to be made for library legislation in this newly formed state.

4.8 Madhya Pradesh

Following are the numerous efforts made for public library legislation in Madhya Pradesh:

In 1946, Central Provinces and Banaras Public Libraries Bill prepared by Dr. S.R. Ranganathan.

In 1950, Madhya Pradesh Public Libraries Bill was prepared.

In 1958, Madhya Pradesh Public Libraries Bill was prepared by Maulana Azad central library committee.

In 1959, Madhya Pradesh Public Libraries Bill was prepared by M.P. Library Association.

In 1968, Madhya Pradesh Public Libraries Bill was prepared by G.D. Bhargava and V.S. Moghe.

In 1970, Madhya Pradesh Public Libraries Bill was prepared by Indore Library Association. This was the result of the 17th All India Library Conference, held at Indore. The Association authorized M.P. Library Association to push the matter further. The bill was presented to the then Education Minister, who could not get the Bill cleared.

In 1978, Madhya Pradesh Public Libraries Bill was presented by M.P. Public Libraries Association to then Education Minister, Mr. Om Prakash Rawal, but before anything could happen, the Minister was dropped from the cabinet.

In 1990, Madhya Pradesh Public Libraries Bill was prepared by K.M. Ujlambkar.

Each time the draft was forwarded and put up for the discussion in the Assembly, but the matter of passing the Library Act got postponed.

4.9 Meghalaya

As regards Public Libraries in Meghalaya State, the first Assam Government Public Library was established in Shillong, then capital of composite Assam in 1903, serving generally the state government officials. In 1956 this library was amalgamated with the state central library, established in 1954 by the composite Assam government and in 1974, the Assam portion was shifted to Guwahati as Meghalaya was bifurcated from Assam in 1970. There are also four district libraries at Jowai, Tura, Nongstain and William Nagar. Personal collection Library like Shillong Records Collection Centre Library(SRCC,1975) is worth mentioning. In Meghalaya no library legislation has been enacted.

4.10 Nagaland

Nagaland has been fortunate enough to have a central university located at Kohima. Its library is yet to be built up. There is one state central library at Kohima functioning under the Directorate of Art & Culture. Besides, there are information centers / Libraries in seven districts without qualified librarians under the publicity department. In addition, there are 108 rural libraries functioning with matching grants from RRRLF. The research library of the North East Zonal Cultural center is located at Dimapur. There is no library association in the state of Nagaland.

4.11 Punjab

Punjab Public Library system has its origin in the Punjab Public Library in Lahore. The library was managed by a committee of 23 members, appointed by Punjab Government. Incidentally, it was in this state, probably only next to Bengal, the Government has invested in establishing and maintaining village libraries, in the early decades of the present century.

Efforts towards public library legislation are given below:

In 1962, Punjab Libraries Bill was prepared by late Dr. R.L. Mittal

In 1964, Seminar was held on "A model library bill" which was circulated by the government and the bill was introduced in the assembly but nothing came out.

In 1982, Punjab Public Libraries Bill was prepared by Punjab library Association

In 1992, Public Libraries Bill was prepared on the basis of Model Public Libraries Act prepared by Dr. Venkatappaiah. Inspite of all these efforts, Punjab couldn't get the legislation enacted as yet.

4.12 Rajasthan

In 1965, Rajasthan Public Libraries Bill was prepared by Rajasthan Library Association.

In 1969, The government accepted the memorandum submitted by the Association containing the proposal of the Public Libraries Bill. The administrative department was asked to prepare the draft bill. The assistance in this regard was provided by late Sh. N.N Gidwani and Mohan Rao. The draft bill was sent to legal department for further assessment. But the result of this was the usual game of postponement. However, the bill after some more efforts finally got enacted in 2007.

In 1972, Public Library Act, Draft Bill was prepared

In 1990, Rajasthan Public Libraries Bill was prepared by K.M. Ujlambkar

In 1991, Rajasthan Public Libraries Bill, Revised draft bill was submitted

In1992, A committee was constituted under the chairmanship of late Prof. S.N. Srivastava.

After a gap of 17 years the government of Rajasthan was able to enact the Public Libraries Act in February 2007.

4.12 Sikkim

The Government of Sikkim realized the importance of public libraries and started a few libraries. But public libraries did not develop in a systematic way. Libraries in schools and colleges are in a very neglected and deplorable condition. Many school libraries and number of other libraries are managed by unqualified personnel. Collections are generally inadequate. Funds are not available for libraries. There is no library legislation and state library committee does not exist. There is poor co-ordination between the libraries at various levels.

4.13 Tripura

Birchandra State Central Library, previously known as Birchandra Public Library, founded by the then Maharaja of Tripura during first part of twentieth century was taken over by the government of Tripura in 1953. There are four district libraries, 14 sub-divisional libraries, 9 block level public libraries and a mobile library under the Directorate of Higher education. In addition all the 704 Panchayats have libraries, and Social Education Directorate has established 200 rural Libraries, receiving matching and non-matching grants from RRRLF since 1973. It is remarkable that 200 Panchayat libraries have reading room facility. The state is yet to have a library Act for regularization and systematization of the public library services. Three library associations have been trying to prepare a draft public library bill for the state to develop library service in Tripura.

4.14 Uttrakhand

The state came into being on 9th November 2000, as the 27th state of the Union of India. The new state comprises of 13 districts. The state of affairs of Uttrakhand libraries is far from satisfactory. It is lacking in quality of manpower, efficiency of services and in maintenances of rare treasures of the past. Though rich in resources, this scarcity of fund flow has dampened the library growth in the newly formed state. In February 2005, Uttrakhand Government enacted Library legislation for Uttrakhand State.

4.15 Uttar Pradesh

In 1949, Dr. S.R. Ranganathan prepared a draft library bill for Uttar Pradesh and submitted to Dr. Sampurnanand, the then Education Minister who showed keen interest in putting the library Act on the statute book. But for some reason the bill could not be enacted. In 1960, the Uttar Pradesh Library Association sent its representatives to then Education Minister to discuss library legislation for the state. Copies of new draft library bill were again sent to the cabinet ministers and to the Director of education.

In 1964, a Model Public Library Bill drafted by the Union Government was sent to the state Government for putting a library Act in the state on the lines suggested by the Model Act. But no action was taken on it. In 1971, Government of UP constituted a Public Library Enquiry committee under the chairmanship of Mr. Radha Krishan Goswamy, the then Education Minister. The Goswamy committee submitted its report to the Government along with the draft library bill. The committee also recommended the opening of library cell in the secretariat to look after the matter of Public Libraries till a separate directorate of public libraries could be set up. Accordingly the government had established a library cell in the education department in 1980. In

1981, government constituted another committee under the chairmanship of Prof. C.G. Viswanathan. The committee re-drafted the Public Libraries Bill and submitted it to the government in 1983. Since then, the U.P. library Association is persuading the state government for enactment of the library bill. A delegation of UPLA also met Mr. N.D. Tiwari (then chief Minister, UP) and apprised him about the in-ordinate delay in enacting the Public Library Bill in the State. Ultimately during the regime of Samajwadi Party government the U.P Public libraries Act was passed on September 4, 2006.

4.16 Union Territories

4.16.1 Andaman & Nicobar Islands (ANI): Though library legislation has not been enforced in ANI, the local administration, directorate of education and the Library Association of this territory have taken initiative for all round development of library services as well as to protect the service conditions and status of the librarians.

4.16.2 Chandigarh: Like many other states, Chandigarh has no library legislation and hence lacks any efforts for the concerned library development. But like many others, it has a tradition of maintaining a State Central Library. It has its own distinguishing features, including its own location in a prime place, its children's section and its mobiles library service.

4.16.3 Dadra & Nagar Havelli: The library services are under the control of Director of Education. There is no public library Act for the Union territory. The expenditure for libraries is provided in the budget of union territory under the head "Education". There is a library committee which consists of 9 official members and 11 non-official members.

4.16.4 Damn & Diu: The library services in the union territory of Daman and Diu are under the control of Department of Education supervised by the Assistant Director of Education. There are 3 municipal libraries one each in Motidaman, Nanidaman and Diu. In Daman and Diu a central library, 2 district libraries and 1 mobile library is proposed to be established in future.

4.16.5 Delhi: In 1955, Delhi Public Libraries Bill was prepared by Prof. P.N. Kaula. The bill received no takers, and hence the Act could not be passed in the assembly.

In 1964, Library Bill was prepared by Kaula and Dr. S. R. Ranganathan. This draft library bill aimed at suggesting a library development plan for Delhi state. It was accepted by the government of Delhi, but not implemented.

In1994, a Model Library Act was drafted by Dr. Velaga Venkatappaiah and the same was submitted to the then Development Minister (Sahib Singh Verma). Nothing came out in this direction.

In 1996, Dr. V. Venkatappaiah Presented the 2nd Delhi Public Library and Information Services Act with a few modifications. For a large city like Delhi, the Public library system has proved to be inadequate.

4.16.6 Lakshadweep: Lakshadweep has well organized public library system in which Lakshadweep serves as the state central library and each of the 10 constituent inhabited Islands are provided with a public library by the administration of Lakshadweep. The island libraries were earlier celled as Reading Room-cum-Library which where renamed as public libraries. There is no membership fee in the libraries. There is no separate department for public libraries in this union territory. The Public Library Act has not been enacted so far.

4.16.7 Pondicherry: The "Bibliotheque Publique" of Pondicherry established in 1827 has been renamed after the French scholar Romain Rolland, on August 27, 1967 during the birth centenary of the great scholar. Pondicherry has chain of government run public libraries headed by the Romain Rolland Library. Since 29th January 1992, the Director of Art and Culture is the Head of the Department for Library services. Pondicherry has always remained in the forefront as far as spending on libraries is concerned. Late. D.R.Kalia had reported that Pondicherry stood as number one regarding the level of expenditure on public libraries in India during 1988-89 According to him, the per-capita expenditure of Pondicherry was Rs. 2.48p. for libraries. Pondicherry has not enacted Public Library Act till date.

5. PROGRESS MADE FOR ENACTING LIBRARY LEGISLATION

The Minister in-charge of the Department of Culture at the Center has been writing to the state governments to legislate on public libraries, but it has not had any effect whatsoever. Neither has the RRRLF, Kolkata - the nodal agency of the Department of Culture, Government of India to promote and support the Public Library movement and to take the library movement to the grass-root level - been able to convince the state governments to do so. All persuasive efforts of RRRLF have failed. So far we have been providing public library service to less than 10% of the total population of the country, that too not as a modicum to the required standard. Compared to this, the Anglo Saxon countries such as UK, USA and Scandinavian countries are million miles ahead of India in the provision of public library service. It is commonly believed in India that these countries being affluent could afford to spare required funds for the provision of high-grade public library services. If we compare the percapita income of these countries with that of India and the percapita expenditure on public library services, it is to be found that India is not spending even one tenth of the amount that it can afford to spend on public libraries. Take for instance the case of Punjab, it has the second highest percapita income in India, but it spends only a paltry sum on public library services. It is not therefore only a matter of lack of resources but also lack of willingness on the part of the state governments to spend the amount, which they can very well afford to spend on public libraries.

The solution lies in placing Public libraries on the Concurrent List of the Indian Constitution, so that a uniform state library system is evolved as was done in the case of education to rectify the mistakes in the Indian Constitution.

6. NEED FOR PLACING PUBLIC LIBRARIES ON THE CONCURRENT LIST

Public Library falls into the State List of subjects assigned to states in item 12 of the State List in the 7th schedule of the Indian Constitution. The Central Government .restricts itself to limited activities in the field of public libraries with the result that the public library legislation in the country is not the same as it should be. The world over, the public library has been conceived of as a local institution and as such it is taken as a responsibility of the local government, partially financed by the state and federal governments. The Madras Act of 1948 instead of entrusting public library service to the local government created ad-hoc local library authorities (LLA) one in each district and one for the city of Madras. The LLAs were made to provide library service both to rural and urban areas. The reason given for ignoring the local bodies was that they lacked financial resources and administrative acumen.

7. AMENDMENTS TO THE CONSTITUTION OF INDIA

In 1992, the Parliament carried out two significant amendments to the Indian Constitution, by which some subjects from the State List were transferred to the List of Local Government. Constitutionally speaking, India has today 3 tiers of governments namely, Federal, State and Local government. The two amendments have turned the tables on the Madras pattern and have nullified it. The 73rd amendment to the Indian Constitution, has entrusted provision of public library services to the Panchayats and it is left to the state governments to decide whether to create a Library Authority at the district level, sub-district level or at the village level. The 74th amendment has transferred certain subjects to the municipalities and urban corporations, including the "Cultural Institutions" Public Libraries in the urban areas as well should go to the urban local governments, but the 74th amendment doesn't specifically mention "Public Libraries" in this regard.

But the State, which have already created painstakingly district library authorities over the years, are not willing to dismantle them and bifurcate public library services into rural and urban areas. The Government of Tamil Nadu has already notified in the official gazette that LLAs will not be dismantled and the Panchayats will be allowed only to maintain reading rooms. Rural libraries will continue to be looked after by the LLAs. This amounts to defiance of the Indian Constitution by the state governments. The Ministry of Culture of the Government of India has not taken any action.

CONCLUSION

Given the appalling state of public libraries in the country, it is necessary and urgent to evaluate the prevailing public library systems in 16 states through an expert committee. In 1998, RRRLF appointed a committee at the behest of Department of Culture, Government of India to revise the Model Public Library Bills drafted earlier in 1983. The committee recommended to the Department of Culture to get public library systems in 16 states evaluated to enable it to draft the Model Public Libraries Bill as per findings of the evaluation report. Late. Prof. D.R. Kalia, the renowned authority on public libraries in the country also wrote a D.O. Letter to Dr. R.V. Vaidyanatha Ayyar the then Secretary, Department of Culture, on this aspects but to no avail.

It is high time that the central government as well as state governments join hands to ensure that the country offers quality public library service to all the citizens. The public libraries should take up the new role and face the challenges and act as the backbone of *Knowledge Commission* of India. The Knowledge Commission has submitted its repot to the Government of India in 2007 suggesting a National Commission on Libraries to look after the organization, development, Modernization, IT application and networking the public library System in the country.

BIBLIOGRAPHY

1. Jain, M.K. Ed. (2001). *Library and Information Service in India, States and Union Territories.* Delhi, Shipra Publications.
2. Kaul, H.K. Ed. (2002). *National Round Table on the Modernization and Networking of Libraries in India.* New Delhi, DELNET.
3. Mahapatra, P.K and Thomas, V.K. Ed. (1996). *Public Libraries in Development Countries: Status and Trends.* New Delhi, Vikas Publishing House.
4. Mohamed Taher. (2001). *Libraries in India's National Developmental Perspective; A Saga of Fifty Years since Independence.* New Delhi, Concept Publishing.
5. Patel, Jashu and Krishan Kumar (2001). *Libraries and Librarianship in India.* London, Green Wood Press.
6. Ramesh Babu, B. ed. (2003). National seminar on new public library in the information age (Chennai, 12-13 Jun, 2003) Chennai, Foundation for Information and Communication, 2003.
7. Roy, Choudhury Prabir, Ed. (2000). *Library and Information Services in India*, Dr. S.M. Ganguly commemorative volume, Kolkatta, IASLIC.
8. Thomas, V.K. (1997). *Public Libraries in India, Development and Finance.* New Delhi, Vikas Publishing House.

Rural Public Libraries as Community and Communication Information Centres: Towards Sustainable Livelihoods

Pradip Kumar Upadhyay*

1. INTRODUCTION

India is a land of diversity with different types of terrain, various agro-climatic conditions, different levels of socio-economic conditions, and varied levels of regional development. There have been concerns about persistent rural poverty, unemployment and inequality, and resulting social tensions at grassroots level in India. The strategies and policies developed by the planners and policymakers, adopted *two approaches*: one focusing on the overall economic development (through percolation, trickle down and spread effect), and the other poverty alleviation (direct intervention). Though these two approaches *reinforce* each other, there has been *no effect* to integrate them. The most important sectors for sustainable national development are agriculture, education, healthcare, water and energy.

As per Planning Commission[1], at the beginning of the new millennium, 260 million people in the country did not have income to access a consumption basket, which defines the poverty line. Of these, 75 per cent were in the rural areas. Agricultural wage earners, small and marginal farmers, casual workers engaged in non-agricultural activities, rural women (especially women-headed households), among the others, constitute the bulk of the rural poor. The growing populations need food, clothing, shelter, fuel and fodder for their livestock.

Science and Technology (S&T) offers tremendous opportunities in the simultaneous achievements of the goals of sustainable agriculture and improving the rural livelihoods[2]. "Doubly Green Revolution" talks about

---

* Technical Director, National Informatics Centre, Department of Information Technology, Ministry of Communications and Information Technology (Government of India), Block-A, CGO Complex, New Delhi-110003(India). E-mail: pku@nic.in

"growth in agricultural production (GAP)" and "improved livelihoods" through:

- Access to land, capital and knowledge;
- Dissemination and sharing of knowledge and technologies (IPRs);
- Improvement of user training and qualification;
- Affordable and accessible technologies;
- Gender equity; and
- Improve/Enable risk/benefit assessment at national, institutional and private level.

The experience shows [Acharya[3]] that rural livelihoods can be improved in a sustainable way if the following conditions hold true: -

- Availability of appropriate technology;
- Availability of *inputs, services* and *credit* to farmer and rural families;
- Availability of market support to farmers and rural households;
- Adequate local institutions and social capital;
- Security of tenure or rights to resources;
- Absence of poor non-friendly macro policies; and
- Good governance.

Sustainable livelihood is thus a multi-faceted concept as against sustainable food security, which is a uni-dimensional concept [4].

There have been both national and international efforts (DOT Force of the UN, the UN/ESCAP Committee on Poverty Reduction, the Millennium Development Goals, PovertyNet of the World Bank, etc) to improve information flows and communication services to eliminate poverty (ICT for Poverty Reduction). Information, knowledge and communication are the lifeblood of economic and social interaction. Developing appropriate ICTs (i.e. a framework) for sustainable development and sustainable livelihoods is, therefore, essential. These deprivations are compounded at the societal level. The poor lack:

- *Access* to information that is vital to their lives and livelihoods:
  - About market prices for the goods they produce,
  - About health, and service
  - About the structure of public institutions;
  - About their rights.
- *Political visibility* and *voice* in the institutions and power relations that shape their lives;
- *Access* to knowledge, education and skills development that could improve their livelihoods;
- *Access* to markets and institutions, both governmental and societal, which could provide them with needed resources and services;
- *Access* to, and information about, income-earning opportunities.

"Networking of People" and "Networking of Information" are essential. Informatics Networks, besides Computer Networks, are increasingly considered as development tools for achieving:

- Reaching the unreached : Public Services.
- From digital divide to digital opportunities for sustainable development and economic growth.
- Fostering agricultural growth, poverty reduction and sustainable resources use.
- Sustainable development and earth care policies[5]—water, energy, education, health, agriculture and rural development, biodiversity
- A Cluster of Villages - sustainable societies in viable rural space

One of the major problems of using ICT for poor is the language barrier. Content development in local languages (more than 22 official languages and more than 1000 dialects spread over 6.25 Lakh villages) is a challenging task ahead. Grassroots level information access (contents) and grassroots level access to information (Networking) are the two essential components for grassroots level development strategies through ICT. Indian grassroots are about 6.25 lakhs villages and about 2.3 lakh panchayats—the grassroot level governance institutions.

Former President of India Dr Abdul Kalam[6] visualizes establishment of Village Knowledge Centers (VKCs) in 2.3 Lakh Panchayats *to empower* the villagers with the knowledge and to act as a nodal center for knowledge connectivity for the villagers, and also identifies a "Village Information Officer" to be "the extended eyes and ears of the villagers to the world of knowledge". The benefits of e-governance, tele-education, tele-medicine, e-commerce and e-judiciary initiatives should be reaped at, through these Knowledge centres.

Rural India thus desires to take advantage of "knowledge-intensive" techniques for its sustainable development and sustainable consumption. Community Information and Communication Centres (CICC) or e-Community Centres, as a concept and model, aim to "boost efficiency and enhance market" integration through Internet/ Intranet technologies for sustainable remote/regional development at grassroot level. In India, NICNET based "Community Information Centres (CIC)" in grassroots level in the North Eastern States (Arunachal Pradesh, Assam, Manipur, Meghalaya, Mizoram, Nagaland, Tripura), Sikkim and Jammu & Kashmir, aim to "boost efficiency and enhance market integration" through Internet/ Intranet through VSATs, for sustainable development at block level (http:/ /www.cic.nic.in).

Community Information & Communication Networks in India empower disadvantaged community for effective information & communication, in view of the stated pronouncement of "India to become Knowledge Society" and also facilitate "social inclusion" of marginalised rural poor to access knowledge and information. Through e-Community centres, rural people can obtain necessary information and knowledge that can improve their livelihoods and lead to their empowerment. However, building e-Community Centre is not only about providing ICT equipment, it is also about understanding the needs of the people who will use them, and providing locally useful content and applications in local languages (i.e. information related to inputs, services and credit to farmers and rural families, etc).

2. DIGITAL DEVELOPMENT AT GRASSROOTS: A JOURNEY STARTED IN 1985 WITH THE ESTABLISHMENT OF NICNET IN DISTRICTS OF INDIA

In India, "district" is the basic administrative unit at the sub-state level and also consistent with the decentralized planning process prevailing at the grass-root. With the establishment of NICNET in districts numbering about 439 in 1985-87, National Informatics Centre (NIC) has launched its "district information system (DISNIC)[7]" in about 27 sectors viz., agriculture, animal husbandry, education, health, industries, rural development, micro-level planning, etc., as an informatics tool for development planning and responsive administration. In the era of e-Governance at grassroots, the relevance of the DISNIC programme has been felt necessary even now, and hence the Planning Commission has desired to re-establish the DISNIC-PLAN Project, with institutional linkages at grassroot level organizations, to provide continuous support to development agencies in districts, during 2004-07. The National Task Force on Information Technology and Software Development (1998) recommended that "*DISNIC-PLAN programme should be made widespread and the database updated online should be made available to the public, the Panchayat among others*" under the Section "*Citizen IT Interface - Empowering people through the use of IT and information availability: Decentralised Planning and Implementation*".

3. WARANA WIRED VILLAGE EXPERIMENT IN 1990S: TRUE REFLECTION OF A PUBLIC-PRIVATE-PARTICIPATORY (PPP) MODEL OF NIC AND WARANA NAGAR COOPERATIVE SOCIETY IN THE STATE OF MAHARASHTRA

Another pro-poor initiative is the Warana Wired Village[8] in Maharashtra State, which has set up information kiosks in 70 villages to enable villagers to access agricultural, medical and educational information through the Internet. About 20 farmers visit each kiosk daily to access information on crop cultivation practices and schedules, quantities harvested and sold net income due to them, pest and disease control, and marketing, among other topics. All information is being provided in the local language (i.e. in Marathi).

The WARANA experiment shows that for farmers, the Internet is a better source of information than traditional sources such as traders, field officers, television, radio and the print media. By providing neutral information, this ICT service also minimizes cheating by unscrupulous traders quoting the prices of farm products. This experiment has also proved that Community-based Telecentres offered a way of providing affordable access to ICT services in rural areas.

A study was undertaken by Moni[9] to find out what type of services, as given below, to citizen are appropriate for ICT applications in governments so as to facilitate good governance at grassroots level. ICT applications in the following areas, wherein interactions between Citizen and Government (Central and State) are higher, *reinforce commitment* for good governance:

(a) Issue of Certificates (a partial list)

- Age Proof certificate
- Allotment of residential plots
- Arms license
- Birth & Death Registration Certificate
- BPL Certificate
- Bus Conductor license
- Caste Certificate
- Certificate of Widow of Ex-Service Man
- Destitute Pension Certificate
- Election Commission Identity Card
- Encumbrance Certificate
- Family Income Certificate
- Fertiliser Dealer License
- Freedom fighters Pension Identify Card
- Handicapped Person Certificate
- Income Tax Permanent Account Number
- Kerosene Dealer License
- Legal heir Certificate
- License for Cinema and Entertainment related
- License for Fair Price shops
- License for oil mills
- License for running Hotels
- License for selling and storing explosives
- Marriage Certificate
- Nationality Certificate
- Nativity Certificate
- Old Age Pension Certificate
- Orphan Certificate
- Passport
- Permanent Resident Certificate
- Permission for cutting trees
- Permission for small savings agent
- Permit for leasing ponds for fishing
- Permit for stamp paper selling
- Pesticide Dealer License
- Pharmaceutical Dealer License
- Property Registration
- Ration card
- Road Transport Driving license
- Sales Tax Registration No.
- Seed Dealer License
- State Excise Registration No.

(b) Developmental Schemes

- Central Sector Schemes
- Centrally Sponsored Schemes
- MP LAD Schemes
- MLA/MLC LAD Schemes
- State Sector Schemes
- District Sponsored Schemes under Untied Funds
- PRI Schemes
- NABARD Development Plan

(c) Resources Information

- Infrastructure Details
- Socio-Economic
- Agro-economic
- Natural resources

(d) Agriculture

- Agricultural Extension Services
- Agricultural Inputs
- Agricultural Commodities Prices
- Agri-Business
- Crop Insurance
- Production System Planning
- Region and Crop Specific Agronomic Practices
- Soil Health Card
- Credit distribution to farmers by Primary Agricultural Credit Societies
- Kisan Credit Card

(e) Animal Husbandry and Veterinary Services

- Animal Disease Information and Advisory Services
- Breed and Husbandry Practices
- Milk Price

(f) Fisheries

- Potential Fishing Zone Information

(g) General Administration

- Public Grievances Redressal
- Citizen's Charter
- Pay-slip for Government Employees
- Service Register of Government Employee
- Government Employees Personnel Information
- Government Pension Payment
- Government Tenders
- Application Forms and Procedures of Government Departments, Public sector and Cooperative sector

(h) Financial Resources

- Payment of Customs Duty, Central Excise, State Excise, VAT etc
- Payment of Direct Taxes (Income Tax, Wealth Tax, Corporate Tax, etc)
- Payment of Municipal Taxes (Property Tax, Property Assessment, etc)
- Payment of Utility Charges (Electricity charges, Water bill, Telephone Bill)

(i) Rural Economy through Cooperative Development

- E-Commerce applications in Cooperative Banks to strengthen agro and rural industries
- E-commerce applications in Primary Agricultural Credit Societies
- Registration of cooperative societies

(j) District Revenue Administration

- Revenue Recovery
- Land Acquisition
- Land Ownership Details
- Electoral rolls

(k) Industries

- Intellectual Property Rights related information to SMEs
- Agro and Rural Industries information
- Wholesale and Retail Price Details of Products

(l) Labour

- Networking of Industrial Training Institutes
- Employment Exchanges Computerisation

(m) Home Finance and Insurance

- General Insurance Schemes
- Life Insurance Schemes
- Postal Life Insurance Schemes
- Private and MNCs Insurance Schemes
- Home Finance Institutions Schemes

(n) Share Market Information

(o) Tour and Travel

- Integrated reservation of multiple Airlines, Railways, Waterways, and Roadways

4. COMMUNITY INFORMATION & COMMUNICATION CENTRE (CICC) / E-COMMUNITY CENTRES: SUSTAINABILITY ISSUES

A Community[10] is defined as "people or a group of people living in a particular local area with day-to-day problem solving and with participation in the democratic process". Information sources of relevance o them will relate to any topics that affect/impact the life of the community. Rose[11] defines Community Information & Communication Centre (CICC) as "a shared community facility, capable of servicing most of the information and the ICT (information and communication technology) requirements of the local population." It may also be called: "Community TeleService

Centre", "Virtual Village Hall", "Telecottage", "Multipurpose Community Telecentre" (MCT), Community Multimedia Centre (CMC), Community Knowledge Centre, Community Learning Resource Centre, Community Technology Learning Centre (CTLC), etc.

Turning easy accessibility into a reality, the two separate programmes of e-*Setu* and CIC (Community Information Centre) have more than made up for the lack of a 'real bridge' between the Majli island (State of Assam) and its the mainland (http://www.teriin.org/terragreen/issue53/feature.htm).

With the advent of e-*Setu*, digital opportunities initiative supported by the Government of India and UNDP (United Nations Development Programme) on the island, hazardous and time-consuming journeys to avail basic government services have been drastically reduced. The case studies related to regional knowledge sharing projects for agriculture, national projects targeted specifically at bring information to the poor, and private-public partnerships aimed at using ICT to generate not just knowledge, but income in local communities by enabling them to set up local franchises. Rose[11] identifies the following applications as "key applications" of "Community Information and Communication Centre":

- Public libraries and access to databases
- Education and e-learning
- Health services to citizens
- Services to economic agents (such as farmers)
- E-government & Citizen participation

Developments in information technology are bringing about a second industrial revolution, but the new drivers are information, data, computer and connectivity and not iron and coal. Library technology is poised to become the new sunrise sector with digital libraries dominating the information service sector while content generation is expected to boom. Information Technology, Biotechnology and Library Technology (IT-BT-LT) revolution would be the route to economic progress for developing countries. Libraries must change from "collection" orineted institution to "service" oriented organisation. The World Information report (1997-98) observes, with respect to South Asia that:

- Bulk of the population is not information dependent in day-to-day work and living;
- A large proprotion of the population cannot consume information, especially if it is delivered in written form;
- The vast majority of the population does not have the means to access information;
- People, in general, are not accustomed to pay, cannot pay, or unwilling to pay for information. In fact, information does not appear in their list of wants.
- The existing pattern of economic activities does not favour a growth in information consumption;

- The countries do not have sufficent capacity to invest in infrastructure development;

Converting "traditional' library into "digital" is essential for self sustainaed growth. The future is undisputedly "digital" and concern has been expressed elsewhere on the effects of digital restructuring in deepening economic, political and social inequalities[12]. Rural poor are now being treated as a resource, whose ideas and experiences form an integral part of the development strategy[13]. According to Dr. Julius Nyerere[14], the former President of United Republic of Tanzania, "Knowledge is not a way to escape poverty. It is a way of fighting it".

5. PUBLIC LIBRARY AS COMMUNITY INFORMATION AND COMMUNICATION CENTRE AT GRASSROOT LEVEL: A MUCH NEEDED STRATEGY

Libraries are considered as the pillars of the democracy and society's memory. Libraries preserve the culture and knowledge of the country. They serve communities as cultural and educational centers – known as 'knowledge institutions'. The cities and urban areas are well identified by the modern library buildings. There are about 4 lakh School Libraries, 18,000 University/College Libraries, and 13,000 R&D Libraries, 56000 Public Libraries (which include 51000 at village level), 35 State Libraries and about 526 District Libraries functioning in India. This means that only 8.4 per cent of the villages have Pubic Libraries in India. Networking of these Government Libraries and converting them into "digital Libraries" will be the step towards India becoming a Knowledge Society[15]. These libraries should take the shape of "Community Information Centres", which should serve as the backbone of "Literacy Mission and Poverty Alleviation". The need of the Library Science is to "empower the people" to improve their working cultures to better their livelihood. Mehra and Ramesh[16] suggest a library-community convergence framework (LCCF) to extend the role of all libraries to participate more fully in community action and enhance their function as proactive catalysts of social change, as compared to a sometimes perceived role of bystanders and highlights deliberations about the involvement of public libraries in their local communities. Indian Libraries and Information centres can be dividied into five sub-sectors: national, academic, special, government and public. It is a fact that both the government and public librray sectors are responsible for library and information sector development. According to International Fedration of Library Associations and Institutions (IFLA), there should be a one public Library for every 3000 persons[17]. Rural libraries lagged behind in the application of ICT. But the library technology is poised to become the new sunrise sector with digital libraries dominating the information services sector, while content generation is booming. Rural Public Libraries are also a part of this revlotuion. Rural libraries, as a concept, exist in India. Professor Chatopadhyay Committee on National Policy on Library and Information system (NAPLIS) (1985) recommended to establish, maintain and strengthen "free public libraries" and in particular, "the rural public library". There have been noteworthy developments for "Libraries and Information Systems Development for Rural Areas" in India, since its independence:

- Advisory Committee for Libraries, 1957
- Public Library Acts in States
- Establsihment of Raja Rammohun Roy Library Foundation
- National level Associations:
  - Indian Library Association (ILA)
  - Government of India Library Association (GILA)
  - Indian Association of Special Libraries and Information Centres (IASLIC)
  - Indian Association of Teachers of Library and Information Science (IATLIS)
  - Society for Information Science (SIS)
  - Association for Government Librarians and Information Specialists (AGLIS)
  - Librarians Cultural Forum
  - Medical Library Association of India (MLAI)
  - Association of Agricultural Librarians and Documentalists in India (AALDI)
  - State Level Associations (A.P Library Association, bengal Library Association, etc)
  - Joint Council of Library associations in India (JOCLAI)
- Delhi Public Library (1951)
- Delivery of Books (Public Libraries) Act 1954 – A mandatory provision for all publishers to send one copy each of their publications to national Library at Kolkata, Connemera Library at Chennai, Asiatic Society Library at Mumbai (and the fourth one was to be delivered to Central Reference Library at Delhi)
- Chatopadhyay Committee on National Policy on Library and Information System (NAPLIS).
- National Knowledge Commission (NKC)

Various Organisations, who played a prominent role in building the rural Library movement in the country, include:

- Raja Rammohun Roy Library Foundation
- Rajiv Gandhi Foundation
- Indian Library Association
- Indian Public Library Association
- Andhra Pradesh Library Association
- Bengal Library Association

A framework for building Community Information Networks in India combining Public Libraries will empower the community for effective information communication, in view of the stated pronouncement of "India to become Knowledge Society". This will facilitate "social inclusion" of marginalised rural poor to access knowledge and information. Rural Digital Libraries will sustain Community Information & Communication Centres, as citizens, business, local governments, and public institutions like schools and libraries take part in the information economy. The goal is to increase the capacity of the community to adapt to a rapidly changing 21st century society and to use technology to solve increasingly complex community challenges. There have been popular suggestions that the public libraries in urban as well as rural areas should be converted to modern community information centers, which could serve as the backbone of Literacy Mission and Poverty Alleviation. The basic infrastructure for rural ICT initiatives includes: electricty, telephony and network connectivity.

6. DIGITAL LIBRARY SERVICES: A PARADIGM SHIFT AND A STEP TOWARDS SUSTAINABLE RURAL LIVELIHOODS

Digital information needs to be achieved and preserved for future use. Digital libraries are not the "Digital Equivalents" of the present day library. Digital library is a new instrument, which can spread the knowledge nearly at the speed of light.

Convergence of print medium, databases and telecommunication has led to the advent of the electronic content industry. The Content industry has come to mean various commercial and non-commercial activities relating to the bibliographic, textual and statistical databases as well as the information, education and entertainment materials in the electronic form including audio, video and multimedia forms. Considering the vast global and domestic market, the content industry has a potential to grow to a size comparable to the computer software industry with enormous opportunities for income and employment generation. Content development being an integral part of any information system, the content industry is recognised as a priority sector for lending and according the same benefits for purposes of promotion and development as given to the software sector.

Connectivity is strength, connectivity is wealth, and connectivity is progress. For enabling knowledge connectivity, in rural areas, it is necessary to have a comprehensive plan for developing new infrastructure for extending the digital library services in regional languages. Large and effective digital libraries are to be built during the 21st century to make "India, a Knowledge Society". Upadhyay, Moni, and Vijayaditya[17] felt necessary to accelerate content creation and development industry in India, and discussed key issues in digital content development and management (viz., migration from traditional to digital, maintenance, interoperability, universal access, localisation, private participation, sustainability, legal & copyright issues, digital divide, standards & formats, and meta data).

Most of schools and colleges are located across the country in rural areas. They lack better communication and transportation infrastructure. These institutions turn out lakhs of students every year. Majority of the students are not even capable of purchasing reference basic textbooks and are mostly dependent on the obsolete/old textbooks. The teachers are really handicapped with the current knowledge due to lack of accessibility to knowledge source. There is need for equitable development of the country through uniform distribution of the natural and ICT resources. These difficulties can be overcome if the Indian libraries Viz., 4 Lakhs School Libraries, 11000 University/College Libraries, and 13,000 R&D Libraries, 56000 Public Libraries (which include 51000 at village level), 35 State Libraries and about 526 District Libraries become the part of "digital library" movement and form the nodes of "Knowledge Management Grid" of India. These Virtual libraries provide extensive information and instant access to users through information networks.

Digital libraries and knowledge management are innovations, the implementation of which is still nascent in developing countries. However, they hold the promise of becoming key technologies for knowledge creation and management in the future. The Long Term Policy (1998) has also envisaged a "National Internet Centre of Excellence (NICE)", to promote standards, assist digital content development in India, devise standards for content building and delivery, and research new technologies. For enabling knowledge connectivity in our rural areas, Upadhyay, Moni, and Vijayaditya[17] stressed the need to have a comprehensive plan for developing new infrastructure (viz., development of OCR Software in all the Indian languages, language independent operating system, database servers, search engines, web servers and messaging servers) for extending the digital library services in regional languages. This will enable the digital library initiative to percolate to the rural masses in the form of e-governance, tele-education and tele-medicine.

7. E-GRANTHALAYA: A DIGITAL AGENDA FOR LIBRARY AUTOMATION AND NETWORKING

According to International Federation of Library Associations and Institutions (IFLA), for every 3000 persons, there should be one public library. With more than 1.2 billion population, there is a requirement of over 330,000 libraries in India. A large majority of the population does not have access to free public libraries and rural areas have been neglected compared with urban areas. There is a need to integrate the functioning of rural libraries with information centres. School Libraries and Public Libraries in villages can function as public libraries where an information facilitation centre can be established; and this integrated infrastructure can take the shape of a digital library[19]. There is a widespread belief that rural information centres with computer networks can create new roads for knowledge, services, money etc., to travel from one node to other one even across long distances. However, there is a need to create appropriate S&T based digital sources in rural areas (i.e. soil map to help the farmer to correctly depicting land capability or land suitability, etc).

In order to make "India A Knowledge Based Society", it is essential to network the 60000 Public Libraries in India for internet access. In view of the importance of bibliographic informatics services, as a knowledge input to S&T services, NIC proposes to undertake programmes for establishing "digital library", strengthening of Bibliographic Services Programme, networking of libraries of Ministries/Departments of the Central Government, and networking of 35 State Libraries and 526 District Libraries, to enrich "bibliographic informatics" programme in the country. In view of economic importance and social relevance to facilitate "libraries" to become "knowledge centres", NIC has envisaged a digital agenda "e-Granthalaya" [which means "electronic book house", in other words "digital library"] during the eleventh plan. The objectives of this mission are as follows:-

- Automation and Networking of Government Libraries and Information Centers;
- Automation and Networking of Public Libraries and Information Centers;
- To provide marginalized villagers opportunity to access knowledge;
- To serve as an integrated Information Center model by creating cost effective and economically viable model to the masses in a timely period;
- Impacting Information Technology on the G2C interface; and
- Providing platform for self-employment.

To strengthen this movement, NIC has developed a library automation package "e-Granthalaya" (http://egranthalaya..nic.in) to suit the needs the requirements of different classes of libraries. Development of an e-Granthalaya Network (Community Information & Communication Centre Network) is conceptualized as in Figure

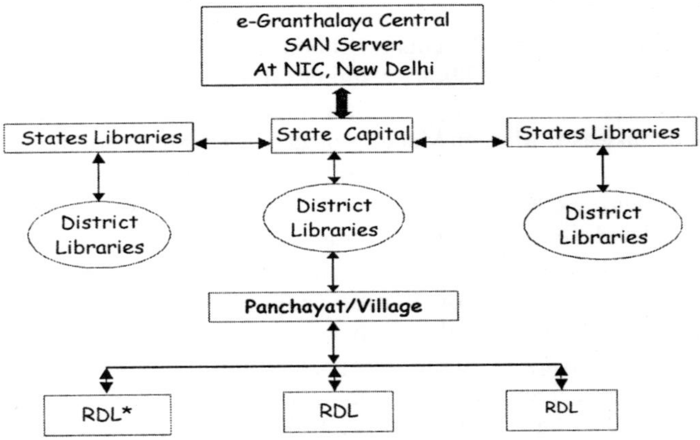

(*RDL means Rural Digital Libraries)

Figure-: e-Granthalaya Network at micro level

National Knowledge Commission[20] , submitted a report to the Hon'ble Prime Minister of India in 2006, in relation to the library segment. The Theme title of the Report is "People's Access to Knowledge can transform India". The Key recommendations of the NKC 2006 run as follows:-

- Set up a National Commission on Libraries
- Prepare a National census on all Libraries
- Revamp Library & Information Science Education, Training & Research
- Re-assess staffing of Libraries
- Promote ICT applications in all Libraries
- Set up a Central Library Fund
- Facilitate donation and maintenance private collections
- Encourage Private-Public-Partnership (PPP) in LIS development
- Modernize Library Management and Encourage Community Participation in Library Management

In the recommendation of the NKC 2006, it is important to underline the theme "People's Access to Knowledge can transform India". This shows a future for Indian Libraries to facilitate "People's Access to Knowledge which can transform India". Rural India thus desires to take advantage of "knowledge-intensive" techniques for its sustainable development and sustainable consumption. Grassroots level information access (Contents) and Grassroots level access to information (Networking) are the two essential components for grassroots level development strategies through ICT. Community Information and Communication Centres (CICC), as a concept and model, aim to "boost efficiency and enhance market" integration through Internet/ Intranet technologies for sustainable remote/ regional development at grassroots level.

8. CONCLUSION

Public Libraries across the country should be developed as Knowledge Kendras / Centres and all library resources should be digitized and shared across the country". Ministry of Culture and National Informatics Centre may undertake as a "Mission Mode" project under the NeGP of the Ministry of Communications and Information Technology. Since most higher education and research institutions in India are funded and controlled by the central and state governments, national plans and polices are on their way for infrastructure, standards, metadata, interoperability, multi-lingual databases, training, co-ordination, copyright, and archiving and preservation methods, so that heritage of knowledge and culture can overcome the ravages of time, and present and future generations can benefit and be guided by them. Public Libraries are relevant today for acting as "bridge" between the COMMON PUBLIC and the e-Governance/ e-Government programmes. All the stakeholders of the e-Governance/ e-Government programmes are required to be exposed to Digital Library Science, which will facilitate "design and development" of "Knowledge Management" in the e-Governance/e-Government Programmes.

Acknowledgement: The Author acknowledge various technical papers available on Internet while writing this article.

REFERENCES

1. Planning Commission, Government of India: Five Year Plans. 10th Plan (2002-2007). Volume2, Chapter3.2. Available at http://plannin.http:// www.knowledgecommission.gov.in/ Accessed on 30th January 2009. gcommission.nic.in/plans/planrel/fiveyr/10th/volume2/v2_ch3_2.pdf . Accessed on 30th September 2008.
2. World Bank (2003). Multi-Stakeholder regional consultation for international assessment on role of agricultural science and technology in reducing *hunger, improving rural livelihoods and stimulating environmentally sustainable economic growth.* Organized by The World Bank, 12-13 May 2003, New Delhi.
3. Acharya S.S. (2004). Sustainable agriculture and rural livelihoods. *In* K.V. Sundaram, M. Moni & Mrityunjay M. Jha (Eds.). Natural Resources management and livelihood security: survival strategies and sustainable policies. Bhoovigyan Vikas Foundation (New Delhi). Delhi: Concept Publishing Company.
4. Maxwell, S. & Franken Berger, T.R. (1992). Household food security: Concepts, indicators and measurement. New York: UNICEF & Rome: IFAD.
5. Bhoovigyan Vikas Foundation (New Delhi) (2002): International Conference on "Sustainable agriculture, water resources development and earth care policies. New Delhi (India); e-mail: bhoovigyan2000@yahoo.co.uk.
6. Abdul Kalam, A.P.J. (2005). Address to the Nation by the President of India, H.E. Dr. A.P.J. Abdul Kalam, on the eve of 56th India's Republic Day–2005.
7. DISNIC http://disnic.nic.in. Accessed on 30th September 2008.

8. National Informatics Centre: Project proposal for Wired Village Project at Warana Nagar, Maharashtra 22 June 1998. Available at http://www.mah.nic.in/warana/. Accessed on 30th September 2008.
9. Moni, M. (2002). Digital opportunities for responsive administration in India: Electronic Administration of Services to Citizens. An Internal Note sent to e-Governance Division of Department of Information Technology, 2002.
10. *World Book Encyclopedia.* V4. pp. 245.
11. Rose John B. (2005). Community telecentres: Assessing their impact and viability. delivered as the Corzonco-Seshachalam Lectures Series (3) (2005), in the National Symposium on «Information and Communication Strategies for Grassroots development », 4-5 March 2005, organised by School of Information and Communication Studies, University of Madras, Chennai, India.
12. Crow, B., Longford, G. (2000). Digital restructuring: gender, class and citizenship in the information society in Canada. *Citizen Studies,* 4 (2), 207-230.
13. Theodore, Rajiv (2005). Rural development. *Yojana, January 2005.*
14. *The Hindu.* December 4, 2001 [Open Page]. http://www.hinduonnet.com/thehindu/op/2001/12/04/stories/2001120400060100.htm. Accessed on 30th June 2006.
15. Moni, M. (2002). Digital libraries in rural India: A digital opportunity for sustainable development. Invited Talk on the "National Technology Day – May 11, 2002" organised by DELNET, New Delhi.
16. Mehra, Bharat and Srinivasan, Ramesh (2007). The Library-Community convergence framework for community action: libraries as catalysts of social change. *Libri,* 57, 123–139
17. Bhattacharjee, R. (2002). Public Libraries Section, Country Report: India. International Federation of Library Associations and Institutions. Available at http://www.ifla.org/VII/s8/annual/cr02-in.htm. Accessed on 30th September 2008.
18. Upadhyay P.K., Moni M., and Vijayaditya N. (2004). Digital library initiatives in India. *Libraries, Information & Knowledge,* 21 (1).
19. Venkatasubramaian K. (2002): Presidential address by Dr. K. Venkatasubramainan, Member, Union Planning Commission, at the Seminar on "Electronic libraries in rural India", 11 May 2002.
20. National Knowledge Commission.

Public Libraries as Social Institution: A Discussion

P.R. Goswami*

1. INTRODUCTION

There are three mutually supportive aspects of India's development process: economic reforms, good governance and democracy. Public libraries are deemed as institutions that can contribute towards creation of an informed citizenry essential for the functioning of democracy. They are also capable of generating new ideas as a public forum. Now the question is how do we assess the impact of a public library? The traditional approach is highly quantitative; i.e. to find out the number of foot-falls and the titles consulted or issued to the borrowers/ members. The purpose of this paper is to look beyond this traditional ways and look for other yardsticks that can be employed to justify the existence or expansion of public library system in a democracy like India.

2. PUBLIC LIBRARIES: USE AND OUTCOME APPROACH

In a seminal work, published in USA way back in 1977, two American Scholars D Zweizig and B Dervin challenged researchers and said that the time for studying 'how much use is made of libraries and by whom' is a story of the past. We should switch our focus from 'the user in the life of the library' to the 'library in the life of the user'. So far, in India, library authorities have been attempting to provide quantitative data to meet the demand for accountability. They fail to identify the contextual benefits of libraries often revealed through qualitative approaches associated with basic research conducted by academicians and NGOs. The following inferences can be drawn from studies done regarding societal benefits of public libraries.

- Users benefit in diverse ways from accessing library services that go far beyond traditional circulation and head counts.

* Director, Central Secretariat Library, Shastri Bhawan, New Delhi – 110 001

- Information use in public libraries is taken as forms of enlightenment, problem understanding, and personal benefit.
- Information consumption experience has also an impact on a person's emotions, activities, thoughts and values within a particular situation.

One can say that current quantitative approaches and tools fail to reflect the depth and breadth of impact of library services that may relate to knowledge, skills, attitudes, values, behavior etc. These tools also fail to appreciate the efforts that have gone into creating well designed information system and services For instance, a well organized library programme in an Indian village with higher level of social intelligence can produce results in the form of knowledge on nutritional needs, improved reading skills, more effective responses to a conflict, getting a job or having greater financial stability.

3. INDIAN LIBRARIES: IMPACT EVALUATION

It is true that countries like USA, UK and Germany which have a larger network of well organized public library system can produce more live cases relating to positive impact of library services. Such cases are very few in India because of two factors: a) people in general (including the library professionals) have a limited (poor) view of library services; b) the beneficiaries often overlook or fail to record the contribution of the libraries in their 'personal achievements' partly due to lower visibility of libraries as institutions of self learning.

As public library system in a country like India is greatly influenced by the culture of the region; and culture generally points to the values, meanings and attitudes people have about anything that influences all human actions and institutions. A region that presupposes a culture emanating from the ideal of equal and universal citizenship deliberates on public issues with active participation and shows a responsibility in public affairs. Kerala and West Bengal which have a higher level of social intelligence, also have a well knit system of public libraries largely under private control i.e. under the aegis of informal local governance institutions (ILGI). These type of organizations i.e. ILGI are prevalent in most of rural India in some form or other. They are institutionalized and they embody stable, recurring, and valued behavior patterns. In varying degrees, ILGI's in India resolve disputes, maintain peace, assist the unfortunate, finance and support temples, organize religious and social festivals, help develop social infrastructure (including libraries) and resources, influence how the village is represented at higher political level and negotiate directly with these higher level.

The result of a research on 'social mobility and poverty reduction' reported in a prominent social science journal points to the importance of information service in a rural area. It says that raising the aspiration of young people in villages will require connecting them better to diverse sources of information about employment opportunities. The provision of public information is associated at the macro level with Olympic success or success in international sports event by stimulating their desire to participate, and at the micro level with individual mobility. The comparative importance of information in two such diverse arenas suggests that it would be worth exploring its effects more broadly in addition to other fields of human achievements.

4. PUBLIC LIBRARY DEVELOPMENT: TOWARDS A ROADMAP

In order to appreciate the impact of certain broad social developments, one could turn to the specific cases like libraries and their impact. As a social science discipline, library science also requires detailed familiarity with the functioning of particular societies. This dependence on detailed access to the everyday life in which society or culture is embedded makes public libraries a regional or state subject. As a result, there are differences in development status of this sector in different States. The states like Tamil Nadu, Karnataka, Andhra Pradesh, Maharashtra, Kerala and Gujarat have well developed public library system under the State government as well as public-private partnership. Some other states have enacted library legislation but their implementation mechanism is sluggish and they also suffer from financial crunch. Moreover, most of the libraries at different levels (i.e. State Central Library, District Library, Village Library etc) do not have the bare minimum infrastructure and facilities like spacious reading room, proper storage system for books and periodicals, almirahs, cafeteria, drinking water, electricity toilets, (in case of village libraries) and trained staff who can communicate with the readers. The educated citizenry needs to have an incentive to use them. And for this, public libraries have to develop a system of need based information service in a pro-active way with a suitable social marketing strategy.

One can take the example of Karnataka state which has a reasonably good library system. A decade ago (i.e. 1998-1999), the effectiveness of the system was studied and evaluated. The result of this study based on a survey showed that there were problems with user population and quality of service. Most of the users of city libraries were young men who wanted to read free newspapers and magazines that they could not afford to purchase personally. Other groups-women, the elderly and children were under represented. However, a large group among the clientele wanted the library to become a component within a multi institutional educational set up that could provide information on job training in different fields. The survey also revealed that there was a continual concentration on serving the current clientele and this isolated libraries from woman, children and both the poor who really needed help and the well to do who could help the system. As a matter of fact, it was basically a problem of expanding services to more varied groups of library users.

Karnataka Public Libraries: A Factsheet (2006)

Public Library Type	*Library Count*
State Central Library	1
City Central Libraries and their branches	17+219
District Central Libraries at Head Quarters	14
Other District Libraries	272
Indira Priyadarshini Children Libraries	14
Public Technical Library	1
Mobile Libraries	15
Gram Panchayat Libraries	2728

In Karnataka, the officials of library department provided insight into the functioning of the system. They said that the main priority remained in rural areas and the objective is to provide daily newspapers and Kanaad literature. In view of the resource constraints achieving even this limited objective all over the State remained an ambitious project. On the other hand, the literate and educated population in rural areas was looking for technical and management information in a liberalized agrarian market economy. In urban areas, the drive towards career advancement was pushing a relatively young clientele toward up to date technical and professional literature. The result of the survey also showed that the public library system was spending a major part of its resources meeting the information needs of a relatively narrow social group and only a few older people, school children and female population were using the services.

A casual visit to the District Central Library (DCL) at Ranchi (Jharkhand) in 2007 has brought out another dimension of public library services. The DCL located at Ranchi is also deemed as State Central Library of Jharkhand. The parking space of this library was full of two wheelers (mostly bicycles) and it appears that the library must be having a very good collection of books and periodicals. However, it was found that the library has been bifurcated into two parts:- one part has a few locked almirahs with books and library staff; and the second part has a sprawling reading room where young learners are preparing for their examinations. A brief discussion with the librarian incharge revealed that there is hardly any library service in terms of lending books, periodicals, reference service etc and library building providing a reading space for the students. However, it was mentioned that the state library is striving hard to expand its services with the help of Raja Rammohun Roy Library Foundation (RRRLF). Though it provided a limited view of library services in the state, one can argue that the reading hall functions as a social space to young aspirants to read and compete for various examinations. It is also apparent that there is ample scope for development of proper need based library services in the state.

It has also been argued that the design of a library building or a reading hall reflects a sense of discipline. Alistair Black[1], a library historian has stressed the point that modern public library not only supports enlightenment to the benefit of the development of the individual as well as the society but also does a supervisory function. There is a mark of discipline in modern library design where the circulation desk as well as the librarian's table, are placed in a way that helps the staff to oversee the entire library room space.

In India, 16 states have so far passed the Public Library Act. The other states which have not yet enacted library Act are developing public library services through a) direct governmental efforts and b) grant-in-aid system. It has been found that bigger States have adopted the grant-in-aid system and Union Territories are establishing government libraries at different levels. It cannot be said that the state of public libraries is quite satisfactory wherever library legislation is in place. During the first half of 19th century, Alexis de Tocqueville had pointed out in his book 'Democracy in India' that good customs contribute even more to the success of democracy than good laws. In India, we are more adept in making laws but our customs hold us back even more strongly. Good laws are indispensible but mere multiplication of laws without any thought of inertia and obduracy of custom is not likely to take us out of the troubled waters.

In India, a village library can be viewed as a form of social capital as it can play the role of a meeting place for educated as well as disadvantage class and can forge unity and cooperation among them. Social capital refers to trusts, networks and norms shared by a group of actors that enable them to work together more effectively. Oral tradition is very strong in India's villages. It is even possible to think that someone reads out a story or a piece of prose to others particularly the neo-literates. This is possible in a library as an extension of the reading of Mahabharata, Ramayana etc. in the villages.

5. CONCLUSION

In India, public libraries should try to gain firsthand knowledge of the social characteristics of their prospective users and aim to reorient the delivery of their services in the context of these characteristics. The provision of reading material as has been the practice in a traditional way will no longer suffice.

REFERENCES

1. Black, Alistair (1998). Information and modernity: the history of information and eclipse of library history. *Library History*. 14(1), 39-45.
2. Basu, K; Foster, James E and Subramannian, S (2000). Isolated and promixate illiteracy and why these concepts matter in measuring literacy and designing education programmes. *Economic and Political Weekly.* 35(2), 35-36.

3. Beteille, Andre (1999). Trials of Democracy: primacy of customs over law. *Times of India.* 29th April, 12.
4. Heitzman, J and Asundi, A.Y. (2000). Evaluation of public libraries in India: Case of Karnataka. *Information Development.* 16(3),.142-155.
5. Krishna, Anirudh and Haglund, Eric (2008). Why do some countries win more Olympic medals: lessons for social mobility and poverty reduction. *Economic and Political Weekly.* 43(28), p.149.
6. Mahapatra, Sitakant (2002). School-cum-village library: taking books to rural India. Paper presented at a conference organized by Planning Commission, 22nd March 2002.

Public Library and Its Role in the Modern Society as a Community Information Service

Devendra Kumar[1], Rajkumar Singh[2] and Krishna Kumar[3]

1. COMMUNITY INFORMATION: AN INTRODUCTION

Community Information (CI) is the combination of two terms i.e. 'Community' and 'Information'. The term 'Information' is used to identify many concepts; hence it is extremely difficult to define it precisely. Normally, information is a message, communicated by a communicator to a receiver. It is the product of human action in mind, which may be abstract or concrete. Therefore, it is the raw material that is used in knowing, making decisions, taking actions, thinking and learning. Reid[1] defines information as "a process rather than as material. Data only becomes information by the act of imparting it." Information can be regarded as data, which can be transmitted between individuals, and each individual can make use of it in whatever form he/she wants. When information becomes publicly recorded, it becomes objective knowledge and is available to all. Community is a body of people in the same locality or a body of people leading a common life or a group of people having common rights or a group of people having a common possession or enjoyment. Giggey[2] defines community as "a group of people who have something in common. This can be their age, education, religion, interest, political affiliation, activities, work, possession or a combination of two or more of these elements." Similarly Usherwood[3] defines community in a comprehensive way as "any geographical community or neighborhood will be made up of a number of communities definable by race, social class, or income group, employment, leisure interest, religion and so on, each with its own informal information

1. Faculty Member, Department of Library & Information Science (DLIS), CCS University, Meerut, UP, Email: dkdeobhu@gmail.com
2. Librarian, Govt. Mahila Degree College, Aurai, Sant Ravidas Nagar, Bhadohi, UP, E-mail: singhrajkumar16@yahoo.com
3. Faculty Member, DLIS, CCS University, Meerut, UP, E-mail: kkbhuvns@gmail.com

network that has grown up without the help of librarians or any other information advice workers." Thus community in general implies a group of people having common interests. However, neither can they be assumed nor they can be created to legitimatize a political programme or support a plan for action. In the context of librarianship, it is a group of people with shared meaning and shared communication.

Community Information (CI) is the information for the survival and growth of the community or it is the information that members of the community require to make effective use of resources available around them. In this context Kempson[4] has rightly defined CI as "information for self-reliance and self-determination". Thus CI is that information which helps to solve day to day problems of community members, in particular problems of their survival such as health, education, housing, legal protection, sound economic development, political rights etc or it is the information that helps to empower them to participate in social, political, cultural, legal and economic activities of the society either individually or collectively. The service by which community information (CI) is rendered to communities is called Community Information Service (CIS).

Besides, libraries are now engaged in the knowledge business[5] and increasingly they are exposed to marketplace pressures in a manner similar to other businesses. Core activities in knowledge management are associated with knowledge creation, dissemination and learning. Knowledge management projects and applications can be categorized in accordance with their objectives. These objectives may be: to create knowledge repositories; to improve knowledge access; to enhance the knowledge environment; and to manage knowledge as an asset.

2. COMMUNITY INFORMATION AND UNESCO'S MISSION FOR PUBLIC LIBRARIES

According to UNESCO[6] Manifesto for Public Library (1994) community information is part of 'the mission of public libraries services'. In overall, public library mission as UNESCO includes the following services:

- Creating and strengthening reading habit in children from an early age;
- Supporting both individual and self-conducted education as well as formal education;
- Providing opportunities for personal creative development;
- Stimulating the imagination and creativity of young people and children;
- Promoting awareness of cultural heritage, appreciation of arts, scientific achievements and innovation;
- Providing access to cultural expressions of all performing arts;
- Fostering intercultural dialogue and favouring cultural diversity;
- Supporting the oral tradition;
- Ensuring access for citizens to all sorts of community information;

- Providing adequate information services to local enterprises, associations and interest groups;
- Facilitating the development of information and computer literacy skills;
- Supporting and participating in literacy activities and adult education programmes for all age groups, and initiating such activities if necessary.

3. PUBLIC LIBRARY IN MODERN AGE

The public library has become a multi-purpose agency with multiple roles such as community information, support for education, life long learning, recreation and leisure, culture and research. Because of their importance, public libraries are at the heart of both the Department for Culture, Media and Sport (DCMS) and broader Government policies: In the present era of information society and knowledge based economy, public libraries are perceived as follows:

- They underpin education, providing essential support for school children, students and lifelong learners;
- They enhance public access to the world's storehouse of knowledge and information;
- They promote social inclusion, by helping to bridge the gap between those who can afford access to information and those who cannot, and by facilitating access to information for socially excluded people;
- They are a vital conduit and access point for the main principles of modernization and delivery of public services;
- They provide information and learning opportunities which underpin creativity, economic regeneration, urban renewal and rural development.
- In addition, their traditional roles in support of literacy, reading and personal and community growth remain undiminished.

4. SCOPE OF COMMUNITY INFORMATION SERVICE (CIS)

Community information service is aimed at disseminating information relating to survival issues such as health, education, and sound economic development as essential for community survival and also relating to citizens action with regard to their political and legal rights. It includes provision of information on the following aspects:

- Information on educational avenues;
- Information on employment opportunities;
- Information on health aspects;
- Information on cottage industries;
- Information on income generation programmes;
- Information on government procedures;

- Information on legal aspects;
- Information on consumer services;
- Information on government welfare schemes; and
- Information on sports activities;

The traditional libraries don't seem to be meeting the changing information needs of today's knowledge society. Library buildings, which were planned on old norms and standards, do not seem to be satisfying the users requirements in today's situation. The modern public library has to be multifunctional providing not only informational or other typical library services but cultural, communicational and other services as well. Such a library will have to be visualized as performing two main functions:

- Provision of library's traditional (informational) services and,
- Cultural and social services.

These non-traditional services (including cultural, educational, commercial, sports, recreational, entertainment etc.) will make the library more attractive and lead to surge in public library clientele. For managing the cultural and social functions suitable premises will have to be planned. We also need new premises to lend library a new image – as of social relevance. The library will become a library information centre, club, and Internet café etc. oriented to the various needs of society, of different user groups and ages. The modern public library will be a synthesis of various informational, social and cultural activities. All these different kinds of activities will stimulate public interest in the libraries. Hence, public libraries in addition to being perceived as community information centres must also be seen as organizing informational, educational, social, recreation and cultural activities.

5. PRE-REQUISITES FOR COMMUNITY INFORMATION SERVICE (CIS)

There is an ample scope for its provision of community information services by the public libraries. The pre-requisites mandated for the purpose are as follows:

- Design and development of computer-aided information system with necessary infrastructure. Such a system performs the activities such as: links speedily appropriate information sources needed for CIS; Provides information through network access; connect the users to the information content and identifies the pattern of utilization of such services.
- Adoption and utilization of Information and Communication Technology (ICTs).
- Establishment of networks at the local, regional and national levels.
- Utilization of the services of National Informatics Centre (NIC), Department of Information and Public Relations of the State Governments, Revenue departments, Agriculture department, etc.

- Formulation of Public Library Policy to strengthen the Public Library System in India.
- Formulation of a better information policy perspectives which includes
  - ❖ remodeling of the existing services;
  - ❖ promote cooperation between agencies associated with publication and information,
  - ❖ promote adoption of system for information processing, organizing, retrieval, modeling
  - ❖ user friendly dissemination services and promotion of ICT.
- Enactment of library legislation in all the states and striving for their implementations.
- Motivation of the library staff towards the provision of money and resources, etc.
- Establishment of close coordination with NGOs and other social organizations, etc.
- Covering the existing rural libraries as Rural Community Resource Centres.
- Establishment of community library for a village or village cluster as suggested by the National Policy on Library and Information System (NAPLIS)[7].
- Identification of human expertise and exploitation of local talents effectively for knowledge base for CIS.

6. ICT IN PUBLIC LIBRARIES FOR EFFECTIVE COMMUNITY INFORMATION SERVICES

The information revolution in communication and information technologies has significantly influenced the concept and role of libraries and librarians. The time is ripe to convert public libraries as community information centres rather than as mere collection centres of books. This can be done by introducing computerization in libraries, networking of public libraries and at all levels. At present computerization of public libraries is already in progress but it pace is still very slow. This activity needs to be accelerated. It is a matter of pride that the public library system of Karnataka is seriously planning library automation programme in a big way.

7. COMMUNITY INFORMATION INITIATIVES IN INDIA

Former President of India A.P.J. Abdul Kalam[8] coined a new term, PURA (Providing Urban amenities in Rural Areas) that describes coherent knowledge and resource distribution across the country. PURA seeks to deliver three types of connectivity: physical connectivity by providing roads in rural areas, electronic connectivity by providing reliable communication network and knowledge connectivity by establishing more professional institutions and vocational training centres. He also envisaged establishing Village Knowledge Centres across India. To implement visions of former President of India and other contemporary social reformists, the Government of India and other agencies have taken up a number of programmes and initiatives across the country. Some initiatives are public-private partnership (PP) between public bodies (like, village Panchayats) and private bodies (like, corporate and NGOs), e.g., e-Choupal, TARA Haat. Some initiatives provide Government to Citizens (G2C) interface to ensure better transparency in governance, e.g., Bhoomi, Gyandoot, Community Information Centres, etc. These community information centres provide various kinds of community information as required by common citizens, e.g. education, health, nutrition, sanitation, agriculture, wholesale prices of agricultural products, village industries, weather, land records, utilities (such as, ration cards, driving licenses, birth certificates, death certificates, caste certificates, income certificates, etc.), and so on. Some projects have coverage in select fields, e.g. Bhoomi (covering land records), whereas others cover an array of fields, e.g. Community Information Centres (covering education, health, utilities, etc.). Most of such initiatives have established information kiosks or cyber cafes in villages and the semi-urban areas, with the infrastructural support for hardware, software, network, telephone and power coming from respective institutions involved, and with the participations of the self-help groups or volunteers who run information kiosks at the doorsteps of the villagers and common citizens. In areas where telephone connectivity is not adequate, VSAT terminals are provided and managed by Community Information Centres and eChoupal, These community information initiatives deliver e-literacy programmes to the common citizens where basic skills of using computers and Internet are imparted. These initiatives also offer information literacy programmes to users of information kiosks, where learners come to know how to use information resources as available through portals of the agencies engaged in such programmes, intranet and Internet, and how such information can be applied in solving problems of the individuals in their vocational (e.g. agricultural know how), personal (e.g. getting a certificate) and social (e.g. sanitation) life.

Community Information Initiatives in India

Name of the Project (with web address)	*Coverage*	*Institutions Involved*	*Type of Partici-pation*
Common Service Centre (CSC) (www.mit.gov.in/default.asp?id=825)	Establish 1000,000 Common Service Centres in 600,000 villages of India	Department of Information Technology; Infrastructure Leasing & Financial Service Limited	G2C

Akhaya (www.akshaya.net)	1 State (Kerala)	Kerala State Information Technology Mission	G2C
Bhoomi (www.revdept-01.kar.nic.in)	1 State (Karnataka)	Revenue Department; National Informatics Centres	G2C
Community Information Centres (CIC) (www.cic.nic.in)	10 States (Arunachal Pradesh, Assam, Manipur, Meghalaya, Mizoram, Nagaland, Sikkim, Tripura, Jammu & Kashmir)	Ministry of Development of North Eastern Region (DONER); National Informatics Centres	G2C
Digital Gangetic Plane (www.iitk.ac.in/mladgp)	1 State (Uttar Pradesh)	Media Lab Asia, IIT Kanpur	G2C
Drishtee (www.drishtee.com)	5 States (Haryana, Punjab, Madhya Pradesh, Rajasthan and Bihar)	Drishtee Ltd.	PP
e-Choupal (www.echoupal.com)	6 States (Madhya Pradesh, Karnataka, Andhra Pradesh, Uttar Pradesh, Maharashtra and Rajasthan); 31,000 villages.	International Business Division of ITC Limited	PP
Gyandoot (www.gyandoot.nic.in)	1 District (Dhar district of Madhya Pradesh state)	Gyandoot Samiti & National Informatics Centres	G2C
Rural e-Seva (www.westgodavari.org)	1 District (West Godavari district of Andhra Pradesh state)	West Godavari District Administration	G2C
TARAhaat (www.tarahaat.com)	4 States (Punjab, Haryana, Madhya Pradesh, Uttar Pradesh)	Development Alternatives	PP
Village Knowledge Centres (VKC) (www.mission2007.org)	600,000 villages across India by the year 2007	National Alliance for Mission 2007, NGOs, Department of Information Technology, Ministry of Panchayati Raj, Ministry of Agriculture, National Bank for Agriculture and Rural Development, etc.	G2C, PP

8. THE FUTURE PUBLIC LIBRARY

In the future we expect to witness tremendous changes in the public library sector. We will witness globalization of information culture facilitating faster access to information - especially through the Internet. Information technology will continue to remain the driving force behind processes of change. People will be exposed to a range of technological challenges and opportunities in the digital age. We will witness change in industrial production, service provision, markets, organizational structures, and professional roles, etc. We only have to look back by few years and see to what extent personal computing has done to us in changing the way we now spend our life and leisure time.

The rapid changes in information technologies during the last two to three decades have altered the activities of information professionals. Existing libraries now cover a multitude of functions. It is certainly evident that the role of the libraries will change quite a lot. To a certain degree the role of the future libraries and librarians is closely linked to the societal structures and degree to which such structures are going to become consumer-oriented or information oriented at individual level.

9. CONCLUSION

Information literacy is an area that seems very important to build information skills of end users as needed to identify, access, and use electronic information from the network. It is also important from social perspective given the widening gulf between the network literate and the network illiterate. In outlining a vision of public libraries in a networked society, libraries and librarians should seek to serve as electronic intermediaries, navigators and instructors helping people to make best use of network resources. The overall changing scenario of libraries from manual to computer based operations and services in different countries and the slow pace at which progress in bringing about such as a change is taking place, underlines the need for continuing education of librarians and information professionals in ICT applications to libraries.

In the present era of knowledge society public libraries must act as community information centres to the citizens. CIS must become an integral part of the public library services. Further, the country needs a network of community information centres for accelerating this activity. The long pending NAPLIS report must be accepted and its recommendations implemented. It is also required that public library legislation must incorporate in it the provisions with regard CIS. In addition, governmental agencies and NGOs should coordinate, supplement and complement their efforts in this regard. The professional associations such as ILA, IASLIC, and all regional and states libraries associations should come forward to formulate guidelines for planning, organizing and operationalizing CIS. On successful implementation of action plans and programmes, the CIS in public libraries in India would certainly become a reality.

REFERENCES

1. Reid, B. (1977). Community Information and the Library. *Australian Library Journal.* 26(2): 30-36.
2. Giggey, Shirley (1988). Rural community resource centres: a guide for developing countries. London: Macmillan.
3. Usherwood, B. (1999). The neighborhood information networking of librarianship, Liverpool Polytechnic, Liverpool. In: Vishwa, M and Raju, A.A.N. Communitinformation concepts. *DESIDOC Bulletin of Information Technology,* 19(1): 5-14.
4. Kempson, E (1986). Information for Self-Reliance and Self-Determination: the Role of Community Information Services. *IFLA Journal.* 12(3): 182-91.
5. Goddard, A (1998). Facing up to market forces. *Times Higher Education Supplement*, 13 November, pp. 6-7.
6. UNESCO (1995). UNESCO Public Library Manifesto, 1994. Paris: UNESCO.
7. NAPLIS (1988). Report on public libraries as accepted by the Empowered Committee, *CLIS Observer,* 5(1-2): 32.
8. Abdul Kalam, A.P.J. (2005). Address to the nation by the President of India Dr. A.P.J. Abdul Kalam on the eve of 56th Republic Day.

BIBLIOGRAPHY

- Adeyemi, N.M. (1991). Issues on the provision of information services in developing countries. *African Journal of Libraries, Archives and Information Science*, 1(1):1-8.
- American Library Association. Community Information Section, Public Library Association (1989). *Guidelines for Establishing Community Information and Referral Services in Public Libraries.* 3rd ed. Chicago: American Library Association.
- Anyim, J.C. (1972). Public libraries as cultural centres. *Nigerian Libraries*, 8(1):15-19.
- Ashok Babu, T. (1999). Automation of public libraries. *Herald of Library Science*, 38 (1-2): 47-52.
- Banach, E. (1989). The role of the public library in a changing society. *Artes Natales*, 7(11):5-11.
- Bench, Allan (1982). Community information services: their origins, scope and development. London: Clive Bingley.
- Buragohain, Alaka (1999). Public library scenario in India: problem and prospects. *Herald of Library Science*, 38 (1-2): 5-14.
- *DESIDOC Bulletin of Information Technology* (1999). Special issue: Community Information Services.

- Ghosh, Maitreyee (2005). The public library system in India: challenges and opportunity. *Library Review*, 54(3): 180-191.
- Ghosh, S.B. and Das, Anup Kumar (2009). Information literacy and emerging knowledge economy in India. In Library Information Systems: from Alexandrian heritage to social networking (Essay in honour of Prof. S. Parthsarathy), New Delhi: Ess Ess Publication, pp. 16-44.
- Jakovlevas-Mateckis, K., Kostinaitë L. and Pupelienë J. (2004). Conceptual Principles of the Planning of Modern Public Libraries. *Library Quarterly: The Journal of European Libraries*, 14(2). (Online Journal)
- Kumbar, B. D. and Krishna Murthy, C. (2004). Public libraries as community information. Ramesh Babu, B. and Gopal Krihan (Ed). In: information, communication, library and community development (Festchrift in honour of Prof. C. P. Vashishth). Delhi: B. R. Publishing, pp. 197-210.
- Lee, Olive "Urban Community Information Center." In Access to Information, op. cit.: 301–311.
- Liew, Cheong Kwai (1983). Community Information Service in the Public Library with Special Reference to Singapore. In: The Library in the Information Revolution: Proceedings of the Sixth Congress of Southeast Asian Librarians, Held in Singapore, 30 May–3 June 1983, pp. 339–347. Singapore: Maruzen Asia.
- Naidu, G. Hema Sunder… et al. (1999). User services in modern libraries. *Herald of Library Science*, 38 (1-2): 70-75.
- Raghavaiah, A. and Venkateswarara Rao, L. (2004). Public libraries community information centres. Ramesh Babu, B. and Gopal Krihan (Ed). In: Information, communication, library and community development (Festchrift in honour of Prof. C. P. Vashishth). Delhi: B. R. Publishing, pp. 211-217.
- Ramesh Babu, B. and Gopalkrishnan (2004). Community information services libraries in India: myth or reality. Ramesh Babu, B. and Gopalkrihan (Ed). In: Information, communication, library and community development (Festchrift in honour of Prof. C. P. Vashishth). Delhi: B. R. Publishing, p. 263-269.
- Ruzaif Adli M.D. and Shukriah Yon (2007). Knowledge Management Implementation Model for Community Information Service (CIS) in the Library: A Case of Perbadanan Perpustakaan Awam Pulau Pinang (PPAPP) International Conference on Libraries (ICOL) 2007 organized by Universiti Sains Malaysia Libraries and Librarians' Association of Malaysia, (pp.-) Gurney Hotel, Penang, 31 October – 2 November 2007.
- Tise, E. (2000). The role of libraries in socio-economic development and the need for information literacy. *Meta-info Bulletin*, 9 (2):55-61.
- Vijay Kiran, A. and Ramesh Babu, B. (2004). CIS in church organization in India. Ramesh Babu, B. and Gopalkrihan (Ed). In: Information, communication, library and community development (Festchrift in honour of Prof. C. P. Vashishth). Delhi: B.R.Publishing, pp. 263-269.

Using ICT Tools for Public Empowerment: Wishful Role for Public Library System in India

USHA MUJOO MUNSHI*

1. INTRODUCTION

The application of ICT has caused significant changes in libraries: While technology was being quickly embraced by the libraries and information centres in the developing countries, the developed countries were relatively slower in adopting, assimilating, and implementing. The reasons are many, but at the core issue is the librarians' attitudes towards implementing information communication technology (ICT) in the library. The areas that were addressed as part of the automation measures were automated cataloguing, circulation, information retrieval, electronic document delivery, and CD-ROM databases. The advent of the Internet, digitization, and the ability to access library and research materials from remote locations created dramatic changes by the end of the twentieth century. The expert systems, wireless networks, virtual collections, interactive Web interfaces, virtual reference services, and personal Web portals have brought changes since the start of the present millennium. There have been fast and significant changes in librarianship, where digital and electronic libraries complement, and in (some) cases are blended with traditional libraries giving rise to hybrid libraries, that are sustainable, acceptable and perhaps most adaptable entities in today's knowledge society.

2. ICT IN DEVELOPING COUNTRIES

Information and communication technology (ICT) can help developing countries tackle a wide range of socio-economic problems. By improving access to information and by enabling communication, ICT can play a great role in reaching to the unreached. However the benefits of ICT are

* Librarian, Indian Institute of Public Administration, New Delhi

not fully realized in many countries as ICT is often out of reach of the poor and those in rural areas.

Any technology that enables communication and the electronic capture, processing, and transmission of information, is considered to be an ICT. Radio, television and print media are vital in many developing countries. And in recent years new ICT, such as mobile phones and the Internet (and associated applications have become available to growing numbers worldwide. The most rapid growth is in mobile phone usage. Total (fixed and mobile) telephone access in developing countries increased from 2 per cent in 1991 to 31 per cent in 2004. Internet usage has also grown rapidly: from 0.03 per cent of developing country inhabitants in 1994 to 6.7 per cent in 2004. However, there are wide disparities between developing countries. In 2004 Zimbabwe had 3.5 mobile subscribers per 100 people, compared with 4.3 for India, 36.3 for Brazil and 102 for the UK. Although levels of access are low in many African countries, growth over the previous five years has averaged 60 per cent a year. In 2004 Africa was the region with the highest mobile phone growth rate. Growth rates in India averaged 90 per cent over the same period, among the fastest in Asia.[1]

The technological developments that have given rise to new technologies, and changes in usage, can increase access to ICT. For example, recent developments in wireless local area network technologies are raising new hopes for Internet diffusion in many parts of the developing countries. Sharing of devices is common in developing countries, and technology supports this concept in global context, more so when we talk in terms of the information or knowledge sharing processes using technology.

Open Source Software (OSS) is an expanding area and so is Open Access to scholarly content. OSS movement is fast gaining momentum. Since there is no licensing fee attached to it, OSS can be cheaper to acquire than proprietary software. Similarly Open Access to scholarly content is based on the premise that access to information should be free or low fee to the end user. This seems to be a step towards true democratization of information that supports the concept of right to information and knowledge and endeavors to lead to empowering people. ICT can help disseminate indigenous knowledge such as herbal medicine, agricultural best practices, primary health issues and the like

The information can reach all nooks and corners with effective use of affordable technology, breaking down the geographic barriers. But this needs willful planning, proper mindset and attitude.

Information Communication Technology (ICT) is increasingly seen as a means of enabling other developmental needs rather than as an end in itself. Technological developments and changes in the way new ICT are used e.g. sharing devices can help bridge this 'digital divide'.

While we are referring to democratization of knowledge, what comes to mind is the societal role of libraries that too of public libraries in making this happen.

3. KNOWLEDGE EMPOWERMENT: ROLE OF PUBLIC LIBRARIES

Public libraries exist in most nations of the world and are often considered an essential part of having an educated and literate population. Public libraries typically are lending libraries, allowing users to take books and other materials off the premises temporarily; they also have non-circulating reference collections. Public libraries typically focus on popular materials such as popular fiction, movies, educational, nonfiction and other materials of interest to the general public; computer and internet access is also often offered, They are expected to have best of best reference services and with ICT in virtual mode.

Public libraries are thus a social institution with a social mission to serve the society and be a torch bearer in empowering the nation by empowering its people through its knowledge disseminating activities. No country in the world can progress without providing free public library services to the citizens. It is imperative on the part of the democratic country like India to establish the service institutions like public libraries in order to strengthen the democratization of information and to promote the social, cultural, historical and scientific and technical knowledge in the public at large. The activity can be further strengthened with the use of ICT. It will ensure access to information for the benefit of the unreached.

Technological change is posing a particular challenge to librarians in developing countries. Librarians in developed countries moved quickly to learn and adopt new information technologies. ICT was introduced to perform library functions and provide innovative user services. Librarians gained knowledge of new technologies through continuing education programs, professional training, and to an extent through revisions to library school curricula, which helped them benefit from the new technologies. Thus the libraries in developing countries became equipped with appropriate hardware and software.

The story in developing nations is not the same. The technology penetration in many sectors has been witnessed particularly in India. The libraries was stretched themselves to pick a punch, some succeeded and got themselves settled in the new environment, while some tried to pick up a pie, a significant proportion is still grappling with ideas for implementation.

The studies have shown that there is a significant co-relation between training/knowledge of ICT and attitude towards ICT.[2] This means that ICT training and knowledge possessed by librarian can influence their attitude toward ICT. As such adequate training and knowledge of ICT are crucial in encouraging librarians to show a positive attitude toward it. Many argue that the major reason for the failure of library automation projects in developing countries is that librarians and funding agencies plan without sufficient knowledge of hardware, software, and power supply requirements. This reaffirms that sufficient knowledge of ICT and its resources are important to the development of a positive attitude to ICT by librarians. Training and knowledge are the sine qua non of a positive attitude toward ICT. In this era, when new technologies are introduced almost daily, it is essential for librarians to keep up with ICT developments.

4. PUBLIC LIBRARY SCENARIO IN INDIA

The current situation of Indian public libraries has been viewed by some as follows: the public library system in India is ordained to remain peripheral to the actual information needs of the masses; that it is in a depressed state, and serves as little more than a depot of recreational reading materials.

How to transform the situation, using new technological developments which may show the potential to change public libraries in rural India for the better is an important issue. The new technological developments that promise to facilitate the establishment of digital library services in rural India suggest possible ways to transform the "digital divide" into "digital opportunities". This needs to be given earnest thought.

But before the new technologies are taken let us talk about growth and development of public libraries in India.

The first landmark in the pre-independence history of the public library system in India is the enactment of delivery and registration of publications Act of Bombay government in May 1808. The other important events were establishment of the Imperial Library - passing of the Imperial Library Act on 31st Jan 1902 and transforming the Calcutta Public Library into Imperial Library in 1906 by Lord Curzon. Similarly, Baroda State Public Libraries Network of late Shri Sayajirao Gaikwad-III of Baroda. The Post-Independent Period marked the growth of libraries in general and public libraries in particular. While the growth of other types of libraries as compared to the development of public libraries more notable. The setting of the National Library that originated from the Calcutta public Library, which came into existence around 1836. The Calcutta public library and an imperial library formed in 1881 were amalgamated in 1903 to become the imperial library of colonial India and finally named the same as a National Library by the central government of India in 1948. Delhi Public Library:

The establishment of the Delhi Public Library in 1951, involvement of the Union Government in Public Library movement, and enactment of Public Library Laws are some of the main issues which contributed towards the improvement and expansion of public libraries after independence. Library Legislation has also brought in some hopes, Madras Public Libraries Act in 1948 and since then less than 50 per cent of the Indian states Current Status having enacted library acts for their respective states.

The establishment of Raja Rammohun Roy Library Foundation at Calcutta on May 22, 1972 is another positive and welcoming step taken by the central government of India. With a number of activities on its cards, the foundation is endeavoring to bring changes and make a difference. Yet much needs to be done in creating a robust public library system in the country.

The need to take the lead and muster all possible resources to develop a model public library which can make use of all modem technologies, at least one in each state, and Union Territory is inevitable . Sooner the better.

4.1 Using ICT for Democratization of Information: Focus on Public Libraries

As indicated above the use of ICT is necessitated for the democratization and universal access to information. Since technology can break all barriers to reach the right person at right time and place.

When we say that ignorance is not our heritage, if we mean what we say then we need to ensure equity and excellence in the public library. That is possible through use of ICT for facilitating various services to the community for its development, empowerment and upliftment Hence we need to revisit and research our public library system so as to fill the knowledge gaps. .

New technologies such as Internet access have transformed the support for public libraries

The areas critical to the public library mission, use of e-books, trends database licensing—use of consortiums, workstation deployment, workstation access and reservation policies, technology centers, internet access policies, internet filtering, automated book check out, automated routing of returned books, catalog enhancements, digitizing of special audio/video collections, web site maintenance and development, virtual reference systems, integrated library software system, size and composition of technology staff, relation of library technology staff to city/county technology staff, help desk policies, wireless access, cataloging, and catalog enhancements and model libraries being built, are the centric issues that need to be addressed in the changing electronic environment.

World over, it has been realized that the mission and vision of Public Libraries in many ways has been transformed by new technologies, particularly internet access. Besides, the key to winning greater support for public libraries is educating the public in the use of these technologies. At the same time the public's appetite for internet and database access is growing and virtually insatiable. The public library's hybridization of free internet access and knowledgeable tutors and guides has made it an indisputable draw, resulting in several success stories in technology-related bond issues in many libraries (both for new libraries or for refurbishing old libraries). Several public libraries are using RFID automated book check out technology grooming their patrons to adjust to the new technology For consortium arrangements, though public libraries,(even larger ones), appear to seriously lag their counterparts in academic libraries in their enthusiasm, but they are astoundingly ahead in their efforts to digitize their special collections. Though initially a slow start, electronic books are making a significant impact.

The social networking concept is catching up in the libraries, expanding in-house telecommunications capacities, enabling librarians to communicate with one another, and with patrons, while they walked around the library, voice over IP application for libraries, is a sort after application in many libraries in the world.

The larger libraries have entered successfully in to the arena of philosophy of handling content development and management. They are also centering their activities around website training for staff and patrons, the website control within the library, website marketing, usability testing, linking, programming, the development of interactive content, site personalization, best use of website statistics, and many other facets of the rapidly developing world of public library website management.

This indicates that public libraries are increasingly seascaping themselves as places to introduce new technologies to the public. The purpose being to facilitate value added services and personalized information services using the latest technological tools and products. Centers that introduce new software and hardware have increasingly become part of the public library mission and are major selling points in raising new funds for libraries.

While we are struggling with the idea of using ICT for the best performance of the Public Libraries. Let us take some world examples to find out bunch of best practices.

4.2 Best Practices for Public Libraries

While we are struggling with the idea of using ICT for the best performance of the Public Libraries. Let us take some world examples to find out bunch of best practices.[3]

- Social Networking and Public Relation : to periodically evaluate training & centralizing certain responsibilities for staff to serve patrons more effectively.
- Friend of Library Group: to assess the extent to which volunteers irrespective of geographic barriers can be effectively used to assist in providing or augmenting library services. Assisting in developing and maintaining library services for the benefit of all. And

undertake activities and projects that are a good match with the services and programs offered by their library.

- Facilities:
  - Collection development - to identify & remove materials not being.used
  - collaborate with other libraries with more extensive materials or specialized collections.
- Services: To best address the changing needs of their patrons. periodically assess & modify their services in order.
- Technology Tools and Products: Encourage use of electronic resources, such as online databases and library catalogs; and participate and facilitate online catalog of library materials to offer their patrons access to material outside their own collections.
- Use technology to inform public, through local media outlets and the Internet, about the programs and services provided
- Drafting and Adherence to Standards: library standards to help assess the adequacy of existing library services and assist in planning efforts by addressing the areas of greatest need.

4.3 Technology: A Wish list

A wish list of new technology tools which one straightaway associates with web 2.0 or Library 2.0 that has great applications for providing effective library services with (somewhat) affordable technology and even less or non technical people. The new technologies are promising innovative public services.

The Public Libraries in the world have started using and providing services in very innovative ways. These libraries have marketed it through their websites and such Library Websites have almost reached to the Hall of Fame. The application of web 2.0 technologies to libraries has great implications for the libraries and library services. Web 2.0 is basically an architecture for participation and collaboration. It is a social environment that facilitates social media communication. Let us examine some of these tools. Some of the public libraries in the world using the new and emerging technologies like Library 2.0 are given below in alphabetical order, however the list is only indicative and not comprehensive. It may be indicated here that the Stockholm Public Library was perhaps the first real Library 2.0. Many of these libraries have introduced a few or many innovative services based on web 2.0 technologies. It may not be important how many applications they facilitate but what is important is that they (library management) have understood the importance of such social networking and participative environment and took a lead in starting a service and developing the practice of using innovative technologies.

Ann Arbor District Library; Arlington Heights Memorial Library; Bedford Public Library, Texas ; Boston Public Library Burlington County

Library System, NJ ; Bibliothèque Nationale de France ;Carnegie Library of Pittsburgh; Central Rappahannock Regional Library (Answer Point); Christchurch City Libraries; Contra Costa County Library; Denver Public Library; DOK Delft Public Library, Netherlands; Library, Institute of Technology Sligo Ireland; Enoch Pratt Free Library, Baltimore, Maryland; Ellensburg Public Library, Ellensburg Washington; Hennepin County Library, Minnesota ; Iowa City Public Library, Iowa; Jackson-George Regional Library System – Mississippi; Johnson County Library, Kansas ; Kalamazoo Public Library; Kansas City Public Library; Morton Grove Public Library ; Mount Prospect Public Library; New York Public Library; Oakville Public Library, Canada; Orange County Library System; Osceola Library System; Palmerston North City : Library ;Phoenix Public Library ; Royal Oak Public Library, Michigan ; Sala Borsa Library of Bologna, Italy ; Salinas, CA Public Library - John Steinbeck ;Seattle Public Library ; St. Charles, IL Public Library ; Stockholm Public Library ; Stockton-San Joaquin County Public Library; Thomas Ford Memorial Library; Toronto Public Library ; Westerville, Ohio, Public Library ; Weld Library District, Colorado ; and West Milford Township Public Library, New Jersey

At this point of time it may be appropriate to dwell on what web 2.0 and Library 2.0 are.

The Web 2.0. concepts have led to the development and brought about revolution and evolution of web culture communities and hosted services.

4.3.1 Web 2.0: The term has been defined, used and interpreted widely. Essentially, Web 2.0 is not a web of textual publication, but a web of multi-sensory communication. A user-centered Web supports a matrix of dialogues and not a collection of monologues. In fact Web 2.0 is a bunch of Web based applications that facilitate collaboration and sharing of information and reuse of data, encouraging thereby users to help build the information environment.

Web 2.0 encapsulates the idea of the proliferation of interconnectivity and interactivity of web-delivered content. Where two players – producers and consumers are involved in the varied activities facilitated by 2.0 applications such as Wikipedia.com; remote applications slideshare.net; open social applications netwrok like Facebook, YouTube,; application program interface like Del.icio.us; or mashup - a hybrid of all or some of earlier examples (examples include attendr.com, SeclondLife.com) and the like.

This depicts that a new and a more collaborative Internet is in vogue. Keeping this in mind, perhaps one could say that Web 2.0 is open social environment facilitating social media conversation.

4.3.2 Library 2.0: The term library 2.0 is attributed to a number of social and technological changes perceived to be having an increasing impact upon libraries and information centres, their resources such as staff, clientele, and how they could interact in the new environment.

Michael Casey in his Library Crunch blog[4] *coined* the term Library 2.0 and stated that whether it is more than technolog He defined the term as web 2.0 concepts and applications in the LIS realm (but there isn't agreement on the definition). But for the argument sake, and in the present context we can put Library 2.0 as a combination of Web 2.0 and Library domain.

Many bloggers have described the Library 2.0" as "the application of interactive, collaborative, and multi-media web-based technologies to web-based library services and collections" It is thus clear that Lib 2.0 is web-based services, and not (traditional) library services so to say.

From the above it is clear that Library 2.0 is absoultuely based on the Web 2.0 applications and services. Therefore at theis point it becomes imperative to focus on various features/functions and applications of Web 2.0, before taking up its implications on libraries. The present document will thus builds on those core ideas and broadly focus on all such key aspects necessary to ascertain overall picture.

4.3.3 Web 2.0 Building the New Library: There are many Web 2.0 applications and Web 2.0-like services that we want to offer our customers. Around 34 web 2.0 icons were identified by the author, yet this number is likely to date any time as every now and then new web 2.0 features pop up on our browsers. The number of these Web 2.0 applications is fine but not much has been discussed about our ability to offer these services to our users in a usable way. Before discussing this issue, let us have a look at the principles of Web 2.0 on which it is based and then see some of the applications that can have bearing on library services.

4.3.4 Web 2.0 Applications: From YouTube to Facebook to Scriblink to StumbleUpon, new Web 2.0 applications are popping up in our browsers daily. But what is all the hubbub really about? Let us find out about it before venturing into what Lib 2.0 can inherit from Web 2.0 applications.

Google Docs (http://docs.google.com)–Free web-based word processor and spreadsheet–which allows you to share and collaborate online. You can upload, create, edit, share, access in real time, from anywhere at any time. The files are stored securely online. Always up to date, compatible and useful for collaboration and remote storage. The use in academic sector could be facilitating :collaborative works ; google book - where groups of students answer questions and post for everyone; tracking request for special need of users/studentsIt works well for synchronous collaboration also. For example: student writing–drafts can be reviewed and edited by instructor with (almost) instant feedback to the student. Such facilities may work well for the library as well.

Twitter.com–can be called a microblog that could be a hybrid of IM plus Blog plus Social network. It facilitates multichannel use to and from in multiple forms like SMS, Voice, Web, Email etc. It is service for friends, family, and co-workers to communicate and stay connected through the exchange of quick, frequent answers. It also facilitates discussion/timely updates in asynchronous mode Twitter puts you in control and becomes a modern antidote to information overload.

Flickr.com–A photo and short video sharing service and hosting service that facilitates online photo management and sharing application in the world. Student use images for presentations as it is a repository for class project images and videos.

Del.icious (http://delicious.com/)–A social bookmarking tool, facilitating folksonomy: that is collaborative classification using tags while describing content, use, or quality. It is useful for knowing current events in your discipline; shared resources contributed by students; and using folksonomic tags as evaluative descriptions of sources and also for discovering sources.

Slideshare.com (http://www.slideshare.net/)–A slideshow sharing site where it is easy to upload slides to share with others. A public link for presentation materials for faculty &student sharing content. A platform for evaluating and critiquing presentations, where you can rate and comment on the slideshows of others. It is a virtual place for discovering information from outside sources.

Netvibes.com (http://www.netvibes.com/)–A content aggregator that facilitates collaborative content sites. Lets individuals assemble their favorite widgets, websites, blogs, email accounts, social networks, search engines, instant messengers, photos, videos, podcasts,& everything else they enjoy on the web -all in one place. It is sort of a global community of users who are taking control of their digital lives by personalizing their web experience. A widget platform that is used by thousands of publishers around the world. Broadly speaking this is a virtual place for (i) aggregating resources for a course. contributed by the students and a community; (ii) one-stop-shop for information you use often igoogle and others offer similar services; (iii) easy to aggregate content from many contributors. However, contributors must know what tags the netvibes page is looking for.

Ning.com (http://www.ning.com/)–The place where you can create your own social network for anything free with ads. A collaboration/sharing tool for coterie, professional networks, event planning, shared collaborative space.

Others–There are others that are of great use and can find applications in library and information services. Mention may be made of facilities like YouTube. http://www.youtube.com/ YouTube is a video sharing website where users can upload, view and share video clips.

So what does all this mean? Does it signal a paradigm shift for all stakeholders? The stakeholders are libraries themselves, their users, content authors, publishers & software vendors. Perhaps , yes , but there are issues to ponder over at the earnest. May be some of the issues raised below have been partially addressed and/or are in pipeline or will be solved in due course. However it may be worthwhile to raise such issues here for discussion purposes. The big issue is how do you move from here to where we ought to be. How do we integrate these tools and applications in to our domain of services? Do we need some sort of integrator to integrate all this into our suit of services? Let us take some examples below for discussion purposes.

4.3.5 Integrator for Services: In order to offer these (web 2.0 based) services to our users in a smooth and highly usable way. we may need some sort of web 2.0 integrator. Let's use an example. And figure out what if library wants to integrate, on its OPACs, the following items: Flickr for image sharing and tagging; Delicious for tagging and bookmarks and Netvibes for RSS aggregation.

How are we going to do that? We can link to these items individually in some prominent way, but our users will need to create some sort of accounts for each service. In Flickr may be users will be able to tag library images and browse other library-user's images. But finding other library user's images may be difficult unless those users systematically identify their images with a common tag. Similarly library needs to craft a method, in Delicious. For instance, where library bookmarks can live alongside customer-created bookmarks – each user's account will be isolated from every other user's account and the library's account.

The library can create a base Outline Processor Markup Language (OPML) (an XML format for outlines and the most common being to exchange lists of web feeds between web feed aggregators) file of RSS feeds for Netvibes, but we cannot then update those lists for individual users

The whole idea of giving these examples is to focus on a point that library is an entity with mega size population to address and hence integration of these serves in a centralized manner is an issue for us that needs to be addressed. There are obviously other issues related to integrating such services. If we want to offer these wonderful tools then we need an integrator – a tool that will allow our users seamless access across the applications we choose to offer. Until we can address this issue, most libraries will be reluctant to officially offer any of these services and will, instead, choose simply to link to them and never take full advantage of all they have to offer.

4.3.6 Essential Elements Library 2.0 and its Implications: Based on the above could be then essential elements of the Lib 2.0. Perhaps, in some ways it is a virtual reality for libraries; or a web manifestation of the library as place. A library's presence on the Web in Library 2.0 includes the presence of that library's constituency and utilizes the same applications and technologies as its community – a concept important for particularly the academic libraries

The concept is expected to bring disruptive change and challenges our considerations of our library services. Also it challenges our current forms of offering our information services to our users. Four essential elements are:

- User Centric: It is user-centric as users participate in the creation of the content and services they view within the library's web-presence, OPAC, etc. The consumption and creation of content is dynamic, and thus the roles of librarian and user are not always clear.
- Multi media Character; It provides a multi-media experience. Both the collections and services of Library 2.0 contain video and audio components. While this is not often cited as a function of Library 2.0, it is here suggested that it should be.
- Social Networking: It is socially rich. The library's web-presence includes users' presences. There are both synchronous (e.g. IM) and asynchronous (e.g. wikis) ways for users to communicate with one another and with librarians.
- Community oriented; it is communally innovative. This is perhaps the single most important aspect of Library 2.0. It rests on the foundation of libraries as a community service, but understands that as communities change, libraries must not only change with them, and they must allow users to change the library. It seeks to continually change its services, to find new ways to allow communities, not just individuals to seek, find, and utilize information.

Therefore Library 2.0" suggests that the changing Web as "Web 2.0" will have substantial implications for libraries It also recognizes that while these implications keep very close to the history and mission of libraries, they still necessitate a new paradigm for librarianship. How Web 2.0 technologies might intimate changes in how libraries provide access to their collections and user support for that access needs to be seen in its totality. However we can at this point of time deliberate on some of the applications of evolving web 2.0 and evolving Lib 2.0.

4.3.7 Web 2.0 to Lib 2.0 Applications: There could be several applications as we have seen some examples in the previous sections of this document that finds relevance to re-engineered library services. However we would pick up a few for the present discussion as indicated below.

- Synchronous Messaging
- Streaming Media
- Blogs and Wikis
- Social Networks
- Tagging
- RSS Feeds
- Mashups

Synchronous Messaging: Library invites participation that is important for a service entity like library and that is the means of its welfare.

Lib 2.0 is about encouraging and enabling a library's community of users to participate, contributing their own views on resources they have used and new ones to which they might wish access. This technology has already been embraced quite rapidly by the library community. More widely known as instant messaging (IM), allows real-time text communication between individuals. Libraries have begun employing it to provide "chat reference" services, where patrons can synchronously communicate with librarians much as they would in a face-to-face reference context.

Hence such an application allows –a user presence within the library web-presence; collaboration between patrons and librarians. A more dynamic experience than the fundamentally static, created-then-consume nature of 1.0 service often allow co-browsing, file-sharing, screen-capturing, and data sharing and mining of previous transcripts.

Under this context mention could be made of a very important concept of librarianship - referencing. It is conceivable that should a user allow such a service, these chat reference services can be prompted when certain user seeking behaviors are detected. Library 2.0 will know when, users are lost and will offer immediate, real-time assistance. The time will almost certainly soon come when Web reference is nearly indistinguishable from face-to-face reference; librarians and patrons will see and hear each other, and will share screens and files. The transcripts these sessions already provide will serve library science in ways that face-to-face reference never did. For the first time in the history of libraries, there will be a continuously collected transcription of the reference transaction, always awaiting evaluation, analysis, cataloging, and retrieval for future reference.

Streaming Media: Social computing enriches the user experience & encourages user involvement. Streaming of video and audio media is another application that many might consider Web 1.0, as it also predates. For libraries to begin maximizing streaming media's usefulness for their patrons, 2.0 thinking will be necessary. Library instruction delivered online has begun incorporating more interactive, media-rich facets. While the static, text-based explanation coupled with a handout to be downloaded is being supplemented by more experiential tutorials. For instance – Association of College and Research Libraries' - Peer Reviewed Instructional Materials Online (PRIMO). – An Instruction Section provides a database of tutorials, many of which are Web 2.0 in their nature. Perhaps these tutorials are first of library services to migrate into more the more socially rich Web 2.0.

Blogs and Wikis: Blogs and wikis are fundamentally 2.0, and their global proliferation has enormous implications for libraries. Most obvious implication of blogs for libraries is that they are another form of publication and need to be treated as such. Though they lack editorial governance and the security but many are nonetheless integral productions in a body of knowledge, and the absence of them in a library collection could soon become unthinkable.

Wikis are essentially open web-pages, where anyone registered with the wiki can publish to it, amend it, and change it, much as blogs. A library wiki as a service can enable social interaction among librarians and patrons, essentially moving the study group room online. Blogs and wikis are relatively quick solutions for moving library collections and services into Web 2.0. This beginning of Library 2.0 makes collections and services more interactive and user-centered, enable information consumers to contact information producers and become co-producers themselves. It could be that Library 2.0 blurs the line between librarian and patron, creator and consumer, authority and novice. The potential for this dramatic change is very real and immediate, a fact that places an incredible amount of importance on information literacy.

In a world where no information is inherently authoritative and valid, the critical thinking skills of information literacy are paramount to all other forms of learning.

There are number of hosted services for getting started to blog, such as Blogger - http://www.blogger.com; DiaryLand - http://www.diaryland.com ; LiveJournal - http://www.livejournal.com; TypePad - http://www.typepad.com ; UThink - http://blog.lib.umn.edu; Movable Type - http://movabletype.org; Wordpress – http://www.wordpress.org ; Blosxom - http://www.blosxom.com ; B2evolution http://b2evolution.com and more.

Similarly for Wiki's there are several installed services, such as Kwiki - http://www.kwiki.org/ ; Twiki - http://www.twiki.org/ ;PhpWiki - http://phpwiki.sourceforge.net/ ;MediaWiki - http://www.mediawiki.org/wiki/MediaWiki; See them all - http://c2.com/cgi/wiki?WikiEngines; and more. Also hosted services, also called wiki farms such as Wikispaces - http://www.wikispaces.com ; JotSpot - http://jotspot.com Other Wiki farms - http://c2.com/cgi/wiki?WikiFarms; Compare Wiki software http://www.wikimatrix.org/ and more.

Social Networks: Social networks are perhaps the most promising and embracing technology and noteworthy as well. No imagination required to begin seeing a library as a social network itself. Much of libraries' role throughout history has been as a communal gathering place, one of shared identity, communication, and action. Social networking could enable librarians and patrons not only to interact, but to share and change resources dynamically in an electronic medium.

To its users it allows them to create accounts with the library network, and see what other users have in common to their information needs. Besides, user can recommend resources to one another, and the network recommends resources to users, based on similar profiles, demographics, previously-accessed sources, and a host of data that users provide. And also enable users to choose what is public and what is not, a notion that could help circumvent the privacy issues Library 2.0 raises

Of all the social aspects of Web 2.0, it could be that the social network and its successors most greatly mirror that of the traditional library. The face of the library's web-presence in the future may look very much like a social network interface. The example under this category could be LibraryThing. http://www.librarything.com/ that enables users to catalog their books and view what other users share those books. The implications of this site on how librarians recommend reading to users are apparent. LibraryThing enables users, thousands of them potentially, to recommend books to one another simply by viewing one another's collections. It also enables them to communicate asynchronously, blog, and "tag" their books.

Tagging: Another importance application of Web 2.0 tools in Lib 2.0 is that of tagging. Tagging essentially enables users to create subject headings for the object at hand and allows users to add and change not only content (data), but content describing content (metadata). Tags and standardized subjects are not mutually exclusive. The catalog of Library 2.0 would enable users to follow both standardized and user-tagged subjects; whichever makes most sense to them. In turn, they can add tags to resources. The user responds to the system, the system to the user. This tagged catalog is an open catalog, a customized, user-centered catalog. Tagging simply makes lateral searching easier. It is library science at its best. Let us see how it can help. For instance -often-cited example of the U.S. Library of Congress's Subject Heading "cookery," which no English speaker would use when referring to "cookbooks," illustrates the problem of standardized classification. Tagging would turn the useless "cookery" to the useful "cookbooks" instantaneously, and lateral searching would be greatly facilitated.

RSS (Really Simple Syndication) Feeds: Syndication of content is another Web 2.0 application that is already having an impact on libraries, and could continue to do so in remarkable ways. RSS feeds and other related technologies provide users a way to syndicate and republish content on the Web. Users republish content from other sites or blogs on their sites or blogs, aggregate content on other sites in a single place, and ostensibly distill the Web for their personal use.

Libraries are creating RSS feeds for users to subscribe to, - updates on new items in a collection, new services, and new content in subscription databases. They are also republishing content on their sites. However libraries have yet to explore ways of using RSS more pervasively. For more details on how libraries use RSS feeds for patron use see RSS4Lib: Innovative ways libraries use RSS. http://blogs.fletcher.tufts.edu/rss4lib/

Mention may be made here of BlogBridge –which is a software to organize the library (not a content) It is conceivable that this syndication will replace browsing and searching through library websites for content.

BlogBridge: Library (BBL), and similar RSS aggregator applications, installed in a library's system and coupled with the social network of the library, will enable users to have a single, customized, personal library page that syndicates all the library content of interest to them and their research, eliminating irrelevant information. Users will, of course, control that page and that content.

Let us see how does one subscribe to a feed? For this briefly use an RSS reader such as Mozilla Thunderbird email client - http://www.mozilla.org/products/thunderbird/; SharpReader desktop application- http://www.sharpreader.net/ ; Bloglines web client– http://www.bloglines.com/ . You can also subscribe to a feed at http://freerangelibrarian.com/

Many people interchangeably use RSS feed with a podcast. Infact a podcast is actually a feed although some people refer to the audio file itself as a podcast.

Mashups: Perhaps the single conceptual underpinning to all the technologies, ostensibly hybrid applications, where two or more technologies or services are conflated into a completely new, novel service. Example includes: Retrivr that conflates Flickr's image database and an experimental information architecture algorithm to enable users to search images not by metadata, but by the data itself. Users search for images by sketching images. Another example is WikiBios, a site where users create online biographies of one another, essentially blending blogs with social networks.

Library 2.0 is a mash up as it is a hybrid of blogs, wikis, streaming media, content aggregators, instant messaging, and social networks.

Library 2.0 remembers a user when they log in... It allows the user to edit OPAC data and metadata, saves the user's tags, IM conversations with librarians, wiki entries with other users (and catalogs all of these for others to use), and the user is able to make all or part of their profile public; users can see what other users have similar items checked-out, borrow and lend tags, and a giant user-driven catalog is created and mashed with the traditional catalog.

Others: Other tools that are good and can be checked out include - jott.com: for voice dictation for twitter, email, and more; scribblar.com for online collaboration and presentation and sharing; rememberthemilk.com for online to do list; coveritlive.com for publishing live content in real time; animoto.com for creating your own movies from photographs; wetpaint.com , wikispaces.com and pbwiki.com: free wiki sites;wordpress.com for great blogging software; pageflakes.com for social, personalized homepage; mogulus.com for multi-user live video streaming; ustream.com for live video streaming with chat. Besides there are other sites also, nonetheless the Complete Web 2.0 Directory can be reached at http://www.go2web20.net/.

4.3.8 Core Competencies 2.0 [Library & Web]: After deliberating various facets of 2.0 technologies, what can be thus the core compentcies of 2.0. Broadly these focus on the following savoir faire so to say:

- Services, not packaged software, with cost-effective scalability
- Control over unique, hard-to-recreate data sources that get richer as more people use them
- Trusting users as co-developers
- Harnessing collective intelligence
- Leveraging the long tail through customer self-service
- Software above the level of a single device
- Lightweight user interfaces, development models, AND business models

4.3.9 How Lib 2 Works in Libraries: As a Collaborative web like MySpace, Protopage, NetVibes, etc for communicating with users. For social bookmarking such as Del.icio.us], and social tagging such as CiteULike, Flickrfor integration with virtual library environments.

The question is how can your library start and incorporate some of these features. May be some of these suggestions could kick start: start a library blog; create an Emerging Technology Committee; train staff to use an RSS aggregator; experiment and use 2.0 Tools; implement IM reference For further information on this, you may refer to Creating a 2.0 Library: available at *www.*collegeathome.com/blog/2008/05/29/100-free-library-20-webinars-and-tutorials/ This webinar discusses how you can create a more interactive library using Web *2.0* technologies.

A good example to worth mentioning here for reference purposes could be LibGuides http://springshare.com/libguides/ - an ideal tool for librarians to share knowledge and publish useful information and promote your library services and resources on the Internet. As of now, over 7,800 librarians at 500 libraries (and it is growing) worldwide use LibGuides to create content, share knowledge and information, and connect with patrons. LibGuides is a fully featured, easy to use, web 2.0 content management and publishing system. It combines the best features of blogs, wikis, and social networks into one package designed specifically for libraries. It features include Email Alerts ; Templates, Collaboration, Reuse of Content ; Tagging and Categorizing by Subjects ; Integration with Del.icio.us and Social Bookmarking and Twitter; RSS Feeds, Podcasts, and Videos on Your Guides; Polls, Resource Ratings, Comments, User Submissions; Full Usage Statistics;Link Checker functionality; Librarian Profiles & Reference Chat Integration and the like.

Also you can share content and collaborate on creating guides through LibGuides Community at http://community.libguides.com Other examples in this category include LibGuides @ Univ. of South Carolina http://www.sc.edu/library/camtasia/LibGuidesSpotlight.html

5. CONCLUSION

Libraries are entropic. Just as living systems, they tend from order to disorder. Without an unremitting brewing of new energy, any system will run down the drain from best to worst. To empower nation, the people of nation irrespective of any barrier, the knowledge society ha to be build, strengthened and sustained. The knowledge society cannot exist without knowledge donors and providers, where libraries that too pubic libraries as social organizations have (the) great role to play. Hence a nation cannot afford to neglect and let public libraries to age and go down the drain. Libraries need to be vitalized, energized and reorganized as they move from one life stage to another. And with age they need to portray maturity with grace and divine.

By knowing how libraries normally thrive and change, mature and decline, professionals and supporters may identify their library's current life-stage by recognizing the characteristics of that stage. Effective management and response to issues, inclusion of good practices based on the current trends for meeting user needs in different flavors and changing environments will exercise a kind of preventative library health management for public libraries and is the most appropriate mechanism for their robust health.

Refurbishing, renovating, recreating, and recognizing the importance of new technologies and their subsequent implementation for facilitating enduring value added information services will ensure sustenance of progressive public library systems.

Many public libraries in the world are using emerging ICT tools like web 2.0 applications for keeping their users intact and also inviting and attracting those who currently are not their core users. Web 2.0 is a convenient label upon which to hang a range of concepts. Library 2.0 is all about library users — keeping those we have while actively seeking those who do not currently use our services. It's about embracing those ideas and technologies that can assist libraries in delivering services to these groups, and it's about participation — involving users in service creation and evaluation, thus creating user friendly services that people expect, and encouraging participation Areas of change: policy, programming, physical spaces, and technology.

Library 2.0 applications will benefit library users by providing rich, peer-generated content that adds value to online library databases and systems. However, not all of this shared content could be worthy for it's possible for library users to abuse Lib 2.0 applications by generating hate speech. For academic libraries to flourish in the new information environment, it becomes imperative to take steps that address such abuse. With appropriate checks and balances, libraries will be able to ensure that user contributions enrich library databases without poisoning them. Now

Web 3.0 is one of the terms that is used to describe the evolutionary stage of the web 2.0.

Therefore for stimulating growth and renewal of public libraries, use of ICT for reaching the unreached is inevitable. Can India and Indian Public Library System fulfill a part of the wish list for empowering the people of nation? Start a service and develop a practice for adoption, assimilation and implementation of ICT tools and products for facilitating effective user services to the general public, thereby ensuring the sustenance of effective social organization.

REFERENCES

1. Adekunle, P A. et.al. (2007) Attitudes of Librarians in Selected Nigerian Universities toward the Use of ICT In *Library Philosophy and Practice.* 2007 (also available at: http://www.webpages.uidaho.edu/~mbolin/tella3.htm)
2. Parliamentary office of science and Technology, UK. ICT in developing countries, March 2006, No 261 (accessed on March 21, 2009 at http://www.parliament.uk/documents/upload/postpn261.pdf)
3. Legislative Audit Bureay, Madison, WI, Best Practices Review. Public Library Services, 2007-2008 Joint Legislative Audit Committee (also available at: http;//www.08libraryservicesfull.pdf)
4. Casey, Michael. Service for the Next Generation Library: A Library 2.0 Perspective. (accessed on March 21, 2009 at http://www.librarycrunch.com/2006/01/post_1.html)
5. Norm, P, Stimulating Growth and Renewal of Public Libraries: The Natural Life Cycle as Framework.. ERIC Digest ERIC Clearinghouse on Information & Technology (accessed on March 21, 2009 at http://www.ericdigests.org/2005-2/libraries.html)

FURTHER RESOURCES

- Williams, D., et. al. (1998). Teachers' ICT skills and knowledge need: Final Report to SOEID. The School of Information and Media, Faculty of Management. The Robert Gordon University, Scotland. Available at: http://www.scotland.gov.uk/library/ict/append-title.htm [Accessed on 30 May 2007].
- Williamson, M. (1993). *Training Needs Analysis*. London: Library Association.
- Winter, S.J., Chudoba, K., & Gutek, B.A. (1998). Attitudes toward computers: When do they predict computer use? *Information and Management,* 34 (5), 275- 84.
- Woodhouse, S., & Baigent, H. (2002). People's network. *Library Association Record* 104 (1), 18.
- Yaacob, R.A. (1990). Attitudes concerning information technology of librarians employed in government-supported special libraries in Malaysia. PhD. dissertation. University of Michigan.

Application of ICT in Public Library Services

B. N. Singh*

1. INTRODUCTION

Public Libraries are called 'People's Universities' for their important role in educating the masses in general and making people conscious internationally. Public library is also acknowledged as the local gateway to knowledge, providing basic conditions for lifelong learning, independent decision-making and cultural development of the individual and social groups. According to the Manifesto of UNESCO, public library is a living force for education, culture and information, and an essential agent for fostering peace and spiritual welfare through the minds of men and women. Public library is the local centre of information, all kinds of knowledge, and makes this readily available to users. The services of the public library are provided on the basis of equality of access for all, regardless of age, race, sex, religion, nationality, language or social status. These services include:

- Creating and strengthening reading habits in children at an early age;
- Supporting both individual and self conducted education as well as formal education at all levels;
- Providing opportunities for personal creative development;
- Stimulating the imagination and creativity of children and young people;
- Promoting awareness of cultural heritage, appreciation of the arts, scientific achievements and innovations;
- Providing access to cultural expressions of all performing arts;
- Fostering inter-cultural dialogue and favouring cultural diversity;
- Supporting the oral tradition;

* Librarian, National Museum Institute of History of Art, Conservation and Museology (Deemed University), Janpath, New Delhi-110011, Email: byanktesh@gmail.com

- Ensuring access for citizens to all sorts of community information;
- Providing adequate information services to local enterprises, associations and interest groups;
- Facilitating the development of information and computer literacy skills;
- Supporting and participating in literacy activities and programmes for all age groups, and initiating such activities if necessary;

2. PHASES OF DEVELOPMENT OF PUBLIC LIBRARIES IN INDIA

The development of public libraries in India has taken place in five phases as follows:

- First phase: Bombay Government initiated proposal to register libraries which were to be given copies of books published from funds for the encouragement of literature in1808. By the middle of 19th century three cities i.e. Bombay, Calcutta and Madras had their public libraries.
- Second phase: It started from the beginning of 20th century to 1937. In this phase Indian Intelligentsia promoted the causes of public libraries.
- Third phase: The Congress party came into power in many provinces. Government promoted to establish villages libraries in Assam, Orissa, Bombay, Punjab, Cochin and other states.
- Fourth phase: This was very important phase, lasted between 1948-1951. In 1948, Madras Public Libraries Act 1948 was enacted. In 1948 itself, the National Library was set up by an Act from the old Imperial Library and 1951, the Delhi Public Library at the initiative of UNESCO was set up.
- Fifth Phase: In 1972, the Raja Rammohun Roy Library Foundation was established to give a push to the development of public library movement in the country.

In India there are nearly 55000 public libraries, consisting of national library, state central libraries, district central libraries, town libraries and village or panchayat libraries. In overall, the following different types of libraries have come up in India:

Library Type	*Estimated Number*
Academic Libraries	8100
Public Libraries	55000
Science and Technology Libraries	1200
Social Science Libraries	450
Government Departments	800
Humanities Libraries	500
National Libraries	19

According to IFLA standards, for every 3000 persons there should be one public library. Accordingly, for Indian population of 1 billion people there is a need for more than 3,30,000 public library units in the country. Therefore, the need of hour is to open more and more public libraries. We must raise slogans 'Education for all' and 'books for all'. Make education as a fundamental right. For this easy access to books and libraries must be ensured. The major deterrent in the development of public library system in the country is lack of resources. The condition of majority of public libraries in India is very pathetic and lacks even the basic facilities. The services provided by them are equally bad. This is perhaps the reason why people are not using these libraries.

3. TRANSFORMATION: FROM TRADITIONAL PUBLIC LIBRARY TO DIGITAL PUBLIC LIBRARY

Information technology has brought about phenomenal change in the way the libraries process their collections, storage functions and delivery of information products and services. In the new scenario, the library building is no longer the central venue wherein users once used to flock in to seek information. Unlike in the past, when information on a wide range of subjects was available under one roof, vast body of information is now becoming available on the desktop, on the network, and on the Internet. Information was never available so speedily and so effectively as it is now. This is mainly due to the transition of traditional libraries to digital libraries. Given the rate of information explosion, the need for ICT applications has become even more urgent otherwise public libraries would not be able to play their role effectively in the emerging knowledge society. We need to apply ICT in libraries mainly for improving operational efficiencies, reallocating the staff for user services, improving the delivery of information and quality of services, managing resources still better, facilitating wider access to information, seeking improvement in dissemination of information products and services, and evolving new frameworks for resource sharing. The top priority in ICT applications should go library automation which includes library functions such as circulation, cataloguing, acquisition, and serial control.

3.1 Acquisition

Computer application in acquisition functions is helpful in selection, ordering and procurement of library materials. The computerized acquisition systems include functions such as preparation of order list for purchasing new books, pre-order search, approval process, order placement to the booksellers, sending reminders for unsupplied books, informing indenter through mail about procurement of requested books, and preparation of list of specialized booksellers on the basis of supplied books. For book selection of new titles either traditional method can be chosen or the websites like www.amazon.com or www.bookfiders.com can be browsed. Nowadays even Indian vendors are putting the list of new arrivals on the websites. So, for the preparation of list of books for purchase their websites can also be consulted. Some vendors are also sending new arrivals through e-mails so this service can also be availed of. With the help of computers, several lists can be prepared to maintain records of all documents on order, booksellers directory and client directory etc. The computerized print out can be taken for the list of books ordered with different suppliers and reminders for unsupplied titles can be generated. Once the requested titles are received in the library the order records become basis for catalogue records in the library.

3.2 Cataloging

The role of computer in cataloguing is to help in production, updating and maintenance of catalogues. The bibliographical information is collected from the relevant sources and acquisition systems. Once the catalogue information is made available on computer, the document can be rearranged, searched and retrieved in the desired format. Once it is decided to computerize the manual data, there are several points to remember to make the data more user friendly and convenient. The basic data available in the software can be adjusted according to CDS/ISIS format, USMARC format or CCF format. The computer software can also generate added entries. It is always good to follow the standard format for the participation in cooperative ventures. The basic processes that can be performed by cataloguing module include generation of bibliographies author wise as well as subject wise, computer generated catalogue cards for standby manual catalogue cards, and listing of new accessions etc.

3.2 Circulation

The application of computers in circulation systems is to have the details of the books issued, the borrowers details on computer files and return dates. This information will give details of books dues on a particular date. Book reservation system will make it possible to reserve a book. The circulation statistics can be readily prepared with the help of computer for better management of borrower's accounts and for efficient management decisions.

3.3 Bar Code Technology for Libraries

Barcodes are accurate and eliminate the possibilities of human errors. The circulation work in automated libraries involves keying in of a large amount of data. Sometimes the information is retyped because of errors committed by staff at the circulation desk. As a result, in big public libraries, there are long queues at circulation desk. This voluminous task can be handled in a smooth manner in short time by the application of bar-coding. It is understood that the speed of barcode captured data would be three times faster than any experienced data entry operator at the counter and the error rate is almost negligible. The public libraries will have to adopt this technology to retrieve and collect data quickly, smoothly, and efficiently and for providing better services to the public.

3.4 RFID Technology for Libraries

RFID (Radio Frequency Identification) is the latest technology to be used in library as a theft detection system. It is a combination of radio- frequency and microchip. RFID can provide cost effective solutions to many key issues faced by most of the public libraries. The annual stock taking through RFID becomes very easy and can be performed in short span of time without disturbance of any kind of library services. Through inventory reader, it can be checked whether books have been shelved in correct areas or not. The library users can themselves perform issue and return function without the intervention of library staff. Any specific documents can be searched by inventory reader, whether lost or misplaced.

3.5 Serials Control

Serials control is a tedious job. The unpredictable nature of serial publications makes this house-keeping job most complicated. The main application in serials control systems include maintenance of the records of serials holdings, accessioning of serials, and other functions like selection for ordering, checking in, renewal of subscription, sending notices for non-received issues, binding etc. Due to frequent changes in the title, periodicity etc. the production of catalogue based serials holdings becomes problematic task However, from master files of serials records available in machine-readable form, the individual listing can be made on title basis, subject basis or publisher basis. The local union lists of serial holdings can also be prepared by the libraries with the help of computers. At the time of accessioning of serials, each record must contain detailed information like number of volumes per year, part volumes per publication, supplementary volumes, frequency pattern etc. The entries should also have the necessary details of suppliers, price per volumes for renewal of subscription and for accounting purposes.

3.6 Resource Sharing in Public Libraries in the Modern Computer Age

The future growth of knowledge will be largely in digital form. Therefore, resource sharing at the local level as well as the global level will create the scope for automated delivery mechanism. In the new situation, there are no barriers in accessing the resources. Reaching for full-text articles from remote work stations is now far easier and speedier. Such emerging trends underline the urgent need for libraries to make resource sharing programme effective in meeting users requirements.

4. THE ROLE OF AUTHORITIES OF PUBLIC LIBRARIES

The librarian's mission is to work towards meeting the information needs of people by providing high quality information systems, services, products, based on the recorded human knowledge of the world, through the utilization of current and emerging information technologies. The management of library and information service is entering a new age of accountability. Disinclination in service is now no longer accepted by the public at large. The library and information professionals will have to justify their existence. The basic concepts of quality management must now be applied to managing libraries for effective performance. The technology alone cannot help to bring about the required changes. The attitudes, management practices and policies also need to be changed, if public libraries are to benefit from the application of new technologies.

5. ISSUES THAT REQUIRE URGENT ATTENTION TO STRENGTHEN PUBLIC LIBRARIES

In order to strengthen the public libraries, the following issues require urgent attention:

- Creation of suitable computerized databases for public libraries,
- Networking of libraries and promoting resource sharing and avoiding duplication,
- Modernization and automation of libraries,
- Setting up of a national level agency to oversee and monitor the library and information system in India,
- Formulation of preservation and conservation programmes for rare books and manuscripts in libraries,
- Training of library professionals particularly, in computer application,
- Promoting awareness among users and library staff regarding the role of libraries in society,
- Mobilization of resources for development of libraries from all channels of society,
- The rural libraries of Bihar, Rajasthan, Madhya Pradesh, Uttar Pradesh etc., need special attention to strengthen the library movement, and
- The Government of India should extend more grant-in-aid to NGOs for organizing public library services.

6. CONCLUSION

The basic objective of any library is to provide the right information to the right person at the right time. The information is valuable only if retrieved in a timely manner. In this age of information explosion the management of information resources is a big challenge before the public libraries. The modern public libraries can meet these challenges by the application of ICT in library operations as well as optimize the value of information to the society. By using this strategy public libraries would certainly emerge as active agent of transformation of our society into a well informed and complete knowledge society.

REFERENCES

1. Bhattacharjee, R. (2002). Public Library Services in India: Systems, modernization, networking and deficiencies. *In National Round Table on Modernisation and Networking of Libraries in India.* Delhi: DELNET.
2. Kaul, H.K. (2002). Electronic Libraries in Rural India. *In National Round Table on Modernisation and Networking of Libraries in India.* Delhi: DELNET.
3. Singh, Byanktesh Narain (2001). Digital Libraries, In H.K. Kaul, ed. *Library and Information Networking.* NACLIN
4. IGNOU Online MLIS Course book, (2008). *Public Library Services.* New Delhi, IGNOU.

University Oriented Electronic Information Services and Their Suitability in the Public Library Context

BHARATI PALIWAL*

1. INTRODUCTION

Information is vital to the success of academic and research activity, and its flow is a two-way process. On the one hand, specialized, updated information is constantly needed by users to keep them informed of the latest developments and updates in their fields of interest. On the other hand, the outputs from their academic and research activities need to be suitably packaged for wider dissemination throughout the world. The above requirements can be met only with a comprehensive library, equipped with state-of-the-art information storage and retrieval systems and having quick access to worldwide sources of information.

In 1928, Dr S.R. Ranganathan defined the five laws of library science, focusing especially on the fifth law, which said, "A library is a growing organism". This couldn't have been more true, considering the pace at which libraries as information storehouses have grown, around the world, from paper-dependent information to the present digital-oriented information. Information is now stored and available online, on CD-ROMs. Electronic mail and video conferencing have cut down all geographical boundaries and made it possible to sit in a remote corner of any country and access information from around the world at the touch of a button.

Libraries are no longer confronted with the question of whether or not to apply this new change to their operations, products and services. The concern now is what technologies to use, the extent to which these should be used, their benefits and impact, and the operational methodologies as appropriate to the library's character. Answers lie in the patterns of IT tools available to libraries, and their overall impact on the services that the libraries offer.

---

* Librarian, TERI University Library, New Delhi

2. ABOUT TERI

Libraries especially designed to meet the customized needs of users are few in this country. Among the highly regarded institutes in the country many are from the non-government sector. One of the such institutes is The Energy and Resources Institute (TERI). It has affiliate Institutes in Washington DC, and London along with overseas presence in Japan, Malaysia and Dubai. Its Centres in India are located in Bangalore, Guwahati, Goa, Mukteshwar and Mumbai.

TERI University contributes globally by serving the society as a seat of advanced learning. The University commits itself to academic excellence and providing an environment that encourages both personal and intellectual growth through teaching, creating, and sharing knowledge. The TERI University offers world-class research facilities to students with its state-of-the-art infrastructure and well-equipped laboratories and library.

The University and the Institute collaborate in research projects; undertake joint studies; and offer mutual support for seminars, symposia, and conferences on subjects of theoretical and practical relevance. TERI has 25 years of research experience and ample case studies, a legacy that is passed on to the TERI University; thus the experience of researchers is translated into unmatched learning with state-of-the art computer hardware and software, a GIS laboratory, videoconferencing facilities, and South Asia's most comprehensive library on energy and environment.

TERI University has academic collaborations with several foreign universities, which provide for joint curriculum development and exchange of faculty and students. The TERI University was established in 1998 and was granted 'Deemed-to-be University' status by the UGC and the Ministry of Human Resource Development. TERI University also entered into a memorandum of understanding with the School of Forestry and Environmental Studies of the Yale University, Donald Danforth Plant Science Centre, USA, University of Nottingham, UK, Michigan State University, USA, New South Wales University, Australia, University of Iceland, Iceland, North Carolina State University, USA, and Brandeis University, USA. TERI University campus was inaugurated by The President of India, Shrimati Pratibha Patil in September 2008.

TERI University faculties are segmented into centres and departments that focus on specific aspects of sustainable development. While the centres carry out doctoral research, the departments focus on instruction at the Master's level as well as doctoral research. The University campus located at Vasant Kunj in South Delhi, is a showcase of the concept of modern green buildings. The campus is aesthetically designed with several features of passive solar design, energy efficiency, water and waste management systems.

3. ABOUT THE LIBRARY

The library is modern and well-stocked, which promotes and disseminates information services. It meets the information requirements of users and institutions in India and globally. The library's services are offered electronically, in IT-enabled and wi-fi environment, CD-ROM collections of bibliographic and statistical resources, Internet connectivity for accessing worldwide scientific information and databases, audio and videos.

The Library maintains South Asia's finest repository of readings on energy, environment, sustainable development, and biotechnology. The library holds over 25, 000 books, reports, and conference proceedings; 1000 CDs; a large volume of miscellaneous literature including annual reports, government documents, maps, newsletters, newspaper clippings, pamphlets, reprints, and standards; and provides access to over 1800 online and print journals (with 14 250 bound back volumes). The Web-enabled integrated library system facilitates access to a wide range of resources and e-services available to users on their desktops.

Institutional membership of some select libraries is obtained in order to provide access to resources through inter-library loan facility. This also helps TERI to promote networking with such libraries. The Library has on an average 2000 visitors every month, which include users from India and abroad. It is the constant endeavour of Library to make this repository easily accessible for meeting the information requirements of all its users.

4. ELECTRONIC INFORMATION RESOURCES AND SERVICES

These are strengthened with quality content and value-added services. The Library provides access to several significant databases, which include JSTOR, Prowess, and Science Direct; various portals such as Indiastat.com, Indiapetro.com, India Trades, and Infraline.com; government documents; reference documents; annual reports; newsletters; theses; and current and archived in-house journals. The Library also undertakes development and management of the in-house databases: Energy–environment literature abstracts, news archives, events, rare documents, the Institute's memoranda of understanding, in-house books, photographs, newspaper clippings, and multimedia resources.

5. INFORMATION DISSEMINATION

The Library also provides information for in-house publications, websites, and reference and information services. The library develops information products and services with specialized focus on needs/preferences of users. Information resources/services available to users include the following:

- Journal content alerts that provide access to the contents pages of journals received in the library

- Access to catalogues of about 1000 libraries of national and international repute
- Access to websites of other institutes for latest publications, ongoing projects, and relevant emerging research topics
- Forthcoming events, recent additions, and daily news headlines
- Access to international news/information from online sources.
- Specialized information service to users in the form of exhaustive literature searches from books, journals, and online resources
- Linkages and networking for resource sharing
- Information exchange programmes with overseas institutes/ universities
- Partnering to strengthen mutually fruitful collaboration
- Alert services
- Call for papers announcements
- Forthcoming sponsored programmes by foreign institutes/ universities
- Resources/websites of relevance
- Subject/Syllabus/Course based information support
- Monitoring catalogues of publishers and online databases
- Tracking information for scholarships/placements

6. USAGE OF LIBRARY SERVICES

Among all the library services, electronic library services are most popular. The library users are satisfied with the Selective dissemination of Information service. The survey revealed that the majority of users came to know about recent information through electronic alert services. The survey revealed that the users feel that the proactive role-played by the library in providing them these services is very useful. Most users weren't aware of CD-ROM collection. However, what was alarming was the poor use of these resources something that needs looking into. Adequate publicity should be given about CDs to improve their usage.

Usage of Library Services (%)

Book requests	85
Library catalogue	79
Literature searches	84
Reference services	87
Bibliographic Databases	76
Inter-library loan	42
Electronic library collection and services	92
CD-ROM collection	36
Reprographic services	11
Alert Services: Selective dissemination of Information	88

The survey also underlined the need for organizing, conducting regular orientation programmes for newcomers, user alert services, adequate publicity about the CD collection, more online journals, strengthening collections in select areas, greater emphasis to be given to latest reference books and promoting library cooperation for resource sharing.

7. CONCLUSION

The Energy Research Institute and TERI University are the excellent examples of knowledge creation, knowledge application, and knowledge utilization. Their contributions symbolize raw knowledge capital that is expected as an outcome form a university environment in the knowledge based economy. The University and Institute both organize several electronic information services customized for the benefit of faculty, research teams, project teams, research scholars and student population. This paper has sought to characterize these electronic information services in the context of the university environment. Having done that, the issue that is being raised here is whether public libraries can justify the provision of such electronic information services for the public in the context of emerging knowledge society. If so, do public libraries have the potential, capacity, infrastructure, organizational structure and mandate to organize such information services with a certain degree of excellence. We need to address such questions before we pass any opinion or judgement on the new roles that public libraries should take in the context of emerging knowledge based economy.

Public Library Services for Children in the Digital Environment

Manpreet Kaur Sohal[1], **Prabhjeet Kaur**[2] **and P. K. Walia**[3]

1. INTRODUCTION

The vital role that public libraries can play in the national development of the country particularly in programmes such as informal education, dissemination of information, and recreational activities as well as in its programmes on socio-economic development, has since been well accepted world over. A public library is an organization established, supported and funded for the community either through local, regional or national governmental bodies or through some other form of community organization. It provides access to knowledge, information and works of the imagination through a range of resources and services and is available equitably to all members of the community regardless of race, nationality, age, gender, religion, language, disability, economic and employment status and educational attainment[1].

The public library, the local gateway to knowledge, provides a basic condition for lifelong learning, independent decision-making and cultural development of the individual and social groups. According to ALA Glossary of Library and Information Science[2] public library is

- Any library which provides general library services without charge to all residents of a given community, district or region. Supported by public or private funds, the public library makes its basic collections and basic services available to the population of its legal service area without charges to individual users, but may impose charges on users outside its legal service area. Products and services beyond the library's basic services may or may not be provided without individual charges.

---

1. M. Phil. Research Scholar, Department of Library & Information Science, University of Delhi
2. M. Phil. Research Scholar, Department of Library & Information Science, University of Delhi
3. Reader, Department of Library & Information Science, University of Delhi

- Earlier a library accessible to all residents of a given community, but not generally free, as distinguished from a private library.

Thus a public library is a library which is accessible by the public and is generally funded from public sources. Public libraries exist in most nations of the world and are often considered an essential mechanism for having an educated and literate population. The public libraries serve the population of a community or region. They meet the needs of all groups in the community regardless of age and physical, economic or social circumstances. Children who are the future of a nation are the most important category of users served by the public libraries. 'Catch them young' is a phrase of great social relevance. Habits picked up at the early impressionable period in one's life are bound to continue throughout life. Reading is a habit that should necessarily be cultivated in the children. Apart from exposing them to the works of knowledge and widening their mental horizon, it helps them to learn throughout their life. Many of the students even at the university level of education where self study becomes more important, find themselves severely handicapped because it is at this late stage that they have their first library experience. Therefore, it is very necessary that children should be provided adequate facilities for reading and this is the responsibility that public libraries need to share with school libraries, by establishing children's wings and maintaining them in an attractive and inviting manner.

2. NEED FOR CHILDREN'S SECTION IN PUBLIC LIBRARIES

Children, who have not been exposed to the world of books at any early age, find themselves at a loss, when as adult they are supposed to do self-study. Public libraries have a special responsibility to meet the needs of children and young people. If children can be inspired by the excitement of knowledge and by works of the imagination at an early age, it will benefit them in their personal development during the rest of their lives as well build their potential to make useful contributions to society.

Children can also encourage parents and other adults to make use of the library. It is also important that young people who experience difficulty in learning to read should have access to a library to provide them with appropriate material. So, to meet the needs and requirement for their children clientele, the public libraries should have a separate section for children. This section should have provision for children's story time or after-school program, and space for homework help programs or other community services. The public libraries should also co-operate with the educational, social and cultural institutions, including schools, adult education centres, and with leisure activity groups and with all those concerned with promotion of arts[1].

Following points highlight the needs for developing a children's section in a public library:

- To inculcate reading habits among children at a young age
- To facilitate the right of every child to:
  - information
  - functional, visual, digital and media literacy
  - cultural development
  - reader development
  - lifelong learning
  - creative programs in leisure time[3] (IFLA, 2003)
- Helps in developing language skills;
- Developing positive habits and learning to socialize;
- To encourage children to become confident and competent people;
- For stimulating their imaginations;
- Understanding the functions of the words and pictures in the books;
- Helps foster the intellectual development- hearing words and music, viewing pictures and text, teaching objects and scanning pages of books;
- To develop a child's knowledge base;
- For better utilization of ideal time: These days, children get easily diverted into activities like watching television for long hours, playing video games etc. They can instead go to the children's section which can help them in utilizing their time in a better way by learning activities like painting, getting an exposure of web based information, etc.;
- For fulfilling their information needs: In the present environment mostly both the parents of children are working and there arises a communication gap between them. In such a scenario the children's section librarian can provide them with answers to their questions;
- For recreation: To provide children with open access to adequate resources and media, and in addition provide cultural and recreational programmes; and
- For developing skills: To provide various activities for children and their parents, children's libraries provide opportunities, outside the school or family environment, for learning about the responsibilities, for acquiring skills necessary in the promotion and protection of rights and freedoms, as well as for living in conditions that reflect them.

3. LIBRARY SERVICES FOR CHILDREN

The children's section in a public library must plan and implement services for children based on their age, development and interests, and the objectives of the library. Some of the essential services that should be provided in the children's section include the following:

3.1 Traditional Services

- **Lending services**: Children can borrow books (for education, information, inspiration and recreation), comics, novels, story-books, text books, etc along with multimedia collection in the form of CDs, DVDs, audio tapes, audio books, etc from the library.
- **Reference and information services**: Children have special information needs that cannot be met through the services traditionally offered by public libraries. It is intended to explore the special needs and requirements of the child as a 'reference client' and identify opportunities for the public library to take a greater role in meeting there information needs. Both school and public libraries should develop partnerships to delivery quality reference services to children. Reference service also provides assistance in the searching and location and using of library material[4].
- **Readers' clubs** for inculcating reading habits among children
- **Group Discussion and Debates** should be carried out to improve communication skills among the children.
- **Creative Writing:** To develop and improve language and writing skills of the children.
- **Storytelling:** Story hours should be organized for different age groups where the library staff or children themselves read out stories for leisure.
- **ICT Awareness:** The children's section should have basic computer and networking facility to provide exposure to various IT applications like Paint, Word, Powerpoint, etc and surfing the internet for useful information. This service aims at bridging the gap between the information rich & information poor, particularly through the provision of ICT resources.
- **Drawing and Painting:** Activities like drawing, painting, art and craft should be conducted to develop their skills.
- **Movie Shows:** Cartoon films as well as culture oriented movies should be planned so as build up the child's interest towards the library.
- **Tours:** Libraries should collaborate with schools for organizing children's group tours to libraries which help in creating the child's interest towards using library as a resource for information.
- **Cultural Programs:** The children's section should conduct programs outside the library for schools, daycares, nursing homes, clubs, and not-for-profit organizations when it is possible to do so at the Library's convenience for cultural and social development of the child.
- **Bulletin Board and Display Case:** The bulletin board and the display cases serve as display areas for the children's section and may be used by other groups at the discretion of the librarian.
- **Games**: Educational games and toys should be kept in the children's section to aid in the intellectual progress of the child. Quizzes should also be conducted.

- **Summer reading programmes:** To develop the child's interest in reading during the holidays.

3.2 DIGITAL SERVICES

The traditional services are likely to remain of vital importance in the foreseeable future. With the advent of digital technology, libraries are becoming the gateway to the electronic information world and every effort must be made to open other doors through which knowledge and information can be provided. Some of the digital services provided by the children section of a public libraries include following:

- **Access to e-books and online reference sources:** The children can pick books from the website on children libraries. A facility to search books using search box can be used for the purpose. These can be downloaded, read for free and anonymously. They can create user account to keep a bookshelf of books they like and set various personal preferences. Also online reference sources like dictionaries and encyclopedia as available on the library website (International Children's Digital Library[5]) should interest children.
- **Digital Story Time:** Parents can read story books to children aloud using a computer projector and a large screen display. This has the advantage of making illustrations (and words) large enough for everyone to see – and the technical nature of the display is often engaging[6].
- **Complete the Story:** Parents can also use the first half of any book to inspire children to complete the 2nd half of the story. The first portion of the book can be read together, and then the child can be inspired to envision how the story ends by drawing pictures and illustrating them.
- **Creative Writing:** This can be used to push the child's creativity, by just looking at a picture book in a language they don't understand at all and then they can be asked to write a story that goes along with the pictures.
- **Learning Languages:** Books can be made available in more than one language on the website. These books can be used to study a language that a child needs to learn and doesn't know properly.
- **Online audio and video material:** Such material helps children to learn by listening and viewing material such as e-books, audio books, movie adaptations of books, etc. This material can be directly accessed and downloaded from the website of the digital library.
- **Online games:** Online games like puzzles, jumble words, crosswords, number games etc. should be added on to a digital library website to aid in child's mental development. Also other fun games can be added for amusement purposes.

By providing such services, public libraries help to bring everyone into this global conversation and thus bridge what is often called 'the digital divide'[7]. However, to fulfill the principle of access for all, they must also continue to maintain services that provide information in different ways, for example, through print or the oral tradition[1].

4. PUBLIC LIBRARIES WEBSITES OFFERING DIGITAL SERVICES FOR CHILDREN

In the present environment, public libraries need to develop library websites to meet the needs of their young clientele. The Web pages serve as centers for reference, educational support, popular materials, and community information. Also, children need to be very well versed with the retrieving information using latest technologies. Thus attempts have been made by the children's section of the public libraries across the world to serve their young clientele with digital services. Some of the examples of incorporation of digital services on the websites of the libraries are as following:

4.1 International Children's Digital Library-Digital Library for the World's Children

The ICDL is a rich resource which can be used in a wonderfully wide range of situations by children, parents, teachers, librarians and others from all walks of life. It functions from Maryland, USA. Using this digital library, children can expand upon the stories to create games; parents can extract themes to help explain important lessons; teachers can utilize the multicultural nature of the collection to teach languages; librarians can enrich community outreach programs with tales from around the world and; of course, anyone can just open a book to read for pleasure. The mission of the International Children's Digital Library foundation is to excite and inspire the world's children to become members of the global community- children who understand the value of tolerance and respect for diverse cultures, languages and ideas- by making the best in children's literature available online. The important features of this library are as follows:

- It offers books in more than 40 languages.
- The collection is available for children of different age groups like three to five, six to nine, and ten to thirteen.
- For easy retrieval, the books are classified under various categories like short books, medium books, long books, recently added books, award winning books, fairy tales and folk tales, picture books, chapter books, kid characters etc.
- One can search books with different options like Simple Search, Advanced Search, Location Search and Keyword Search.
- One can read books with the help of Standard and Clear Text Readers, Comic Reader, Spiral Reader.

- One can also create his/ her own personal bookshelf. (International Children's Digital Library).

4.2 New York Public Library – On the Lion

The New York Public Library is a unique and complex institution. Through its Research and Branch Libraries it provides free and democratic access to information on a scale unmatched by any other institution in the world. Its holdings have also played a vital role in the creation of innumerable works in the arts, literature, and history. Through its On the Lion for Kids section it provides special services for Kids. Its services includes:-

- Access to different catalogs on Lion for kid's site like LEO Catalog - for checkout, LEO Telnet, PAWS Catalog - Braille & Talking Books
- LEO Line - Renew books & check holds
- eNYPL- Download books, music & video
- Book Flix - Video Storybooks (PreK - 3)
- NYPL's Best of the Web
- CATNYP Catalog - For Research
- NYPL's Google Books
- Articles & Databases
- Digital Collections- NYPL Digital Gallery & more
- Webcasts, Audio & Video

On the Lion also offers the following digital services from its website:

- Tumble books- Animated Talking Picture Books
- Story time
- Reading Aloud & Story Telling
- Games @ the Library
- Theater Performances
- Art & Craft
- Myths & Magic
- Music
- Activities like: Book plates, Chinese calligraphy, spy riddles, puzzles etc. (New York Public Library).

4.3 Joplin Public Library

The Joplin Public Library District was established in 1902. In 1999, the Library introduced its Web site and provided access to its catalog on the Internet. Joplin Public Library has a different section for children which come under The Rosemary Titus Reynolds Children's Library in the Joplin Public Library i.e. the Children's Department. The objectives of this department are: to introduce as many children as possible to the public library environment in order to create lifetime readers and library users; to provide children with access to current information and quality literature;

and to provide children with access to current information and quality literature; and to provide complete and accurate answers to reference questions to all patrons of the Department.

Patrons of any age may use the computers in the adult department, but the computers in the children's department are reserved for those patrons age 12 and younger. Computers in the Teen Department are reserved for teens, patrons in grades 6-12, and do not provide Internet access. They are available for office applications like word, games, music and movies. Specialized Children's Services include:

- Children's Reference
- Storytimes, Summer Reading Program
- Children's Programming
- Collection Management
- Materials Inventory
- Online reference catalog including encyclopedias, dictionaries etc. (Joplin Public Library).

4.4 StoryPlace

StoryPlace, an interactive web site, provides children with the virtual experience of going to the library and participating in the same types of activities as the Preschool Library and Elementary Library of Public Library of Charlotte Mecklenburg County, North Carolina. It is provided in two languages: English and Spanish, so that children can choose the one they are more familiar with and work on improving the other one. Services provided to children are categorized into:

- Pre-School Library: These services are provided under different themes like animals, colours, music shapes, etc and include the following
  - On-line story
  - On-line activities
  - Take-home activities
  - Activities for parents
  - Suggested reading list
- Elementary Library: These services are also theme based and have themes like Riddles etc suited for this age group. They include the following:
  - Print-out activities
  - Topsy-turvy tales
  - Suggested reading lists. (StoryPlace).

5. INDIAN SCENARIO

With regard to growth and development of public libraries in India, Delhi public library deserves special mention. It was founded in 1951 as the first UNESCO Public Library Pilot Project under the joint auspices of

UNESCO and Government of India. The purpose of the library was to adapt "modern techniques to Indian conditions" and to serve as a model public library for Asia. The establishment of Delhi Public Library, the involvement of union government in the public library movement, and the enactment of public library legislation in some states are the main factors which contributed to the improvement of public libraries after independence. Although the Government of India allotted funds for public library development in its five-year plans, this funding was not connected to effective planning.

The Government of India took various steps from time to time to report on the status of public library development in the country such as Sinha Committee (1957), NAPLIS (1986) under chairmanship of Prof. D.P. Chattopadhyay. Another positive step taken by the Central Government was the establishment of the Raja Rammohun Roy Library Foundation (RRRLF) at Calcutta. Among the various current programmes of assistance of RRRLF is 'Assistance to children's libraries or children's sections of general public libraries' (Wani)[8].

In India the condition of children sections in public libraries is not satisfactory. British Council Library offers a well put up children's corner within its premises. Delhi Public Library in Sarojini Nagar, Patel Nagar and Central Library Branches also have revamped Children's Section with addition of new collection, games and furniture. Dr. B. C. Roy Memorial Children's Reading Room and Library, which come under Children Books Trust caters to children of Delhi and provides a healthy environment for their development with colourful ambience and collection. A new venture by the name of Out of the Box' situated in Bangalore, also aims at providing services to children.

But, in the name of providing digital services only Department of Public Libraries, Karnataka, have put a small step ahead and have developed "Children's Virtual Library Portal". It is a service of its first kind in Indian Public Library Scenario. On this portal free literature for children that are in the public domain links is listed; which is simply called "Khuljaa Sim Sim" and clicking on this link will take the child to the treasure house of knowledge. It is one of the good efforts for encouraging good reading habits in children.

The Mission of Children's virtual Library Portal:

- Internet World Wide Learning Resource Center for children;
- Providing free literature for children that are in the public domain;
- Children's Virtual Library is not just for children who can read, but also beginning readers, disadvantaged and non-readers; and
- Every child can know and appreciate the richness of children's literature from the world community. (Department of Public Libraries).

Apart from this, there is no other adequate effort taken up in India and there is still a need for extending them for meeting the requirements of future generation. For this, the public libraries should give a face-lift to their existing collection, services and infrastructure. They should also develop their websites to impart specialized digital services for fulfilling the needs of their young clientele. Incorporation of collection and services for imparting cultural and mythological understanding is also essential.

6. RECOMMENDATIONS AND SUGGESTIONS

Owing to the present scenario of the digital library services being provided for children in India, there is a dire need for Children's Section in Indian public libraries and children's libraries to develop digital services for their clientele. Some of the recommendations and suggestions have also been made in an attempt to stimulate more and more digital library services in India:

- For children it is very necessary that the physical format of the book should be attractive. It should have an attractive jacket, nice layout so that the child is irresistibly drawn towards it.
- Poetry hour and story time may sometimes be held during the week.
- The collection should include books, CDs, audios, DVDs, etc for stories on heroism, folk tales, myths and legends, biography and autobiography, history, culture etc. along with encyclopedias like children's Britannica, Hamlyn Junior Science Encyclopedia, Understanding Science, Visva Bharti, Children's Book of Knowledge and oxford junior Encyclopedia must be included.
- The children should occasionally be taken to visit book fairs and book exhibitions.
- Some free time should be given to children for browsing things of their interest on the internet accessing digital services of the library.
- To create a happy and healthy environment, rooms may be decorated with cartoons, toys, models, and paintings on walls and windows.
- Some prizes may be awarded to the best readers and best users of the library. This will definitely encourage other children to read.
- Special courses for reading faster and better which are highly popular in USA and UK can be started.
- Libraries may also request schools to organize debate and essay competitions, chat shows, and exhibitions, quiz hours, etc., at regular intervals so as to generate reading interest and information gathering habit.
- Present environment and incorporation of ICT in libraries calls for a need to provide online and digital services to the children via their websites so that they can also have access to the library

services from anywhere and at anytime. These may include online interactive learning environment including audio and video stories, puzzles, games etc according to different age groups.

7. CONCLUSION

Public libraries have always been regarded as the gateways to knowledge and learning for a large majority of the population. As children are the future of a nation, they must be given adequate library facilities to build sound information and knowledge base. It is therefore important that children sections in the public libraries, which are like knowledge centres and contributing to lifelong learning, must be transformed significantly. Children librarians should take initiative to encourage students to improve their knowledge base by reading more and more books, newspapers, magazines and journals. They also provide them necessary guidance as to what to read, how to read and how to make profitable use of the library. Provisions should also be made for providing sufficient digital library services.

REFERENCES

1. Gill, Philip, Ed. (2001). *The Public Library Service*. München: Saur, 2001.
2. *ALA Glossary of Library and Information Science* (1983). ALA, Chicago.
3. IFLA. The background text to the Guidelines for Children's Libraries Services. 2003. Accessed on 6 March 2009 <www.ifla.org>.
4. Brown, Anita.(2003). Reference services for children: information needs and wants in the public library. *Australian Library and Information Association.* 53 (3). Accessed on March 6, 2009. <http://alia.org.au/publishing/alj/53.3/full.text/brown.html\>.
5. International Children's Digital Library. Accessed on 6 March 2009. <http://en.childrenslibrary.org/icdl/ >.
6. Story Place. Accessed on 6 March 2009. <http://www.storyplace.org/storyplace.asp>.
7. Pateman, John (2008). Public libraries and digital divide. *Information for Social Change.* 26, 52-55. http://libr.org/isc/issues/ISC26/26%20Public%20Libraries%20and%20the%20Digital%20Divide.pdf
8. Wani, Zahid Ashraf (2008). Development of public libraries in India. *Library Philosophy and Practice.* 1-10. Accessed on 6 March 2009. <http://www.webpages.uidaho.edu/~mbolin/wani.pdf>.
9. Department of Public Libraries, Karnataka: Children's Public Library Portal. Accessed on 6 March 2009. <http://164.100.80.120/karpublib/Childrens%20Virtual%20Library/Childrens%20Virtual%20Library.htm>.
10. Out of the Box. Accessed on 9 March 2009. <www.outofthebox.org>.
11. Joplin Public Library. Accessed on 6 March 2009.<http://www.joplinpubliclibrary.org>.
12. New York Public Library: On-Lion for kids. Accessed on 6 March 2009. <www.kids.nypl.org>.

Training of In-Service Manpower in Public Libraries: Issues and Strategies

SEWA SINGH*

1. INTRODUCTION

Information is considered as the fifth need of human being. It is the basic resource at par with other types of resources such as capital, land and manpower, playing a significant role in the national development of the country in all sectors of economy. Information is recognized as a commodity in this Information Society to be acquired, organized, preserved, and managed for use in evolving strategies for the overall development of the country.

2. PUBLIC LIBRARY

The UNESCO Public Library Manifesto 1994 defined a public library "as a living force for education, culture and information, and as an essential agent for the fostering of peace and spiritual welfare through the minds of men and women." Public libraries therefore need to play significant role in processing and dissemination of information for educational, cultural and recreational purposes. Public libraries are therefore meant for all the citizens of the society, touching the lives of all under social strata, viz., young and old, men and women, children and housewives, urban and suburban, poor and rich, literate and illiterate, on equal basis. This is why a public library is still considered a place where one can search freely for whatever one wants from its vast resources.

3. MANPOWER

Manpower is the sum total of knowledge, abilities and skills they possess, and the quality of work it is capable of carrying out. It is the quality of manpower which is crucial for this purpose. The quality of manpower is determined by such factors as education and training, work experience, work environment, human relations, etc. Public libraries, in order to fulfill

---

* Former Prof & Head, GND University, Amritsar

the objectives, make every endeavor to recruit manpower with knowledge and competencies in the professional techniques.

4. CHANGE FACTORS

The recent developments in the ICT and its library applications have brought about significant changes in the scope and dimension of the profession as well as underlined the need for professional staff to build new skills and competencies. Every individual harbors the urge to enhance his/her social status, build material wealth, or influence the society in some way or the other. Such social factors are difficult to address adequately within the formal system of library education. However, technological factors can be well covered. Besides, such efforts must also be complemented by organizing continuing education programmes for the benefit of the library staff that were recruited long time back and are lacking in skills and competencies for effective performance. It is in this context that training of in-service staff becomes all the more important in particular to improve and build potential of in-service staff and motivate them for better performance.

5. OBJECTIVES OF TRAINING

In order to make libraries function effectively, not only the proper utilization of manpower is important, but at the same due attention has to be given to in-service training. The in-service training may be defined as a process of acquiring and transmitting professional knowledge and practical skills during working life. The main objective of training is to bring a change in the knowledge, skills, and behavioural attitude of the staff to meet the user needs satisfactorily. Training is aimed at changing the behaviour of the staff to new patterns as specified by the organization and considered necessary for effective performance.

6. IMPORTANCE OF TRAINING

Training should not remain as one time affair, it should rather be a continuous programme. The importance of in-service training lies in the fact that it helps to:

- improve the quality and quantity of services;
- facilitate better utilization of resources; and
- reduce costs and boosts morale of the manpower;

In view of the fast technological changes and the need to keep abreast with such developments, in-service training on regular basis becomes even more essential. It will be in the interest of the library as well as its staff if some budget is earmarked for organizing training programmes on regular basis.

7. BENEFITS OF TRAINING

Some of the benefits of in-service training for library personnel may be as under:

- **Better Performance:** A well designed training programme will help to provide high quality services to the users by acquiring latest IT knowledge.
- **Economical:** Training of in-service staff should make them learn as to how to make the most economical use of the money, material, equipments.
- **Less Supervision:** The staff trained under such training programmes are likely to become more responsible, hence need less supervision from the seniors.
- **Stability:** The availability of trained manpower will bring long-term stability and flexibility in their working.
- **Improvement in Human Relations:** The training programme will enhance confidence in the staff which will result in improving relations with the authorities, coordinates and subordinates.
- **Uniformity of Procedures:** Manpower will help in standardizing the best available method of performing the work to achieve uniformity of procedures.
- **Career Advancement:** With in-service training the library staff have enhanced their knowledge and skills which will help them in career advancement.
- **Job Satisfaction:** There will be greater level of job satisfaction among the staff of the library after the training.

8. TYPES OF TRAINING

The following types of training programmes are most commonly organized in the libraries:

8.1 Internship

Internship is generally developed to provide practical experience and training to professionals with the purpose of acquainting them with the functioning and organization of various library systems and sub systems as well as to strengthen their theoretical knowledge as acquired during formal education. It is possible to organize internship programmes only with the active cooperation of libraries where students are required to be sent for practical training.

8.2 Apprenticeship

One of the traditional methods of training is apprenticeship which aims to impart sufficient knowledge and skills to improve the competence level of trainees to execute professional and technical tasks of the library.

8.3 Orientation

Orientation as a training programme seeks to provide new library staff with the basic background information to enable them to perform their jobs satisfactorily. New staff need to be initiated about the library rules and regulations; different sub systems of the library system; various services designed for users; and human resource management policies and practices; etc.

8.4 Refresher Courses

Refresher courses in library and information science are aimed to acquaint the working library personnel with the latest trends and developments in the discipline and also IT application to libraries, and so on. The knowledge and skills of in- service staff do become irrelevant and obsolete over time as a result of fast technological changes. Refresher course is thus an important method to keep the staff abreast with the latest developments in the field. Therefore, staff must be encouraged and motivated to participate in the refresher courses.

9. METHODS OF TRAINING

Some important methods of training for library manpower are given below:

9.1 On-the-job Training

It is one of the oldest and most popular methods of training the staff. A senior and well experienced staff member is given the responsibility of training the new recruits. In this process the new staff may acquire necessary skills for meeting the user requirements. In this method, the staff learns while working within the library hence it is relatively inexpensive.

9.2 Simulated Training

In this method the trainees learn on the actual equipment they will use on the job. But training is given in a separate room/area by experienced staff. The advantage is that the fresh staff is trained on the same equipment they will be using in the library.

9.3 Workshop Training

It is like classroom training, and hence associated with knowledge rather than skills. The host institute will invite eminent resource persons and professors from universities and libraries to impart the latest knowledge in the subject.

9.4 Electronic Training

In the present electronic environment, the library is playing the role of electronic 'gateway' to information located at various places. Thus it provides access to electronic resources such as:

- online access to government, agricultural, educational, social, political information;
- online journals and serials, electronic databases, and other information resources.

In order to make use of vast pool of resources in e-format effectively, it is imperative that training in the use of computers, browsing Internet, etc. is provided to make them familiar with these IT software applications, hardware and other related equipments.

10. CONCLUSION

In-service training is the cornerstone to rebuild the potential of library staff enabling them to meet the challenges of the electronic environment. Individual libraries may consider using any one or more of training methods as indicted in the text to meet their specific and special requirements. The key point is that training component should be an integral part of the library as a means to improving the existing library and information services and to initiating new ones. In-service training conducted in an unorganized manner may not yield dividends. It is therefore important that it must be organized in a planned manner, and as a long term programme for the benefit of public library staff creating thereby a responsive system for meeting the future challenges. The Librarians Cultural Forum may take such an initiative.

BIBLIOGRAPHY

1. Dessler, Gary (2004). *Human Resource Management*, New Delhi: Pearson Education.
2. Lawrence, Allen (1971). Education for librarians. In: *Encyclopedia of Library and Information Science*, edited by Allen Kent, et al., New York: Marcel Dekker, Vol 5.
3. Penland, Patrick R. (1974). In-service training. In: *Encyclopedia of Library and Information Science*, edited by Allen Kent, et al., New York: Marcel Dekker, Vol 12.

Total Quality Management in Public Libraries

Mange Ram[1], Rajbir Singh[2] and Satish Yadav[3]

1. INTRODUCTION

Ranganthan defined library as "public institution or establishment charged with the care of collection of books and the duty of making them accessible to those who require them for use."[1] The public library supports under privileged in the society as well as it is a means of continuing education for people who have had no opportunity for formal education. Thus, the public library is most relevant for the weaker section and working class of the society to pursue formal education. Unesco Manifesto[2] defines a public library:

- which is established under "the clear mandate of law";
- which is "maintained wholly from public funds";
- which levies no "direct charge" (few) from its users for any of its services; and
- which is open "for free and equal use by all members of the community" regardless of nationality, language, status, and level of educational attainments.

Total Quality Management (TQM) is a management approach that originated in the 1950's and has steadily become more popular since the early 1980's. In the aftermath of the Second World War, American industry, basking in success, did not want to listen to Dr. Edward Deming's quality philosophy. In 1950 he was sent to explode post-war Japan by the MacArthur Government- as an adviser to the Japanese census. The Japanese industrialists listened to Deming and Juran and learned from their teaching. The result was that they captured markets all over the world. Today, Japanese companies are not just competitive but they dominate the world market and, true to Dr. Deming's predication' the rest of the

---

1. University Library Incharge, Dayalbagh Educational Institute (Deemed University), Dayalbagh, Agra-5 (UP), E-mail: mram721@rediffmail.com/ mram72ster@gmail.com
2. Librarian, Vaish P.G. College, Rohtak (Haryana)
3. Librarian, Bhadhawar P G College, Bah (UP)

world is seeking protection from them. In the true sense, then, TQM was launched providing an ultimate way of quality thinking as shared by everyday in the organization. In general, TQM is defined as follows:

- Quality: to satisfy agreed customer requirements continually.
- Total quality: to achieve quality at low lost.
- Total quality management: obtain total quality by involving everyone's daily commitment.

There are 14 principles of TQM as stated by Edward Deming in 1986[3], which may be applied in any service organization like libraries. These are as follows:

- ***Constancy of purpose***: create constancy of purpose for continual improvement of product and service.
- ***The new philosophy***: adopt the new philosophy. We are a new economic age, created in Japan.
- ***Cease dependence on inspection***: eliminate the need for mass inspection as a way to achieve quality.
- ***End 'lowest tender' contracts***: end the practice of awarding business solely on the basis of price tag.
- ***Improve every process***: improve constantly and for every process for planning, production and service.
- ***Institute training on the job***: institute modern methods of training on the job.
- ***Institute leadership***: adopt and institute leadership aimed at helping people and mechanics to do a better job.
- ***Drive out fear***: encourage effective two-way communication and other means to drive out fear throughout the organization.
- ***Break down barrier:*** break down barrier between department and staff areas.
- ***Eliminate exhortations***: eliminate the use of slogans, posters and exhortations.
- ***Eliminate targets:*** eliminate work standards that prescribe numerical quotas for the workforce and numerical goals for people in management.
- ***Permit pride of workmanship***: remove the barriers that rob hourly workers, and people in management, of the right to pride of workmanship.
- ***Encourage education:*** institute a vigorous programme of education and encourage self improvement for everyman.
- ***Top management commitment***: clearly define top management's permanent commitment to ever-improving quality and productivity.

2. TQM AND PUBLIC LIBRARIES

A general misunderstanding about quality is that it is only concerned with objects. This is not true, as we know that banks, hotels and retail shops have already recognized the fact that quality of service is an essential factor in the customer's decision to be a regular customer. Manufacturing companies are also beginning to understand the necessity of quality of service to retain customer, and the need for well-trained, obliging and well-informed staff to maintain quality of service. Not only the persons having direct involvement with the customer has to demonstrate these qualities, but also the support staff who must have the same goals of fulfilling customer needs.

Now, public libraries are also beginning to understand the necessity of quality of service to retain customers, and the need for well-trained, obliging and well-informed staff to maintain quality of service. The main focus of a public library is service, and service quality is most studied topic in marketing research during the past decade. A repeated theme in the marketing literature is that of service quality. As perceived by consumers, it is a function of what users expect and how well the firm performs in providing the service. In public library we may see the following areas where TQM may be applied.

2.1 Acquisition

There should be proper allocation of library budget for its optimal utilization even if quality library services may have to be provided at a nominal cost. Library suppliers and vendors selection should be based on quality rather on discounts offered. Book selection should be based purely on users' requirements. Time to time user surveys should be conducted in a library to know the problems and needs of users. Library collection should be developed as per defined "acquisition policy" ensuring quality (rather than quantity) and balanced (rather than uneven) growth of library collection may be through joint efforts with respective users community. Delay in book available to users directly or indirectly, affects users satisfaction.

2.2 Process

Classification, cataloguing, subject key-word and indexing are the processes that should be performed with user's approach in mind, so that user could retrieve his/her document in an easy way. Given the fact that most libraries are using computers and Internet in their operations. OPACs (Online Public Access Catalogues) are replacing card catalogues. Users now rush to OPAC more often for searching documents. We should no longer be fussy about punctuation marks and such other little aspects as prescribed by the cataloguing codes. Rather such trivial matters can be handled automatically by machines. Librarian should take the help of staff members and users in designing new processes and dropping the obsolete ones. They should provide chance to individual employs to improve the processes of his/her work. Users should not be made to wait more than three minutes at circulation counter for document transactions. Public library should adopt latest technology (e.g. bar-code) for quicker transactions in circulation function.

2.3 Human Resource Management

2.3.1 Leadership: Leadership also plays a significant role in accomplishing the desired level of efficiency in the library. Librarian should consider the importance of team management for improving processes, procedures and practices. Librarian should believe in that all of us have more or less equal potential. Praising staff verbally in public for their outstanding performance and condemning in private for their poor performance is an example of raising team morale. Library manager should support open decision making through brainstorming.

2.3.2 Policy and Strategy: The vision, mission, goals, objectives and values of the library should be conveyed during staff orientation programs. All information should be provided by the librarian to all subordinates and let them jointly be given the opportunity to find the solution to the problem. Library policy and strategy should be made clear to all the staff by library manager. Librarian should take help of focused groups, user surveys and personnel interviews for assessment of users information. User education programme should be carried out round the year because the new users keep visiting the library throughout the year. The new readers of public library may be varying in age and socio-economic background, so the user education programme should be tailored to individual's needs and profiles.

2.3.3 Staff Management: Library manager should consider library staff as an asset to be developed rather than commodity to be used, and place focus on their education, training and re-training for continuous improvement. Librarian should not hesitate to delegate the responsibilities and authority to matured subordinates and should not consider seniority as the best criterion for promotion. There should be intercom telephone service in each section of the library for horizontal and vertical communication.

2.4 Reference Service

In TQM approach, it is no quality if, for example reference queries attended to by a library increased this year to 500 from 300 in previous year, if all the extra 200 queries were attended incorrectly. Mere statistics have no value in terms of quality. Raina advocates for "better" services rather than "more" services.[4] TQM will, in fact, come once the library does stocktaking (by using methods like flow charting ,etc.) of all the 200 incorrect responses to enable the staff to understand the specific problems associated with the process of providing the service.

2.5 Inter-Library-Loan

Though Inter library loan is an old concept in libraries, why are the figures of such transaction very low in libraries? In fact the figures in most of the cases continue to go down day by day. The situation in the West is somewhat different. Some of the reasons responsible for low profile of such figures in our situation are 1) the lack of adequate and up to date locational tools, 2) lack of knowledge of the learning resources of other libraries, 3) poor communication and document delivery mechanisms, and 4) lack of appreciation and understanding on the part of our public libraries.

2.6 Reprographic Services

Experiences has shown that liberal photocopying services rendered by the libraries have not only minimized document losses, page tearing, scrubbing, marking etc but have also attracted users to the libraries when assured of the document or its photocopy. Efforts to provide the services with minimum lead time and quality copy would be the elements that TQM approach would be looking forward to within this service.

2.7 Documentation Services

The one way traffic cannot go further even in the library and information environment, when competition has crept in from outsiders, users have become more information conscious and are willing to pay for quality information products and services. It is therefore high time that libraries wake-up, accept this challenge and take it up in all earnestness, employ new management concepts, marketing techniques and generate quality products and services to meet the need of their respective users rather than continue with issuing, ill designed, less appealing, illegible, routine products like in the form of "current contents," "current addition", "bibliographies," and so on.

3. GENERAL SUGGESTIONS FOR TQM

The following are some suggestions for public libraries to bring about quality in their services in the electronic environment:

- Library should be fully computerized and well equipped. Internet access speed should be high.
- Libraries should be sound proof and Mobile phones should be in silent mode in libraries.
- Libraries should subscribe to more journals especially e-journals to facilitate their users in digital environment. Library should also start the e-book service.
- Libraries should be user oriented.
- Material should be properly shelved if possible stock rectification should be the daily practice of libraries.
- Libraries should display the current material acquired by them.
- Libraries should provide the service of CD/DVD-ROM search.
- Libraries should be provide printing and photocopy services.

4. MEASURING THE QUALITY

There are many tools and approaches to measuring the quality, some of easy tools are as follow[5]:

- **User Survey:** These surveys can be made with questionnaires, interviews and observations etc. to know the merits and demerits of library services.
- **User's complaints:** User's complaints are indicators of quality and suggest the direction for improvements.
- **Suggestion Boxes:** Suggestion boxes should be provided in the libraries so that users express their suggestions. This would help improve library performance. There should be full freedom to user to indicate their suggestion for improvement of library.
- **Organization Culture:** The culture of a library depends on the culture of parent organization. The culture creates a common understanding amongst the organizational members. The culture of academic library should be related to education and learning.
- **Human Resource management:** There should be elimination of fear, social involvement, responsibility on job, participation in decision making and team building of employees. The success of any management depends upon employee's commitment. Now libraries are spending the money on books, furniture, hardware, software and on building etc. They should make investment in human resources.

5. CONCLUSION

In India even after fifty five years of independent rule the status of public library is still very pathetic. Many of the States of India have not introduced library legislation as yet. The development of public libraries has not reached the required stage necessary for our country. Libraries are ideal place to implement total quality management. They are service organizations dedicated to their customers and patrons. By formulating a strategic plan, and following it with a commitment to continuous quality improvement, library managers can transform and improve their organizations. (Riggs 1992)[6] summarizes the notable principles of TQM: 1) manage by fact: make library decision after careful analysis of data gathered with tools; 2) eliminate rework: library work is often labour intensive-simplify it and make sure it is done properly the first time; 3) respect people and ideas: staff are the library's most valuable resources, and they should be encouraged to point out problems without fear of management; and 4) empower people: trust library staff to act responsibly and give them the appropriate authority to make decisions that can improve the quality of work they do. Finally, remember that TQM is not a "quick fix". It needs to be implemented gradually over two–to-three years period.

REFERENCES

1. Ranganthan S. R. (1950). Library Development Plan: a thirty year programme for India. Delhi, University of Delhi, 1950.
2. Unesco Manifesto, 1972.
3. Edwards, Deeming W. (1986). Out of Crises, Cambridge, MOT Press.
4. Raina, R (1995). TQM in Library and Information services, *University News* 33, 4-6.
5. Sharma, U.C. and Mange Ram (2003). Need of quality assurance in services of Central Library, DEI: A case study. *Library Progress (International)* 33 (1), January-June. 59-66.
6. Riggs, D.E. (1992). TQM: quality improvement in new clothes. *College & Research Libraries* 53 (6), 481-483.

Marketing of LIS Products and Services of the Public Libraries in India

U.C. Sharma[1] and R.K. Bhatt[2]

1. INTRODUCTION

Public libraries are considered to be the back- bone of any civilized society worldwide no matter whether these are established, supported and funded by the community either through local, regional or national government or through some other form of community organization.[1] They provide services to all members of the community without considering any barrier of race, nationality, age, gender, religion, language, disability, etc.. In fact, freedom, prosperity and the positive growth of individuals and society depends on access to information and knowledge. It is, therefore, important that every person in a society must be well informed, literate and maturely developed. The main purpose of the establishment of public libraries throughout the world is to provide information resources and services in a variety of forms to meet the needs of individuals and groups for education, information and personal development including recreation and leisure. It is an undisputed fact that the public libraries played significant role in India's freedom movement. In India, one can witness the phenomenal growth and development of public libraries despite limited financial resources. After independence, the Government of India took lots of initiatives for the development of higher education, literacy and supported the role of libraries in principle as the integral and indispensable part of the higher education and learning institutions and organizations which in turn resulted into the establishment of so many higher education institutions, institutions of national importance and establishment of social welfare organizations. In addition, particularly, for public libraries, Unesco being one of the pioneering international organizations working for the

---

1. Head, Department of Library and Information Science, Dr B.R. Ambedkar University, Agra
2. Reader & Head, Department of Library and Information Science, University of Delhi

development of public libraries in the developing countries, also became instrumental in founding of Delhi Public Library in India as its Pilot Project in 1951.[2]

2. MARKETING

The library managers are using marketing techniques and strategies for the promotion of library services and products throughout the world. Before we attempt a definition of marketing let us first understand and differentiate between the two terms called 'Marketing', and 'Selling'. Marketing differs from the concept of selling and the difference between the two needs to be understood clearly to understand the philosophy of marketing. In selling, the basic objective of the seller is to sell his/her goods irrespective of the costumer(s) satisfaction. For example, while you are traveling in a bus or a train you find a hawker shouting "One calculator and a watch in rupee fifty only". Many a times we buy goods and the hawker disappears immediately. What did he do?. He sold his goods by exchanging our money and with this ends his mission. Neither of the two are going to meet each other again. Despite this knowledge, we tend to buy goods without verifying the product quality whether the calculator and watch are in working condition or not. But had we bought these goods from a shop, the shop keeper would not only sell his goods but would also try to initiate a lasting relationship with us and would expect us to visit his shop again and again. His efforts involved in doing so would also be caring for our satisfaction as well from many angles such as quality, price, behaviour etc. This is where selling differs from marketing The Chartered Institute of Marketing, U.K. defines marketing as the management process which is responsible for identifying, anticipating and satisfying customer requirements profitably.[3] The management Guru Philip Kotler opines that marketing is an act of analysis, planning, implementation and control of carefully formulated programmes designed to bring about voluntary exchanges of values with target markets for the purpose of achieving organizational objectives.[4]

3. WHY MARKETING OF LIS PRODUCTS AND SERVICES

Libraries are part of a highly competitive service industry. Competition comes from mega-bookstores, online book dealers, consultants, the Internet community, and individual customers. Thus it is necessary that one provides correct and timely information to sustain oneself in the competitive environment. Libraries of all type have also to compete with other departments within the organization for funds. Libraries need to market themselves to remain connected with their communities and create goodwill, sustain their existence and improve the image in the society. Libraries need to convey what is unique about the access and services they provide. The people need to be made aware of the services and products that are provided and their comparative value. This will solve the problem of under utilization of existing resources. Library users expect recognition, attention, and appreciation for their individual information needs. Customers also have ever-changing needs and wants, which makes the library market as dynamic as retail markets. Marketing helps to create an environment in libraries that fosters customer consciousness among employees. Libraries depend on the support of others for their existence. A library must communicate and work with its customers and governing/ funding entities to provide information about what the library is doing and to enable the library to learn about the community it serves. Effective marketing can among other things: increase library fund, increase usage of services, educate customers and non-customers, change perceptions, and enhance the clout and reputation of the library and its staff.[5] In addition, substantial hike in cost of publications, hike in the foreign exchange rates and devaluation of rupee, Information explosion and increasing demands of users for information and availability of modern information access facilities etc. also necessitate the adoption of marketing approach for the promotion and use of library products and services.

Marketing, thus, is a management process[6], which includes the following:

- Marketing plan: In marketing plan mission analysis, resource analysis, strategic planning and monitoring and evaluation of the tasks performed is to be done.
- Marketing research: It is done to assess market information needs, stating research objectives, developing a research strategy, knowing target market characteristics, and population to be studied etc. Thus, relevant data is to be collected and analyzed.
- Market segmentation: It is defined as a group of customers with similar or related characteristics who have common needs and wants and usually divided into: (i) Demographic Segmentation, (ii) Socio-Economic Segmentation, and (iii) Geographic Segmentation. In case of public libraries segmentation includes the following: Donors, Volunteers, Civil organizations, Board of Trustees, Political community, Friends, Mass media, Researchers, Writers, Government agencies, Business people, Students, Children, Senior citizens, Information brokers, Blind and deaf, Staff, and Competitors.
- Marketing Mix: which includes Products (such as books, periodicals, literal programmes, bibliographies, annual reports, statistical surveys and compilations and services like CD-ROMS etc.); Price (which is in form of credit, discount, cash etc.); Place (includes coverage, distribution channels, inventory, locations and transport.) and Promotion (which is done through (i) advertising, (ii) personal selling, and (iii) public relations)

4. LIBRARY SERVICES IN A PUBLIC LIBRARY

Public libraries can consider rendering traditional and computerized current awareness services (CAS) The traditional CAS services include telephone queries, individual notifications, routing periodicals, documentation lists of micro-documents, accession lists, news bulletin, table-of-contents service, and utilizing commercial current contents service. Computerized CAS includes services such as in-house CAS service using library databases, and commercial CAS (also known as external CAS) from BUBL, ISI (http:/alerting.isinet.com), ACS (American Chemical Society, Sage (content.alert@sagepub.com), and Springer, Elsevier Science etc.

In addition public library can consider offering other types of services such as reference service, translation service, information consolidation, information repackaging, document delivery service, audio-video services, reprographic service, indexing and abstracting service, referral service, online search services, OCLC, and British Library Automated Information Services (BLAISE).

In the context of knowledge society, the services that public library might be required to offer include state-of-art reports, reviews, current content files, distribution of well-designed informative and printed pamphlets, specifically prepared package of information for special groups of users, newsletters/bulletins/brochures, profiles of specialists, compilation of need based bibliographies, web services and home page designing, compilation of indexes and abstracts, and in-house generated information products

5. LIBRARY PROMOTION

Broadly, promotion activity covers all aids to sales. Promotion stimulates demand and increases sales. Usually promotion moves the product towards the customers. It involves mechanisms that inform the target groups about the resources available, services and products offered by the libraries / information centers. The motivations for promoting library products and services are:

- User awareness otherwise people would hardly know what services the library offers
- For targeting passive library users not visiting library often.
- Promoting library services and collections.
- Building stronger relationship with staff in the organization.

There is a need to evolve suitable strategy for library promotion. It includes:

- Ensuring full support from the top management for funds.
- Clearly outlining promotional plan and its purpose.
- What is to be communicated or offered?
- Who are the recipients of services and products?

- Media and channels that are going to be used for this purpose.
- Who is responsible for promotional activity?

The main tools for promoting library products and services include brochures, flyers or companywide e-mails, reading lists and bibliographies, newsletters, annual reports, bookmarks, posters, videos, calendars and directories, and web pages. Exhibits constitute an excellent medium of promotion. However, following aspects need to be taken into consideration while using exhibits as a promotional tool for promoting the library:

- Always communicate important, factual information.
- Emphasize the significance of the task.
- Give accurate facts.
- Use best possible visual markets.
- Cost factor.

Another strategy to promote library is to make presentations to selected groups, guests in the library/institute, organizing open house or information fairs that exhibit services to all interested user, library orientation for new employees/users, organizing special training for employees, and organizing seminars that educate customers on the products and services. Utilizing TV and mass media may not be of much relevance due to diversity of culture and environment in India. Secondly this mode of promotion is expensive and not cost effective. However, word of mouth is the cheapest and most effective means of promoting any kind of library service. The satisfied user will always have a positive attitude towards the library. The following aspects may be taken into consideration for rendering quality services:

- Always be polite and courteous.
- Try to have convenient hours.
- Try to provide users every possible help. For example, scratch paper or pencil etc.
- Make the library client-centered.
- Know the users, and try to anticipate their information needs.

6. CONCLUSION

Library marketing is for promotion of library products and services. It involves using marketing techniques for identifying target users, understanding their needs, their socio-economic profile and developing thereupon appropriate products and services and evolving frameworks for delivery of LIS products and services to the target users. LIS marketing is fast gaining importance in the contemporary librarianship. Given the poor state of public libraries, there is an urgent need to improve their library and information services. It is in this context and in the context of roles that public libraries are expected to play in the emerging knowledge society, application of LIS marketing techniques to public libraries becomes an issue of strategic importance. LIS marketing in public libraries is thus the need of the hour.

REFERENCES

1. IFLA-UNESCO (2001). The public library service: IFLA/UNESCO guidelines for development. Saur, Munchen.
2. Bhatt R. K. (1995). *History and Development of Libraries*. Mittal Publications, New Delhi.
3. Chartered Institute of Marketing, UK. An Official Definition.
4. Kotler, Philip (1982). *Marketing for Non-Profit Organizations*. New York, Prentice-Hall.
5. Dragon, Andrea C. (1979). Marketing the Library *Wilson Library Bulletin,* 29-31.
6 Cronin, Biaise (1982). New Technologies and Marketing – the challenges for Librarians. *Aslib Proceedings.* 34(9); 377-393.

Collection Development in Delhi Public Library System

P.K. WALIA[1], ESMAT MOMENI[2] AND MONIKA GUPTA[3]

1. INTRODUCTION

Today every human activity requires knowledge and information. No progress in any socio cultural endevour could be imagined or achieved without access to knowledge and information. Information must be available to everyone in the society irrespective of religion, caste, nationality, age, sex, language, social and economic status, educational attainment, physical or mental condition, etc. Of all types of libraries, it is perhaps the public library that has the mandate for community development while other libraries seek to influence specified sections of the society as per their target groups. Public libraries have been appropriately called as people's universities as they have the potentials to provide equal opportunities to one and all to develop intellectually.

A public library with rich information sources carefully built up to meet the information needs of its clientele is a boon to them. "The strength of a library's book collection lies first in its quality and second in its size and the strength of a library's service depends on the strength of its' book collection, second only to the ability of its staff, because an able staff builds an excellent collection"[1] .

The public library has the mandate to meet the needs of its users for education, information, leisure and personal development. It is the source for access to the heritage of the society, its cultural resources and experiences. One of the roles of the public library is to build well informed, skilled individuals and it tries to achieve this role in a democratic manner.

---

1. Reader , Department of Library and Information Science, University of Delhi, Delhi; Email: pkwalia2002@yahoo.com
2. Research Scholar, Department of Library and Information Science, University of Delhi, Delhi; Email: esmatmomeni@yahoo.com
3. Research Scholar(M.Phil), Department of Library and Information Science, University of Delhi , Delhi; Email: monikaaupta @gmail.com

A well planned collection development program is thus essential to satisfy not only the current needs but the near future needs of their users as well[2].

India is a large country and an emerging democratic power in Asia, having public libraries scattered all over the nation including National Capital Territory of Delhi, 28 states, and 6 centrally administered union territories. The total population of India as per Census of India, 2001 is 1,027,015,247. The overall literacy rate was 64.84 percent[3].

Delhi was the Capital city of India during the Mughal period and also during the British period after the British shifted the capital back from Calcutta to Delhi in 1911. Delhi became Union Territory on 1st November 1966. Its population as on 1st March, 2001 was 13.78 million as against 9.42 million in March, 1991. The total population of Delhi is 1.34 percent of the All-India population. The total area of NCT of Delhi is 1483 Sq. Kms. In 1999, its literacy rate was 75.29 percent which rose to 81.82 percent in 2001 (Table 1).

Table 1: Literacy Rate for Delhi and its Districts

S.No.	*State/Districts*	*LITERACY RATE*					
		Persons		*Males*		*Females*	
		1991	*2001*	*1991*	*2001*	*1991*	*2001*
1	*2*	*3*	*4*	*5*	*6*	*7*	*8*
	NCT of Delhi	75.29	81.82	82.01	87.37	66.99	75.00
1.	North-west	72.22	80.79	79.59	86.89	63.06	73.30
2.	North	75.87	79.88	80.83	84.53	69.69	74.20
3.	North-East	67.83	77.85	77.08	84.52	56.52	69.97
4.	East	77.50	85.10	84.14	89.91	69.52	79.38
5.	New Delhi	80.59	82.54	86.33	88.70	73.19	74.64
6.	Central	75.42	79.52	79.85	82.55	70.26	75.90
7.	West	79.01	83.24	84.17	87.68	72.85	77.87
8.	South-west	78.40	83.63	85.95	89.53	68.66	76.00
9.	South	75.69	82.57	82.9	88.73	66.67	74.71

Source[4]: Economic Survey of Delhi, 2001-2002. Accessed on 6th March

2. SCOPE AND OBJECTIVES OF THE STUDY

Delhi Public Library was started as a UNESCO project in the year 1951 by the Government of India. At present Delhi Public Library System (DPLS) has network of 61 libraries comprising central library, zonal Library, 3 branch libraries, 27 sub-branch libraries, 22 re-settlement Colonies(R.C) libraries, 6 community libraries, and a Braille library. In addition, it has 26 mobile service points and 30 deposit stations within the Union Territory of Delhi[5].

This paper looks at the adequacy of library collection of DPLS keeping in view the total population of Delhi and its actual number of library users. This paper also looks at the collection development process of DPLS to understand its strengths and weakness.

3. DATA COLLECTION

Data has been collected through questionnaire method. The other sources of data as used in this study are Annual Report (2006-2007)[6] and Collection Development Policy Document of DPL[7].

4. PUBLIC LIBRARY SYSTEM IN INDIA

In India, libraries is a State subject in the Constitution of India and the Central government has jurisdiction only over libraries established by it and the institutions of national importance as declared by it .However the central government does provide financial assistance to all libraries through Raja Rammohun Roy Library Foundation (RRRLF). It is the duty of the state Government to enact library legislation to facilitate library service to the public. India comprises of 28 States and 6 Union Territories. So far only 16 States have enacted Library Acts in their States.

5. DELHI PUBLIC LIBRARY SYSTEM

Delhi Public Library is an autonomous organization under the Ministry of Tourism & Culture, Government of India and is governed by Delhi Library Board, fully financed by the Government of India. Delhi Public Library was established as a UNESCO project in the year 1951 by the Govt. of India. It was inaugurated by the first Prime Minister of India Hon'ble Pandit Jawaharlal Nehru, as a small unitary library in Old Delhi, opposite Old Delhi Railway Station. It has since developed into a premier Public Library System in the metropolitan city of Delhi.

5.1 Organizational Structure of DPLS

The Delhi Public Library describes itself as one of the busiest libraries in Southeast Asia. It has a network of zonal libraries, branches and sub-branches, resettlement colonies libraries (R. C. libraries), community libraries, deposit stations, mobile library, Braille library, etc. spread all over Delhi.

The Library currently comprises central library, zonal library, 3 branch libraries, 26 sub-branch libraries and 6 community libraries. The system includes 23 units serving former slum inhabitants, and a Braille library. In addition the library system provides 54 service points with its mobile services and has 30 deposit stations. Deposit stations are small libraries run by local societies or associations under the supervision of the Delhi Public Library, which provides a training program for their workers.

5.1.1 Departments: The DPL library system has been organized into following departments, branches, service units:

- Book Purchase & Process Division
- Delivery of Books Act Division
- Stock Review Department

- Reference Section
- Social Education Department
- Serial & Binding Section

5.1. 2 Libraries under DPLS: The following libraries are under the DPLS

- Central Library(S.P. Mukharjee Marg Old Delhi) : 01
- Zonal Library Sarojini Nagar) : 01.
- Branch Libraries(Patel Nagar, Karol Bagh and Shahdara) : 03
- Sub-Branch: 26
- Community Libraries: 06
- R.C. Libraries: 23
- Braille Library : 01

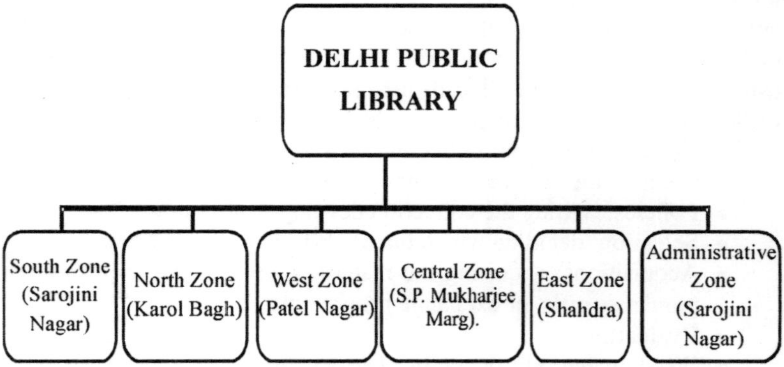

Fig. 1: Organizational Structure

Table 2: Library Membership of DPLS

Section	*Adult*	*Child*	*Male*	*Female*	*Grand Total*
Central Lib.	4937	418	4074	1281	5355
Zonal Lib.	5444	570	3798	2216	6014
Patel Nagar	1875	196	1203	868	2071
Karol Bagh	1420	106	965	561	1526
Shahdara	2744	550	2165	1129	3294
SubBranches	8289	2956	7200	4045	11245
Braille Lib.	513	373	690	196	886
Com.Lib.	713	363	742	334	1076
R.C. Lib.	2794	2008	3851	951	4802
Extension Services					
Mobile Vans	1296	675	1082	889	1971
Deposit Sec.	1842	693	1886	649	2535
Total	31867	8908	27656	13119	40775

Note: *Lib-Library, Yr.- Year, Sec.- Section, Dept.- Department, Com.- Community.

*DPL Annual Report 2005-06

5.2 Library Membership

Delhi Public Library System serves the city with a total population of 13.8 million. Currently it has a membership base of 40,775 registered users. The membership is free of charge. Members pay a refundable security deposit of Rs. 50 unless their membership is verified by a suitable guarantor such as a public official professional.

6. COLLECTION DEVELOPMENT

The important resource of a library is its collection. Collection development is a vital process in creating and building library collection, be it in an institution, college, school or a public library. It is a well planned activity for which a well defined policy is written with due diligence. Evans[8] defines collection development as the "process of meeting the information needs of the people (a service population) in a timely and economic manner using information resources locally held as well as from other organizations. Collection development is a process which has the following components".

- Needs Assessment: collecting data to determine the information needs of the service community.
- Policies: writing the collection development policy.
- Selection: deciding which materials to buy for the library.
- Acquisitions: acquiring the materials for the collection through purchase, gifts, or exchange programme.
- Evaluation
- Weeding: periodic or continual evaluation of resources so that items that are no longer useful are removed.

6.1 Collection Development Policy

In many institutions collection development policies exist for providing necessary guidance and direction in the selection process. Collection development, therefore, has a direct effect on access to library and information resources. It determines first of all whether or not the collection contains the kinds of materials that the user need. It also assesses whether or not the collection should continue to hold the kinds of materials that are there in the collection. A collection development policy is a written statement of your library's intentions for building its collection. It describes the collection's strengths and weakness and provides guidelines for the staff. Producing one is a commitment; it takes time and careful consideration to develop a useful and relevant document[8] (Evans 70). A collection development policy should be written document, adaptable to change and growth. It provides guidelines that can be modified as a library's collection needs change. Collection development policy is a planning document[8].

7. COLLECTION DEVELOPMENT IN DELHI PUBLIC LIBRARY SYSTEM

7.1 Collection Development Process

Delhi Public Library has centralized purchase policy for books' meant for the entire Library System. The books are purchased by inviting quotations on discount rates for books for the current financial year. The quotations are then processed and the Tabulation Chart is placed before the Delhi Library Board. The Board approves the rate of discount for Indian and foreign publications. The approved suppliers submit one copy of their books from time to time on approval. These books are inspected by Deputy Directors (Technical). They recommend the purchase on the basis of the general trend prevailing in the particular unit of DPL. These recommendations are further reviewed by the Director who then places before the Book Selection Committee consisting of language experts in the particular language. Book Purchase and Processing Division is responsible for acquisition and processing the books for the entire system on the basis of selection done by Book Advisory Committee. The members of Delhi Public Library can request for any book available in any other unit of DPL through Book Suggestion form. It is mandatory for each Delhi Public Library unit to have copies of Book Suggestion form. (DPL Collection Management Policy)[7].

7.1.1 Responsibility for Collection Development Programme of DPLS: DPL has the authority and responsibility for selection and management of all collection. According to the DPL Collection Management policy, the Delhi Library Board delegates such powers to the Director,

7.1.2 Selection Criteria: DPL collects and provides access to a wide variety of materials which may include books, periodicals, DVDs, music CDs, audiocassettes, CD-ROMs, pictures, maps, games, electronic databases etc. and ensures that any material selected has the potential to meet the informational, educational, or recreational needs of the community the DPL is expected to serve.

DPL collection development policy states that selection of any resources for the library will be guided by one or more of the following factors (DPL Collection Management Policy)[7].

- Relevance of the information/contents to immediate user requirements
- Popular demand from users
- Present and potential needs of the community of users
- Listing in professionally recognized selection tools
- Favorable reviews in professional, literary or general periodicals/ newspapers
- Reputation of author/creator

- Suitability of physical form for library use (size, paper, print, binding)
- Price, in relation to total budget
- Availability of funds
- The extent to which the supplements, or supports the existing collection
- Accuracy of information and /or presentation
- Collection of other libraries within the neighborhood

7.1.3 Priority Subjects: DPL emphasizes on the subject areas in which it should develop its collection keeping in view the actual and anticipated interests of its user within the community and indeed the objectives of DPL. It prepares in the beginning of every financial year, the percentage of book stock held by each library, subject-wise (broad DDC number-wise), and the proposed percentage addition for the year. This procedure ensures in building a balanced collection, as well as balanced annual additions.

Though DPL acquires resources in all subjects, it, however, avoids selecting resources that can be used only by specialists or researchers. It also does not acquire books as well as resources of very advanced nature, even if these are recommended by users.

7.1.4 Selection Tools: DPL uses the following tools to select information resources:

- Reviews in journals and newspapers
- Review publications such as Indian Book Chronicle
- Publishers' catalogues
- Book sellers' catalogues
- Appropriate websites
- Special lists, e.g. Top Ten books listed in newspapers
- Title short listed for awards
- Catalogues/Accession lists of other libraries
- Suggestions from users
- Suggestions from library staff
- Suggestions from SLB members
- Book received under Delivery of Books Act
- Books supplied by book seller on approval basis

7.1.5 Foreign Publications: DPL focuses more on material published/ produced in India and also on material by Indian authors. However, it makes all efforts to identify key publications from outside, on subjects that are important to the user community. DPL earmarks not more than 20 per cent of its annual budget for foreign publications.

7.1.6 Reference Stock: The level of use of reference books is declining progressively as more and more users access the Internet to find answers to queries. This trend is happening world over and in all types of libraries. DPL monitors the usage pattern of its Reference collection closely and its procurement of reference sources.

7.1.7 Multiple Copies: Libraries restrain from procuring multiple copies of any item, unless there is demand from users to warrant the necessity for procurement of a second copy of any title, except in special circumstances.

7.1.8 Year of Publication: A minimum of 80 per cent of the annual budget on resources is spent on current publications, i.e. resources published in the current year or the previous year. The remaining 20 per cent is used to procure replacement copies, additional copies, missing titles, etc.

7.1.9 Withdrawal: To ensure an active and live collection of continued value to the community, materials which have outlined their usefulness are withdrawn. This necessitates removal of items on a systematic and continuous basis. An item will be considered for withdrawal in DPLS when it is:

- Obsolete or outdated
- Superceded edition (new edition available in the library)
- Worn out/damaged
- No longer in demand
- Unwanted duplicate copy.

Identification of an item for withdrawal is treated on the same lines as selecting a new item for purchase, and hence this activity is carried out by professional staff. Approval for the disposal of withdrawn items is given by the competent authority on the recommendations of a three member committee (from amongst the Books Advisory Committee members) appointed by the Chairperson. A work chosen for discarding may be replaced with another copy of the same title or another title on the same subject.

7.1.10 Book Advisory Committee: DLB has a seven member Book Advisory Committee, one member each for English, Hindi, Punjabi and Urdu languages, to help DPL in the final selection of books. The Committee members in the respective languages are nominated from the following categories of institutions

- One member from University of Delhi.
- One member from Indian Council for Social Science Research (ICSSR).
- One member from the Council of Scientific and Industrial Research (CSIR).
- One member from a national level institution from cultural or humanities or literary field.
- One member from any School of repute in Delhi.
- Two members from amongst the users of DPL, who have members at least for the last five years continuously, nominated by the Director, DPL.

In addition to these external members, each language group has a senior DPL staff as a member, nominated by the Director. These Committees will meet once in every three months to ensure that procurement procedure is spread evenly over the year

7.2 Library Collection in DPLS

Library collection is obviously one of the most important basic resources upon which the utility of library depends. Library collection is a precious treasure of library. Delhi Public Library provides a wide range of books, journals and other reading materials in Hindi, English, Urdu, Punjabi & other Indian languages for everyone.

7.2.1 Book Collection: Library stock consists of over 13 lakh books on variety of subjects including books for competitive examinations, computer science, information technology, philosophy, religion, Hinduism, social

Table 3: Language wise Distribution of Library Collection

S.No.	*Name of Branch*	*Hindi*	*Eng.*	*Urdu*	*Panj.*	*Sindhi*	*Bengali*	*Total*
1.	Central Library							
(i)	Lending Sec.							
	(Adult)	62936	65727	15244	8078	0	0	151985
(ii)	Reference Sec.	3996	2257	619	58	0	0	27230
(iii)	Children Sec.	21568	14393	2309	410	0	0	38680
	Extension Sec.	129682	40338	11958	6073	0	600	188651
2.	Zonal Library							
	(Adult)	44353	30946	3923	3992	2192	1002	86408
	(Child)	20564	12594	70	317	0	41	33586
3.	Branches							
(i)	Patel Nagar							
	(Adult)	37487	20270	9455	4472	0	0	71684
	(Child)	14846	6042	33	386	0	0	21307
(ii)	Karol Bagh							
	(Adult)	34238	16697	6940	4228	0	0	62103
	(Child)	15556	6305	44	25	0	0	21930
(iii)	Shahdara							
	(Adult)	38147	14792	8036	2716	0	0	63691
	(Child)	11453	4200	139	17	0	0	15809
4.	Sub-Branches							
	(Adult)	132027	67646	9665	4548	0	0	213886
	(Child)	99280	49510	97	0	0	0	148887
5.	R.C. Libraries							
	(Adult)	89492	6618	316	1186	0	0	97612
	(Child)	183909	23144	471	0	0	0	207524
	Total							1357982

Note: Punj.- Panjabi, Sec.- Section, Eng.- English, R.C. Library- Resettlement Colony Library

science, economics, political science, international relations, language and linguistics, science, physics, chemistry, zoology, botany, medical science, engineering, literature, fiction, history, geography etc. All of public libraries are subscribing newspaper and magazines.

Maximum numbers of books are procured in Hindi Followed by English, Urdu, Punjabi, and Bengali.

According to Census of India, 2001 the total population of Delhi is 1.38 crore. In this study, we assume that all the 61 libraries of DPLS in different zones serve an equal population of 2.3 lakhs. Therefore the books per capita population available in central library at Chandni Chowk comes out to be 1.76. As per IFLA Standards for Book Collection in a public library the books per capita should be between 1.5 to 2.5 books per capita. Also Central library has a membership of 5355 users. The number of books available per member in Central Library is 75.9. Therefore, the per capita figure of 1.76 (Books available per capita population) and 75.9 (books available per member of central library) highlight the fact that the current collection is underutilized and that only a very small fraction of the total population in Delhi are members of Central library. The per capita figures for books for the other DP libraries show a similar trend of low membership base which is an indication of the underutilization of their collection.

Table.4: Library Book Collection and Membership of DPLS

Section	*Member (A)*	*Member (Ch)*	*Total*	*Collection (A)*	*Collection (Ch)*	*Total*
C. Lib	4937'	418	5355	151985	38680	190665
Z. Lib	5444	570	6014	86408	33586	119994
P. Ngr.	1875	196	2071	71684	21307	92991
K.L	1420	106	1526	62103	21930	84033
SH.L	2744	550	3294	63691	15809	79500
Sub-Br	8289	2956	11245	213886	148887	362773
R.C.Lib	2794	2008	4802	97612	207524	305136
Total				Total		

* A- adult, Ch- children

7.2.2 Non-Book Material: Central Library of DPLS has a Social Education Department which is responsible for maintaining, gramophone and music cassette library and organizing social education programs. Gramophone and music cassette library comprises the records of classical instrument and light music, bhajans, ghazals, film songs etc. This section has 4000 gramophone, 5542 audio cassettes and 5542 video cassettes.

7.2.3 E-Resources: One of the important resources of the collection in a library is e-resources and the Internet today gives access to an overwhelming amount of information, data and electronic information services. For providing the access to e-resources DPLS started Internet access services from 15th Feb 2008 in Central Library and now this facility is available in its three units i.e. Central Library, Zonal Library (Branch) and Patel Nagar Library (Branch) for members free of charge.

8. FINDINGS

The findings of this study are as follows:

(i) The DPLS has a very comprehensive collection development policy which is quite similar to policy guidelines laid down by international organizations like IFLA. Moreover the CDP has been properly documented. However it is highly unfortunate that in spite of having well laid down CDP, the collection of DPLS has not proven to be an asset for attracting large number of readers. This is essentially due to ineffective implementation of CDP. The inefficiency can be judged from the fact that a user survey conducted by the authors showed that the members believed that the collection did not contain new titles. This is in complete variance with the stated objective in CDP which requires the DPLS to maintain a collection which fulfills the needs of the population it serves.

(ii) It has been found that the DPLS has not been able to keep itself up to date with the changing information needs of users in today's digital environment. E-resources are very relevant in view of users changing information seeking behavior. But DPLS has very few e-resources such as online databases, DVDs, Videocassettes, etc.

(iii) DPLS has not been able to adapt to electronic environment. Personal computers having intent access were introduced in DP libraries only in 2008. Even now only 10 PCs are available in each of Central library, Zonal and one branch library of Patel Nagar. This is very discouraging for users. Special material for special categories of users is quite insufficient such as Braille books etc.

(iv) The public library has a role in maintaining and promoting collections of resources as related to the culture of indigenous people and local history resources. Nothing has been mentioned in this regards in the CDP of DPLS.

(v) Keeping in view the total population of NCT of Delhi, the membership base of DPLS is very low .The reasons which can be primarily cited for the low membership of DPLS may be lack of promotional policies and activities pertaining to library and information resources and services which are provided by DPLS. This has resulted into lack of awareness among the public about the collection and services. DPLS having a network of 61 libraries has been able to build up a membership base of only 40,775 users. This is in stark contrast to the British council library, New Delhi which is having approximately 8000 users in spite of the fact that it charges membership fee of Rs 1450 per annum.

9. CONCLUSION

Keeping in view the total population of Delhi, there is an urgent need to increase the membership base of the DPL by adopting promotional policies. More libraries at different levels such as Zonal, branch etc should be set up. More emphasis should be given to children section. Each library should have a separate section for children below 15 years having very good collection consisting of toys, games and puzzles, computer games, short stories collection and other information sources meant for children.

There is a very urgent need in this age of information and communication technology that the whole DPLS should be modernized and fully automated and properly linked as a network in view of the latest developments and changing information requirement of the users. One of the first steps which could be taken is to provide OPAC in all the libraries at various levels, as at present OPAC is available only in a few DP Libraries.

The essence of any public library is its collections, consisting of different categories of material in various formats that a modern public library includes. The public library should provide a wide range of materials in a variety of formats and in sufficient quantity to meet the needs and interests of the community. The culture of the local community and society must be reflected in the resource collection. Public libraries must keep abreast of new formats and new methods of accessing information. All information should be as readily available as possible, irrespective of format. The development of local information sources and resources is vital.

REFRENCES

1. Wheeler, Joseph L., and Goldher Herbertl. (1962). *Practical Administration of Public Libraries*. New York: Harper & Row, 462.
2. Senapati, Susanta Kumar. (2007). Public Library and Tourism Information: A congenial approach. *Library Herald,* 45 (2), 153-161.
3. India. Ministry of Information and Broadcasting, Research and Reference Division. *India (2005): A Reference Annual*. New Delhi: Director of Publications, 2005.
4. Economic Survey of Delhi, 2001-2002. Accessed on 6th March 2009 .http://delhiplanning.nic.in/Economic%20Survey/Ecosur2001-02/PDF/chapter3.pdf>.
5. Delhi Public Library. Annual Report, 2005-06.
6. Delhi Public Library. Annual Report, 2006-07.
7. Delhi Public Library. Collection Management Policy. Delhi: DPL, 2007
8. Evans, G. Edward. (2000). *Developing Library and Information Collections*. 4th ed. Colorado: Libraries Unlimited.
9. Gill, Philip, (2001). *The public Library Services: IFLA/ UNESCO Guidelines for Development.* Munchen: K. G. Saur. <http:// unesdoc.unesco.org/images/0005/000538/053868EB.pdf >.

Public Library System and Services in North East India

IBOHAL SINGH[1] AND N. GIRIDHARI SINGH[2]

1. INTRODUCTION

Libraries are repositories of recorded human knowledge, ware houses of wisdom and a bridge between past, present and future. Public Library is a people's university, a living social force that serves the entire community without any discrimination of caste, creed, sex and status. Shera has rightly remarked that knowledge is the life blood of human civilization and libraries of tomorrow will remain instrumental as flood-gate of human knowledge for distribution and culturing the human knowledge further. An effective Public Library System is a prime need for the social, political, cultural, economic, scientific and technological development of any democratic set-up.

2. MISSION OF PUBLIC LIBRARIES

The UNESCO Manifesto adopted first in 1949 modified in 1972 and remodified in 1994 attempts at capturing the current global aspiration of all the nations in freedom, prosperity and development through public libraries. It is the duty of public libraries to organize reading materials to enable the users of all age groups to find their way and right choice that may happen for promotion of reading habit. Education is a science of creative intelligence for an ideal society. Quality education seeks to inculcate a set of values that would equip the young minds for effective and individual living in the society. If the society is obliged to feed, clothe and house people then it must be obligatory on its part to feed people intellectually through reading in libraries and information centres. Francis

---

1. Lecturer, Department of Library and Information Science, Manipur University, Imphal – 795003, Manipur, India;
E-mail:cisingh@indiatimes.com

2. President, Ranganathan Society for Book Culture and Informatics Studies, NE Chapter, Imphal Sagolband Lukram Leirak, Imphal-795001, Manipur, India

Bacon has rightly said: "Reading makes a full man; conference a ready man; and writing an exact man." The UNESCO Mission also stipulates equality of access to all, has proposed to include all types of appropriate media and modern technologies in the public libraries. Besides, it recommended creation of a mission to facilitate the development of information and computer literacy. So the purpose of public libraries goes beyond any technology invention today. Since new technology brings changes in society and to remain active in the process of being "living force" library must also change[1].

3. PUBLIC LIBRARY AND NORTH EAST INDIA

The North Eastern Region of India comprises of eight states – Arunachal Pradesh, Assam, Manipur, Meghalaya, Mizoram, Nagaland, Sikkim and Tripura. It covers an area of 2,62,500 sq.km representing 8 percent of total area of the country with a total population of 3,90,35,582 (according to 2001 census) which constitutes 3.8 percent of the total country's population. Ninety eight percent of its border lies with other Asian countries – Bhutan, China in the North, Myanmar in the East, and Bangladesh in the South and West. The region is connected with the main land of the country by a small land-strip of 22 km through Siliguri in the North of West Bengal. The region presents a diverse and distinctive identity with respective traditionally rich culture and heritage. The region has wide variations in physical features ranging from the Brahmaputra valley and Barak valley in Assam up to highly dissected mountains of Eastern Himalayan range in Arunachal Pradesh. Other remaining areas of Manipur, Meghalaya, Mizoram, Nagaland, Tripura and Sikkim are mostly hilly.

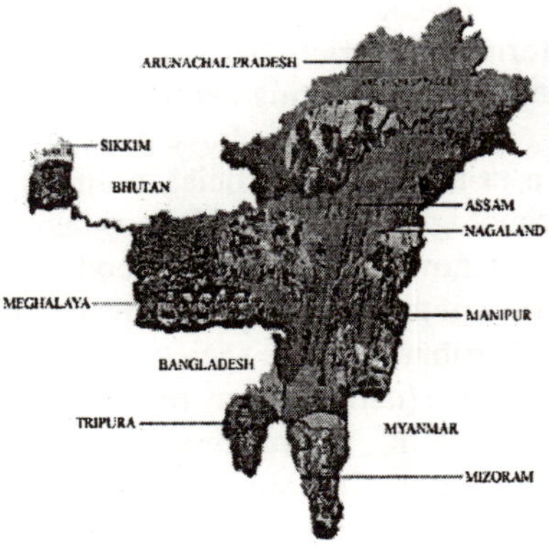

The entire region is not viable economically due to a number of factors. Normal life of this Region has been disturbed and affected many months by natural calamities like land slide, flood, earthquake very frequently. The region has also been suffering since the last many years from insurgency, ethnic feudalism, corruption and other anti-social activities like band and economic blockade, etc. Illiteracy, Unemployment, social injustice, regional disparity, economic inequality, etc. also have been prevailing in the region. The development in the North Eastern Region has been lagging behind the rest of the country. The per capita income of the region is Rs. 3530/- only as compared with the National average of Rs. 5440 at 1989-90 price index.

Special forces had been laid on economic development of the North Eastern Region during various plans and formulations have been made for removal of inadequate infrastructure, bottle necks, provision of basic minimum services, creating conducive environment for private investment etc. The continued efforts of the Government of India to remove impediments have strength/hopes for all round development of the region.

In such a problem prone region of the country development of libraries mostly of public libraries to carry out several programmes of promotional and developmental activities and make the public aware of reading is quite essential because the whole region requires to be improved upon in many respects in which public libraries are expected to play key roles.

To-day social and economic life is becoming more and more knowledge driven. But in the NER we have just only begun to explore and understand the everyday activities and its consequences. Quick scanning of the recent literature on what is happening, what may require in the information society become a considerable force of viewing, predicting, shaping and directing the future trends of the society.

Augmenting the above para, an effective Public Library Networking is a prime need for social, political, cultural, economic, scientific and technological upliftment for any democratic setup. Shera rightly remarked that "Knowledge is the life blood of our civilization". It is also a fact that library of to-day and to-morrow will function as flood-gate of knowledge for distribution to the society. Ranganathan also said "The mode of life of the people (nation) in any region is not accident but the result of its library development". A rural library is a community based centre for 'Information Culture and Communication Mechanism' through which all human relations develop and exist in space and time.

4. SCOPE OF THE STUDY

The present study was attempted to assess the status of automation of the public library system in the entire North East India. This study was undertaken as a part of the research project on Public Library Using Habit in North East India, sponsored by the Raja Rammohun Roy Library Foundation (RRRLF), Kolkata, Ministry of Culture, Government of India. Here the State Central Libraries of the eight states of the region including Sikkim were covered in the study.

5. METHODOLOGY

In order to collect information a semi-structurally designed questionnaire was distributed to the respective State Central Libraries of the region during 2004-05. Co-operation from almost all libraries was received but one or two libraries took much longer than desired, even 1½ years, to provide the sought information despite our repeated visits. The information collected from the libraries was analyzed into tables for interpretations.

6. MANIFESTATION

The following sections and sub-sections constitute a part of the findings of the project, the report of which has recently been submitted[2].

6.1 Types of Library

RRRLF provides grants to 1406 NGO libraries in the NER. Importantly, these libraries need to be governed properly by the State Central Libraries of the respective region. State wise Arunachal Pradesh has 12 district libraries, Assam-22, Manipur-6, Meghalaya-7, Mizoram-5, Nagaland-7, Sikkim-3, Tripura-3 district libraries. Out of 8 NER states only Arunachal Pradesh, Assam and Tripura each have sub-divisional libraries. Arunachal Pradesh and Tripura also have block level libraries. In over all the public library system in the region is not found to be working satisfactorily.

Table 1: Types of Library

State	*Central*	*District*	*Sub-Divisional*	*Block*	*Circle*	*Rural*	*Branch*	*NGO Library with RRRLF Grant*	*Total*
Arunachal Pradesh	1	12	13	18	38	–	–	84	166
Assam	1	22	14	–	–	–	–	174	211
Manipur	1	6	–	–	–	–	1	120	128
Meghalaya	1	7	–	–	–	–	–	15	23
Mizoram	1	5	–	–	–	–	–	410	416
Nagaland	1	7	–	–	–	–	–	244	252
Sikkim	1	3	–	–	–	–	–	159	163
Tripura	1	3	7	10		2	–	100	223
Total	8	65	34	28	38	2	1	1406	1582

Source: Returned Questionnaire
Note: RRRLF = Raja Rammohun Roy Library Foundation
NGO = Non – Governmental Organization

6.2. Background Information on State Central Libraries

Tripura State Central Library is the oldest public library within the NER. It was established in 1896 and the largest collection of documents in the region. It leads in terms of annual additions to the library. Manipur ranks second but the library suffered losses due to fire on 13.4.05. Arunachal Pradesh State Central Library and Sikkim State Central Library occupy 1st and 2nd position in Hindi collection. Meghalaya and Sikkim States regularly subscribe to journals and magazines in Hindi and other languages.

Table 1: Background Information on State Central Libraries in North East India

State	*Estd Year*	*Collection as on 1.4.04*	*Yearly collection during 2002-03*	*2003-04*	*Hindi collection as on 1.4.04*	*No. of Journals subscribed*	*Latest issue of journals received*	*Journals in Hindi*	*No. of Magazines/ Newspapers*	*No. of newspapers in Hindi*
Arunachal Pradesh	1956	43,520	976	1051	4,532	NIL	NIL	NIL	21/15	NIL
Assam	1954	88,500	NA	NA	NA	NA	NA	NA	NA	NA
Manipur	1958	1,35,845	NA	NA	NA	42	24	-	NIL/38	NIL
Meghalaya	1974	1,56,508	3,658	5780	NA	5	June 2004	2	2/20	2
Mizoram	1974	53,977	5,880	3500	NIL	21	NIL	NIL	NIL/14	NIL
Nagaland	1981	50,000	NA	NA	NA	NA	NA	NA	2/7	-
Sikkim	1964	23,300	3000	NA	2600	5	2004	NA	26/10	4
Tripura	1896	1,80,000	16,876	14,426	578	34	NIL	NIL	NIL/18	2

Source: Returned Questionnaire

6.3. Technical Processing

All the State Central Libraries follow same classification and cataloguing schemes uniformly. None of libraries use computers for technical processing of publications. Only two State Central Libraries, Nagaland and Tripura, provide abstracting/indexing services.

Table 3: Processing Work of the Libraries

State	*Classification Scheme*	*Cataloging Scheme*	*Use of Computer*	*Books classified per day*	*Books catalogued per day*	*Filing System*	*Preparation of abstracts/ indexes*	*No. of staff involved*
Arunachal Pradesh	DDC – 20	AACR–2	NO	50	50	Dictionary Catalogue	NO	02
Assam	NA	NA	NA	NA	NA	NA	NA	NA
Manipur	DDC	AACR–2	NO	30-40	30-40	NA	NO	5
Meghalaya	DDC – 21	AACR–2	NO	75	75	Alphabetical	NO	3
Mizoram	DDC – 20	AACR–2	NO	40-50	25-40	NA	NO	2
Nagaland	DDC – 20	AACR–2	NO	30	30	Classified & Alphabetical	YES	3
Sikkim	DDC	AACR–2	NO	12	12	Cat cabinet	NO	2
Tripura	DDC	AACR–2	NO	30	30	Classified	YES	7

Source: Returned Questionnaire
Note: DDC = Dewey Decimal Classification
AACR = Anglo American Cataloguing Rules

6.4. Library System and Facilities

Arunachal Pradesh and Assam are the only two states within NER that have come to set up Directorate of Public Libraries. In Assam, one Assam Civil Service Cadre person is heading the Public Library System as Director.

Table 4: Library System and Facilities

State	*Existence of Directorate*	*If exists date of commencement*	*If no, initiation in this regard*
Arunachal Pradesh	Yes	25.10.95	NA
Assam	Yes	NA	NA
Manipur	No	NA	NA
Meghalaya	No	NA	NA
Mizoram	No	NA	Library Act yet to be implemented
Nagaland	No	NA	Drafting of legislation yet to start
Sikkim	No	NA	Proposal is underway to have library legislation
Tripura	No	NA	Action has taken to initiate

Source: Returned Questionnaire

6.5. Existence of Children Section

Libraries in Manipur, Meghalaya, Nagaland, and Sikkim states are maintaining separate sections of children library (Table 5).

Table 5: Maintenance of Children Section

State	*Children Section*	*Yr. of Estd.*	*Total Collection*	*Registered user*	*Visitors per day*	*Seating Capacity*
Arunachal Pradesh	No	Nil	NA	NA	NA	NA
Assam	No	NA	NA	7999	NA	NIL
Manipur	Yes	NA	NA	13,917	30-40	60
Meghalaya	Yes	NA	NA	6089	50	30
Mizoram	No	NA	NA	NA	NA	NA
Nagaland	Yes	NA	5000	NA	10	20
Sikkim	Yes	2002-03	1740	150	15-20	15
Tripura	No	NA	NA	NA	NA	NA

Source: Returned Questionnaire NA = Not Available

6.6. Library Services

Regarding library services provided by the State Central Libraries of NER, the emphasis is mainly on reference service, CAS service, reprographic facility, book loan for home use, and reading room services. Only two state libraries have taken the lead in providing access to Internet facilities. Some other services are also rendered by the State Libraries of NER.

Table 6: Library Services

State	*(a)*	*(b)*	*(c)*	*(d)*	*(e)*	*(f)*	*(g)*	*(h)*	*(i)*	*(j)*	*(k)*	*(l)*	*(m)*	*(n)*	*(o)*	*(p)*
Arunachal Pradesh	✓	×	×	✓	✓	×	×	×	×	×	×	×	✓	✓	×	×
Assam	✓	✓	×	×	✓	×	✓	✓	×	×	×	×	✓	✓	✓	✓
Manipur	✓	×	×	×	×	✓	×	×	×	×	×	✓	✓	✓	×	×
Meghalaya	✓	×	×	×	×	×	×	×	×	×	×	×	✓	✓	×	×
Mizoram	✓	×	×	×	✓	×	×	×	×	×	×	×	✓	✓	×	×
Nagaland	✓	×	×	×	✓	×	×	✓	×	×	×	×	✓	✓	×	×
Sikkim	✓	×	×	×	✓	×	×	×	×	×	×	×	✓	✓	×	×
Tripura	✓	×	×	×	×	×	✓	×	✓	✓	×	×	✓	✓	✓	×

Source: Returned Questionnaire

Note: *(a) Reference (b) Referral (c) SDI (d) CAS (e) Reprography (f) Bibliography (g) Extension (h) Internet (i) Documentation (j) Indexing & Abstracting (k) Translation(l) ILL (m) Book loan for home use (n)IT-based (o) Reading room (p) Any other.*

6.7. Existence of Library Committee

With the exception of Assam, all states within the NER are having State Library Advisory/Planning Committees. However, their terms of references are not spelt out properly. One state remained silent in this respect.

Table 7: Existence of Library Committee

State	*Arunachal Pradesh*	*Assam*	*Manipur*	*Meghalaya*	*Mizoram*	*Nagaland*	*Sikkim*	*Tripura*
Yes	✓	×	✓	✓	✓	✓	✓	✓

Source: Returned Questionnaire

6.8 Automation Status

None of the State Central Libraries of NER by and large computerized their functions and services and this situation is attributed mainly, as indicated by libraries, to lack of funds, manpower and necessary infrastructure (Table 8).

7. CONCLUSION

The paper seeks to describe the scenario of existing system of public libraries and their services in the North Eastern part of the country. The study reveals that there are many areas on which steps are required to be undertaken for the overall development of the public library system in the region. Though library planning/advisory committees have been recommended for all the states in the North-East region but their functions are mainly limited to making recommendations for utilizing funds as provided by RRRLF. Thus the functions of these committees should be made broad-based including overall planning of the State Central Libraries. The Public Libraries Acts in Manipur and Mizoram are yet to be implemented. The remaining states in the region also require sound library legislation for which the concerned states must make necessary efforts. Besides, the NER Vision 2020 document must incorporate specific clause pertaining to public library development programme for the North East.

REFERENCES

1. Thomas, V.K. (2005). Computerisation of Public Libraries in India: A Study. *Library Today,* 28, 2&3.
2. Report on *Public Library Using Habit in North East India: A Case Study of Manipur.* RRRLF, Kolkata, Ministry of Culture, Government of India, 2008.

Table 8: Library Automation Status

State	*Arunachal Pradesh*	*Assam*	*Manipur*	*Meghalaya*	*Mizoram*	*Nagaland*	*Sikkim*	*Tripura*
Auto mated	×	×	×	×	×	×	×	×
Not automated	✓	✓	✓	✓	✓	✓	✓	✓
If Automated								
a) Date of commencement								
b) Hardware facility	NA	NA	NA	NA	NA	NA	NA	NA
c) Software facility								
d) Manpower involved								
e) Areas of automation								
f) Present status								
If not automated								
a) The reason	Lack of staff, fund, software	NA	NA	NA	Lack of staff	Lack of software fund, manpower.	Lack of space, building, staff, infrastructure	NA
b) Planning in process	Under process			Under process	Under process	Yes		
c) Any problem	RRRLF would not take any appropriate action.			NA		NA	Infrastructure, staff is in need of.	

Source: Returned Questionnaire NA = Not Available

List of Contributors

Narendra K. Bar, Secretary, GILA, and Head, Library & Resource Centre, Election Commission of India, Ashok Road, New Delhi 110001.

R.K. Bhatt, Reader & Head, Deptt. of Library & Information Science, University of Delhi, Delhi 110006.

Devendra Kumar, Faculty Member, Deptt. of Library & Information Science, CCS University, Meerut, UP.

Kirsten Drotner, Founding Director, Danish Research Centre on Education and Advanced Media Materials, University of Southern Denmark, 55 Campusvej, DK 5230 Odense M, Denmark.

Geeta G. Gadhavi, Sr. Lecturer & Head, Deptt. of Library & Information Science, Gujarat, University, Ahmedabad 380009.

P.R. Goswami, Director, Central Secretariat Library, Shashtri Bhawan, New Delhi 110001.

Monika Gupta, Research Scholar (M. Phil), Deptt. of Library & Information Science, University of Delhi, Delhi 110006.

Kiran Kathuria, Lecturer, Deptt. of Library & Information Science, Punjabi University, Patiala, Punjab.

Prabhjeet Kaur, Research Scholar, Deptt. of Library & Information Science, University of Delhi, Delhi 110006.

Krishan Gopal, JNU Library, New Delhi 110067.

Krishna Kumar, Faculty Member, DLIS, CCS University, Meerut, UP.

Mange Ram, University Library Incharge, Dayalbagh Educational Institue (deemed University), Dayalbagh, Agra 5, UP.

Manish Kumar, Lecturer, Deptt. of Library & Information Science, University of Delhi, Delhi 110006.

Esmat Momeni, Research Scholar, Deptt. of Library & Information Science, University of Delhi, Delhi 110006.

Usha Mujoo Munshi, Librarian, Indian Institute of Public administration, New Delhi.

Bharati Paliwal, Librarian, TERI University Library, New Delhi.

M. Sankara Reddy, Member, Raja Rammohun Roy Library Foundation, Kolkata, University Librarian (Retd.) Potti Sriramulu, Telugu University, Hyderabd 500004, AP.

M.P. Satija, Professor, Deptt. of Library & Information Science, Guru Nanak Dev University , Amritsar 143005.

Moorttimatee Samantaray, Deputy Librarian, NCERT, Sri Aurobindo Marg, New Delhi 110016.

U.C. Sharma, Head, Deptt. of Library & Information Science, Dr. B.R. Ambedkar University, Agra.

B.N. Singh, Librarian, National Museum, Institute of History of Art, Conservation and Museology (Deemed University), Janpath, New Delhi 110011.

Ibhol Singh, Lecturer, Deptt. of Library & Information Science, Manipur University , Imphal 795003, Manipur.

M.P. Singh, Senior Lecturer, Deptt. of Library & Information Science, Bundelkhand University, Jhansi 284128.

N. Giridhari Singh, President, Ranganathan Society for Book culture & Informatics studies, NE Chapter, Imphal Sagolband Lukram Leirak, Imphal 795001, Manipur.

Rajbir Singh, Librarian, Vaish P.G. College, Rohtak (Haryana).

Rajkumar Singh, Librarian, Govt. Mahila Degree College, Aurai, Sant Ravidas Nagar, Bhadohi, UP.

Sewa Singh, Former Prof. & Head, GND University, Amritsar.

Manpreet Kaur Sohan, M. Phil, Research scholar, Deptt. of Library & Information Science, University of Delhi, Delhi 110006.

A.C. Tikekar, Retd. Professor & Librarian, University of Bombay, Mumbai.

Pradip Upadhyay, Technical Director, National Informatics Centre, Department of Information technology, Ministry of Communications & Information Technology (Govt. of India), Block A, CGO Complex, New Delhi 110003.

Velaga Venkatappaiah, 4-54-49, Ithanagaram, Tenali 522201, AP.

P.K. Walia, Reader, Deptt. of Library & Information Science, University of Delhi, Delhi 110006.

Satish Yadav, Librarian, Bhadhawar P G College, Bah, UP.

Index